BASIC
The Time-Sharing Language

BASIC

Second Edition

The Time-Sharing Language

Nesa L'abbe Wu

Eastern Michigan University
Ypsilanti, Michigan

wcb

Wm. C. Brown Company Publishers
Dubuque, Iowa

QA
76.73
B3
W8

30,123

Second Printing, 1980

TO Andin
Anita
Antony
Natalie

Contents

Preface

This is a book on BASIC (**B**eginner's **A**ll-Purpose **S**ymbolic **I**nstruction **C**ode), the time-sharing language. The author approaches the teaching of BASIC by the use of "practical applications" in the field of science and business. Exemplary situations are thoroughly explained, demonstrated, and programmed for execution on remote terminals as a tool to implement learning by means of practical application.

The author recognizes that flowcharting is the most effective tool for programming logically. Flowcharting is used to demonstrate the procedure for logical solution for all examples and cases included in this book. The text can be used regardless of the computer in use on location, since various implementations of the BASIC language (thirteen in all) are summarized in Appendix B.

Chapter 1 gives a brief history of computers and time-sharing, explains how time-sharing works and indicates several time-sharing languages of which BASIC is the most popular. That chapter also explains what a computer is and how it works. Flowcharting concepts are illustrated in the second chapter. Chapters 3 through 10 represent the principles of BASIC, which are illustrated through numerous examples, problems, and exercises at the close of each chapter. It is important that these first ten chapters be followed in order of presentation. Chapter 11 discusses sorting routines, whereas chapter 12 covers advanced BASIC programming techniques, such as formated output, plotting and file processing. Chapters 13 through 15 contain special topics: Simulation, Business Cases, Cases in Operations Research and Quantitative Methods, and Interactive Programming in BASIC. These topics can be covered in any sequence.

An attempt has been made to make the exercises appealing and interesting. Besides some simple one-statement problems throughout the text, other business and science-oriented problems have been included at the end of each chapter. The appendixes are especially designed to provide quick reference on (1) flowcharting symbols, (2) the implementation of BASIC statements, and (3) a guide to the flowcharting included in this book.

It is a difficult task to make, in a satisfactory way, all acknowledgments. Special thanks goes to Professor Stephen Mecca at Providence College, Providence, Rhode Island who did a thorough job reviewing the first edition of this book and who offered many excellent suggestions which are incorporated in this text. I also wish to thank Dr. Richard Nelson, Clemson University and Dr. Richard Cheng, Rochester Institute of Technology for their valuable suggestions in reviewing the text.

And last, but by no means least, I am most of all grateful to my husband—for his patience and constructive criticism during the development of this text—as a constant source of great inspiration and encouragement.

Nesa L'abbé Wu

1

Introduction to Computers and Computer Time-Sharing

A Brief History of Computers and Their Components

Generally speaking, the oldest known "computer" dates back more than thirty-five hundred years. The circular arrangement of the huge stones in England, called Stonehenge, is referred to by many scientists as the first computer. Coordinated, with the sun, these stones were used to predict astronomical phenomena. The description of another old "computer" can be found in the June 1959 issue of Scientific American. It deals with a machine, believed to be a Greek computer, which was discovered off the Greek island of Antikythera. It has been estimated that this machine is slightly over two thousand years old. Another ancient computing device, the abacus, was developed and used by the Chinese. This simple device for computing was introduced into Europe during Marco Polo's time.

The first adding machine was invented by the famous French mathematician B. Pascal in 1642. This calculator was improved in 1673 by a German mathematician Leibnitz, who made the calculator capable of use not only for addition but also for the multiplication operation.

Charles Babbage is often referred to as the father of the computer. A noted English mathematician and professor of mathematics at Cambridge University, he conceived the machine (1812) that could take and act on instructions. His first machine, the Difference Engine, was a gigantic, monster computer that was supposed to weigh approximately two tons. It was never completed, due to the lack of tooling technology at that time. Later he developed the Analytical Engine. Financial problems, however, prohibited him from finishing this work. This genius envisioned that his machine would carry out arithmetic operations, one at a time; would receive instructions and data from keypunched cards; would store data and information; and would be able to make decisions between two alternatives. The stored program concept of the Analytical Engine is very close to that of the modern computers.

The Harvard Mark I Computer was the first computer, completed in 1944. It had all started in 1937, when H. Aikens of Harvard University began designing the machine that would perform a sequence of arithmetic operations automatically. Though the size of the Mark I was only one-tenth that of Babbage's machine, it was still a huge electro-mechanical calculator, consisting of adding accumulators, mechanical relays, switches, buttons, wire plugs, and punched tape. Soon thereafter the ENIAC (1945) and the EDVAC (1952) by J. P. Eckert and J. W. Maughly of the Moore School of Engineering of the University of Pennsylvania, were completed.

The binary number system, to represent data and instructions, was introduced at Princeton University by Dr. J. Von Newman (after his stay at the Moore School), and the IAS computer was completed in 1952. With the EDVAC and the IAS computer, the electronic stage of the computer was entered, leaving the electromechanical stage behind.

Developments in computing have occurred in both the hardware (equipment) and the software (programs). Hardware developments are reflected in major changes of the equipment itself and have taken place in four steps or generations. First generation computers (1946–59) used vacuum tubes and were rather slow. Second generation machines (1959–65) used transistors and were smaller and faster. Third generation computers (1965–70) are characterized by integrated circuits and time-sharing capabilities. The transition to the third generation equipment meant a major change to the computer industry. Though these machines exhibited sensational increases in speed, the price of many computers dropped. This reduction in price perhaps explains why approximately 65 percent of the computers in operation today were installed in the sixties. Fourth generation computers (1970–) are the microtechnology devices being introduced today. Minicomputers and many other expected developments, such as: satellite transmissions, microcomputers, laser and fluidic computers, and others, will characterize this generation.

Software developments are reflected in the various changes in computer programs and procedures, which are necessary for the operation of the computing systems. The first generation computers used a machine-oriented language. This language soon appeared to be unpractical, since each computer had its own program—one that could not be used by other systems. Symbolic assembly language was introduced during the second generation computers. Even though this language was easier to write, lack of conformity in the symbols used by the various programmers hindered the development of the symbolic assembly language. Finally, compilers of high-level languages were introduced. High level languages have the advantage of being independent of the computer in use, and are easier to write than the previously mentioned languages. The FORTRAN programming language is one of the first of the high-level languages developed by IBM, and was published in 1957. Less than ten years later, in 1964, a new language "BASIC" was developed at Dartmouth College under the supervision of Professor John G. Kemeny and Thomas E. Kurtz. This language gained in popularity during the fourth generation computers with the introduction of minicomputers and time-sharing. Now it is the language of the personal- or the minicomputer. It is this BASIC language that is considered in this text.

There are two major types of computers: the analog computer and the digital computer. The analog computer deals with continuous quantities, whereas the digital computer works with discrete quantities. In the early 1600s the first widely used analog computer, called the slide rule, was developed. In 1872 Lord Kelvin built his large-scale analog computer to be able to predict the changes in tides in the English harbors. Analog computers are not as widely used as digital computers and cannot be programmed in BASIC.

What Is a Computer? How Does It Work?

A computer can be visualized as a black box device that performs computations automatically, accurately and at high speed, given a set of instructions. The set of instructions combining reading, writing, arithmetic (addition, subtraction, multiplication, division, exponentiation), and data testing are aimed at the solution of some problem and are written in a language the computer can understand or translate. These instructions are in general referred to as the program. BASIC is one of the languages that can be used to write a program.

There are five basic components in a computer system:

1. the **INPUT** unit
2. the **STORAGE** unit
3. the **ARITHMETIC/LOGICAL** unit
4. the **OUTPUT** unit
5. the **CONTROL** unit

These components are shown in figure 1.1.

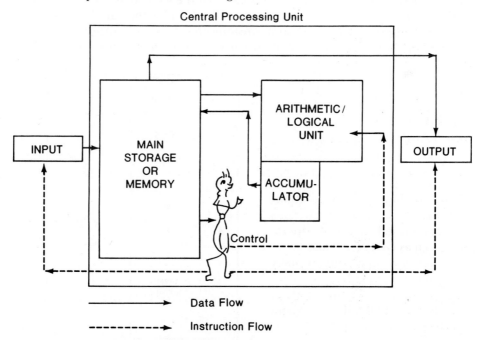

Figure 1.1. *Internal Organization of the Computer*

The **INPUT** unit places the program and the data in storage. The **OUT-PUT** unit gives out the results which are in **MEMORY.** This is accomplished through the command of the **CONTROL** unit. As soon as a computer program is in memory or in main storage the control unit takes the first instruction, analyzes it, and makes sure that the instruction is executed properly. Depending upon the nature of the instruction, the arithmetic/logical unit, the input unit, or the output unit is commanded to perform certain duties, or the control unit brings data from the storage to the arithmetic/logical unit, or from the arithmetic/logical unit to the central storage. As soon as the first instruction is properly executed the control unit fetches the second instruction out of central storage, and so on, until a HALT instruction is reached or an invalid instruction (i.e. garbage, misplaced data) is encountered, until there are none left or until the instruction becomes impossible.

Note that the **MAIN STORAGE** unit is the heart of the system since it bridges all other units of the system. Also, it is not physically possible, in reality, to separate the arithmetic/logical unit from the control unit.

To illustrate how the central processing unit works let us assume that the following statement needs to be executed

$$\text{LET } A = A + B$$
$$\text{where } A = 2$$
$$B = 3$$

The above is a valid Basic statement and means: get the value that is stored under the variable name A and add to it the value that is stored under the variable name B. The result must be stored under the variable name A. The following six cartoons illustrate in fourteen steps the process of execution, under the assumption that all instructions are ready in the central storage.

Step 1

The BASIC statement:

LET A = A + B (assuming that A
                is equal to 2 and
                B is equal to 3)

is broken down into instructions and operands. The instructions are predefined machine operations such as GET, ADD and PUT, whereas the operands usually refer to the storage locations containing the data to be operated on. The translated BASIC statement may be placed in storage as shown.

These instructions read: get the

Loc.	Content
0	GET 4
1	ADD 5
2	PUT 4
3	BRANCH 6
4	2
5	3
6	(next operat.)

CENTRAL STORAGE

ARITHM. UNIT

| ACCUM. | COUNTER |

contents of location 4, add to it the contents of location 5, put the result back in location 4, tell the control data unit where the next instruction is, data, data, . . .

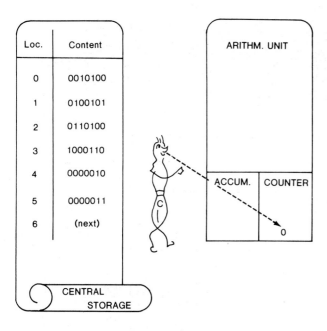

Loc.	Content
0	0010100
1	0100101
2	0110100
3	1000110
4	0000010
5	0000011
6	(next)

CENTRAL STORAGE

ARITHM. UNIT

ACCUM. | COUNTER

0

Step 2

Note that in our "mythical" computer we are able to store an instruction and an operand in each storage location. In reality the instructions in central storage are stored in binary code. For the sake of illustration, let us imagine that each location can store a string of seven ones or zeroes. Furthermore, if that location happens to contain an instruction with its operand, the instruction is represented by the first three digits (or bits), and the operand by the last four. Assuming that the manufacturer has defined the GET instruction to be 001, ADD instruction to be 010, PUT to be 011, and BRANCH to be 100, the contents of location 0 through 5 is as shown in the second cartoon. Note that 000 has never been defined by the manufacturer and is, therefore, an invalid instruction. This should not cause a problem since the BRANCH instruction in location 3 makes sure that the control unit does not try to interpret that data as an instruction.

Step 3

The instruction in location zero (0) is analyzed by the control unit. The control unit must copy the content of location four (4) on his workbench, called the accumulator.

Step 4

The data item "2" is placed in the accumulator.

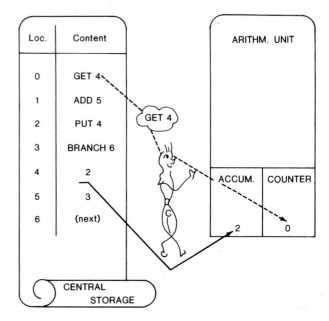

Step 5

As soon as the control unit has analyzed the above instruction, the counter value moves to "1" (one).

Step 6

The control unit analyzes the instruction in location one (1). He must add the content of location five (5) to whatever he has stored in the accumulator.

Step 7

The addition is performed in the arithmetic unit.

Step 8

The result of the addition is stored in the accumulator.

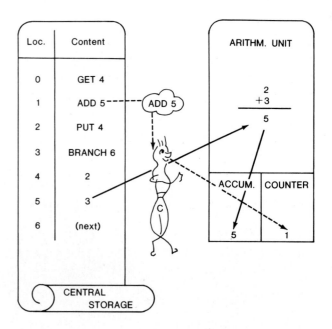

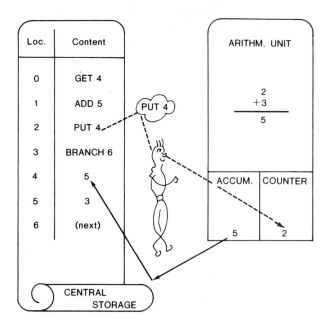

Step 9

Meanwhile, the counter value moved to "2" (two).

Step 10

The control unit analyzes the instruction in location two (2). He must put the content of the accumulator in location four (4).

Step 11

The control unit puts five (5) in location four (4).

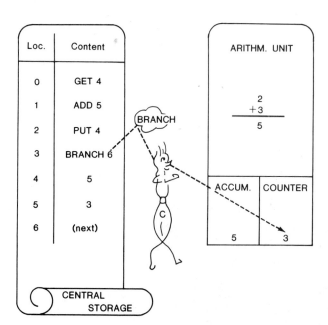

Step 12

Meanwhile, the counter value moved to "3" (three).

Step 13

The control unit analyzes the instruction in location three (3). He must branch to location six (6).

Step 14

He continues with the next operation.

In conclusion, the previous six cartoons illustrated the following interesting characteristics of computers and computing:

1. Data and instructions are stored in binary code.
2. The instructions to be executed must be stored in a logical sequence.
3. All necessary data must be stored in specific locations and in accordance with the instructions.
4. Neither instructions nor data are wiped out. Data values can be replaced by other values (Step 10).
5. At the end of the execution of all instructions, the arithmetic unit shows all arithmetic functions performed and the accumulator contains the last accumulated values. In short, nothing is wiped out.

Computer Time-Sharing

TIME-SHARING—BACKGROUND BRIEFS

The first operational computer time-sharing system was introduced at Massachusetts Institute of Technology only about a decade ago. Called the Compatible Time-Sharing System (CTSS), this system was developed for an IBM 709 computing system in 1961. Other time-sharing systems were developed during succeeding years and were installed by many other end-users, computer manufacturers, and commercial time-sharing vendors. Some early systems are:

CTSS—developed by Bolt, Beranek, and Newman for the Digital Equipment Corporation's PDP-1 computer.
JOSS (Johnniac Open Shop System)—developed by RAND Corporation in 1963.
CAL (Conversational Algebraic Language)—developed by the University of California in Berkeley in 1963.
MAC (Multiple Access Computer)—the beginning of large time-sharing systems (160 terminals at MIT and other institutions of higher learning) in 1963.
BASIC—developed at Dartmouth College in 1964–66.

Many time-sharing systems were developed by major computer manufacturers, such as Burroughs, Control Data Corporation, Digital Equipment Corporation, General Electric, Hewlett-Packard, IBM, RCA, Scientific Data Systems, and UNIVAC.

In 1970, over 100 million dollars were spent for computer time-sharing which now has become the fastest growing section of the computer industry. Users of time-sharing systems are colleges and universities, scientists, engineers, manufacturers, managers, executives, bankers, and many others.

Terminals, such as teletypes, displays, and plotters, are found in many offices and even some private homes. They have numerous applications in business, such as for investment analysis, transportation, rate of return, project evaluation and review, financial analysis, merge analysis, inventory control, purchasing, forecasting, budgeting, production analysis, even payroll processing, and for many other objectives. Time-sharing has also enjoyed great acceptance in educational institutions, public and health service organizations, and many other sectors of our society.

Time-sharing may have special appeal for smaller corporations to whom the initial investment is often of major concern; however, the primary users are still in the larger corporations, where the turnaround time is the major factor.

HOW DOES TIME-SHARING WORK?

The basic characteristic of a time-sharing system is the simultaneous access to a computer system by many users via their individual terminals. Since the central processing unit (CPU) of a computer system performs its operation at an extremely high speed, it takes only a very small portion of time to process each user's data as compared to the time required for data input and output on the terminal. Therefore, though only one user at a time can enter the CPU, each user receives response from the system almost instantaneously. Each user enters his program and data into the computer system or calls out the stored program and data input and output from the system through a keyboard printer. If the keyboard printer is a Teletype, the information transmission actually occurs via a public telephone line. The alphanumerical data and a set of selected symbols can be converted into different voice signals and electrical impulses through a portable coupler connected with the teletypewriter (Fig. 1.2).

The system often uses a sophisticated scheme to allocate computer time to each set of input signals which are temporarily stored in the buffer before gaining entry into CPU. (A buffer is like a secondary memory bank.) The program already in CPU is also transmitted in and out of CPU many times during processing in order to make room for other users. The unfinished programs may be stored temporarily, waiting for their next turn to reenter. Information swaps in and out of the system between CPU and buffer thousands of times, to the effect that each user receives his share of CPU time almost as soon as he is able to react to the information that is already processed.

TIME-SHARING LANGUAGES

Several conversational time-sharing programming languages have been developed as follows:

BASIC: **B**eginner's **A**ll-purpose **S**ymbolic **I**nstruction **C**ode, a rather simple language that has been implemented by almost all major computer manufacturers.

CAL: **C**onversational **A**lgebraic **L**anguage, developed at the University of California in Berkeley, is less popular. It is available on the Scientific Data 940.

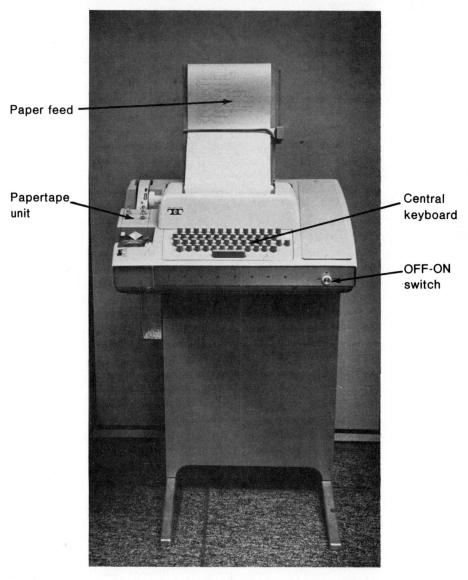

Paper feed

Papertape
unit

Central
keyboard

OFF-ON
switch

Figure 1.2. *Caterfone 33ASR Data Terminal (Courtesy of Caterfone Communications Corporation)*

Figure 1.3. *Acoustic Coupler and Central Keyboard of a Teletypewriter Terminal*

LISP: a **LIS**t-**P**rocessing programming language available on many systems.

QUIKTRAN and XTRAN: variations of the FORTRAN programming language that have been developed for specific time-sharing systems.

Some existing non-time-sharing languages are used for time-sharing purposes. These are:

ALGOL: a specific **ALGO**rithmic **L**anguage.

COBOL: this **C**ommon **B**usiness **O**riented **L**anguage is available on many systems.

FORTRAN II and FORTRAN IV: scientific programming languages that stand for **FOR**mula **TRAN**slation II and IV. The first one, FORTRAN II, is implemented on many systems, whereas FORTRAN IV is implemented on almost all major systems.

PL-1 and PL-C: a **P**rogramming **L**anguage that combines all good features of ALGOL, COBOL, FORTRAN, and LISP. It is implemented on several systems.

SNOBOL: a **S**tri**N**g **O**riented sym**BO**lic **L**anguage; especially convenient for string operations.

This book discusses the syntax and application of the BASIC language. It is the easiest time-sharing language to learn and to use from a terminal.

Exercises

PROBLEM #1

The function of a computing system is described in this introduction with the aid of the skeleton diagram below. Identify the functions which correspond to each of the boxes in the diagram and describe each very briefly.

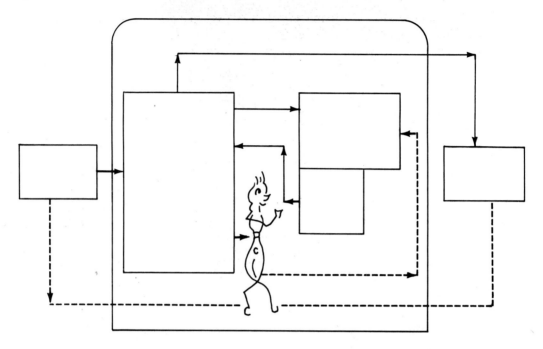

PROBLEM #2

Answer each of the following Review questions.

1. The most dramatic advances in processing information occurred

   _____.

   a. 3,000 years BC
   b. during the sixteenth century
   c. during the last 25 years
   d. during the nineteenth century

2. True or False

   The significant hardware development in the third generation of computers is the use of transistors

3. True or False

   The digital computer, rather than the analog computer, is used for business data processing

4. _____ is often referred to as the father of the computer
   a. B. Pascal
   b. Leibnitz
   c. C. Babbage
   d. H. Aikens
   e. J. Von Newman

5. The binary number system for representing data and instructions was introduced by _____
   a. C. Babbage
   b. H. Aikens
   c. J. Von Newman
   d. J. P. Eckert

2
Flowcharting

The flowchart, or block diagram, is an important tool for programming which allows the programmer to plan the sequence of operations in a program before writing it.

Flowcharting serves to pictorialize a process. A flowchart is made up of a set of symbols (the shapes of which indicate the nature of the operations being described) connected by lines and arrows that indicate the "flow of control" between the various symbols.

The standard flowcharting symbols can be classified within the following groups:

1. Processing group
2. Decision group
3. Input/Output group
4. Connectors and Terminal Group

5. Linkage group
6. Predefined process group
7. Preparation group
8. Comment group

Appendix A summarizes the different symbols within each group, and their usage.

There are two basic kinds of flowcharts: the systems flowchart and the program flowchart. The systems flowchart is general and broad. It emphasizes data flow among machines and does not emphasize how the data has to be converted to obtain desired outputs.

The program flowchart is very detailed, as compared with the systems flowchart. It indicates the logical sequence of events for transforming the input to the desired output. At this point we are basically interested in program flowcharting. The symbols used for program flowcharting are indicated in Table 2.1.

TABLE 2.1
Program Flowcharting Symbols

PROCESS. Any processing function; defined operation(s) causing change in form, value or location of information.

DECISION. A decision or switching-type operation that determines which of a number of alternative paths to follow.

INPUT/OUTPUT. General I/O function; information available for processing (input), or recording of processed information (output).

TERMINAL, INTERRUPT. A terminal point in a flowchart—start, stop, halt, delay or interrupt; may show exit from a closed subroutine.

CONNECTOR. Exit to, or entry from, another part of the chart.

PAGE CONNECTOR.

ARROWHEADS and FLOWLINES. In linking symbols, these show operations sequence and dataflow direction.

PREDEFINED PROCESS. One or more named operations or program steps specified in a subroutine or another set of flowcharts.

PREPARATION. Instruction modification to change program —set a switch, modify an index register, initialize a routine.

COMMENT. Additional descriptive clarification, comment. (Dotted line extends to symbols as appropriate.)

Use of Symbols for Program Flowcharting

INPUT/OUTPUT SYMBOL

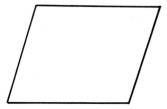

This symbol represents any Input/Output function. Through this symbol, information can be made available to the computer (example: read in payroll data) or processed information can be made available by the computer by printing it on an output medium (example: print out payroll checks).

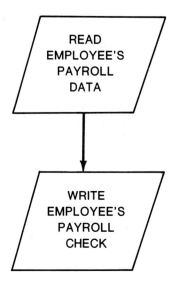

READ
EMPLOYEE'S
PAYROLL
DATA

WRITE
EMPLOYEE'S
PAYROLL
CHECK

PROCESSING SYMBOL

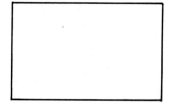

This symbol is used to represent any processing, defined operations(s) which cause change in form, value, or location of information. Arithmetic instructions and instructions for data movement are placed in these blocks.

In the payroll example the PAYROLL DATA must be processed to obtain the output PAYROLL CHECKS. This transformation requires three steps:

1. Compute wages

   WAGES = HOURS·RATE

2. Compute Federal Witholding Tax

   FEDERAL TAX = (WAGES−13·DEPENT).18

3. Compute the Net Income

   NETPAY = WAGES−FEDERAL TAX

Assuming the above change in the PAYROLL DATA, the flowchart can be redrawn as shown here:

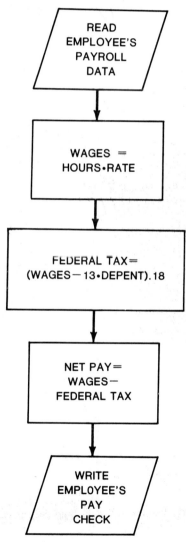

The previous flowchart can be reduced as appears here:

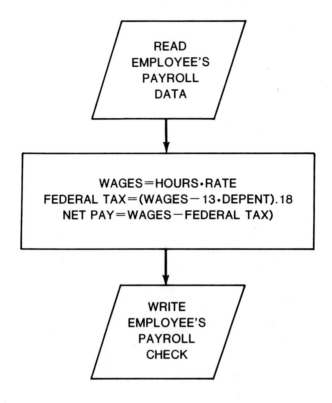

DECISION SYMBOL

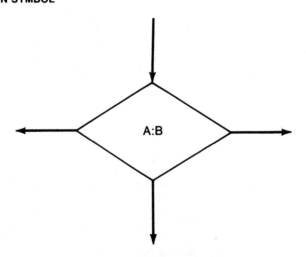

As is the case with the Input/Output and the Processing symbol, the diamond-shaped Decision symbol has one entrance line. However, since the Decision symbol results in a number of alternatives to be followed, there are at least two exit paths or branches. In the case of more than three exit paths, the exits are often represented as shown.

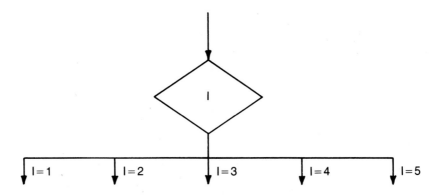

Notice that it is assumed that I can take on five different values and that for each value of I, a different path has to be chosen.

Comparisons made with the Decision symbol are often shown with a colon [:]. For example: compare I with 0 (zero). As compared to zero, I may be equal (=) to zero, or I may be larger than (>) zero, or I may be smaller than (<) zero. So for these three possible cases, three different paths are appropriate. Later it will be indicated that decisions might be written differently in a Decision block.

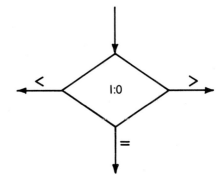

In the PAYROLL EXAMPLE, the calculation of the FEDERAL TAX

$$FEDERAL\ TAX = (WAGES - 13 \cdot DEPENT).18$$

may become negative if there are many dependents and if the weekly WAGES are very small. In that case the FEDERAL TAX should be equal to zero, rather than negative. Therefore, to avoid subtracting a negative income tax from the wages, it might be wise to investigate whether the calculated FEDERAL TAX is negative, zero, or positive before calculating the NET PAY, as follows:

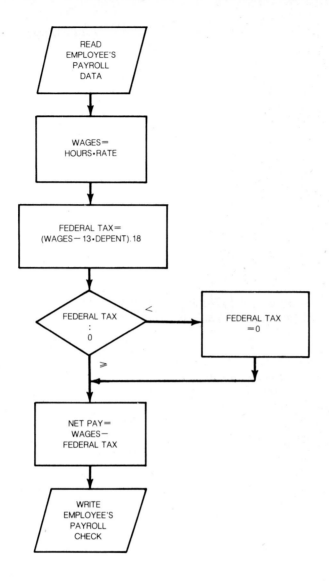

CONNECTORS AND TERMINAL GROUP

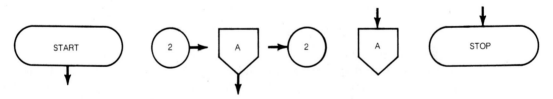

The Terminal symbol and the Starting symbol represent the ending and the beginning of a flowchart respectively. Connectors are used where a single flowline is broken because of page limitation or where several flowlines pin together. With this in mind, we can complete the payroll flowchart as follows:

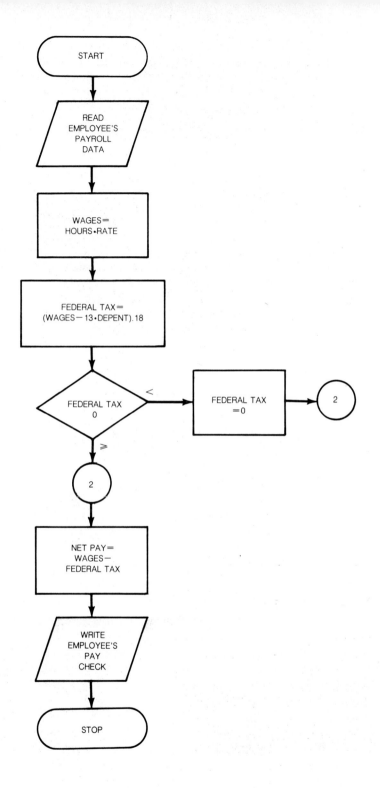

"A picture is worth a thousand words" is certainly true when flowchart symbols are connected in a correct and orderly fashion. The flow direction, as shown in the payroll example, is indicated by an unbroken line between successive flowchart blocks. Arrowheads favor the readability of the flowchart direction path. The arrowheads are not always necessary, but in case of doubt, they should be used as follows:

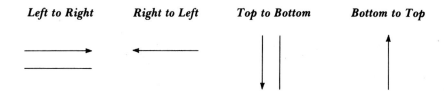

| *Left to Right* | *Right to Left* | *Top to Bottom* | *Bottom to Top* |

It is not necessary to use arrowheads in a "left-to-right" flow and in a "top-to-bottom" flow.

Through flowcharting, essential facts of any problem can be communicated to those who have the ability to find the solutions to the problem. Later on it will become clear that flowcharting is extremely helpful in efficient coding. Flowcharts also aid in the debugging of programs. When errors occur in programming in an initial test run, the flowchart can be useful in detecting and removing these mistakes.

Practical Examples of Program Flowcharting

EX. [1] PAYROLL WITH FEDERAL TAX AND SOCIAL SECURITY

Reconsider the payroll example which is developed in the previous section and let us introduce Social Security tax. In 1977 Social Security laws prescribe 5.85% tax deductions on all income earned. No deductions are made after the cumulative income has reached $16,500 as illustrated in the next flowchart. Therefore, before calculating the Social Security tax one must check whether the previous cumulative income was larger than $16,500. If it was, then no Social Security tax will be deducted. If the previous cumulative income is less than $16,500, then one of two things will happen:

1. The earned wages will accumulate with the previous cumulative earnings to exceed the $16,500 level. In this case only 5.85% Social Security tax must be paid on the difference between $16,500 and the previous cumulative wages.
2. The new wages will not bring the new cumulative earnings over the $16,500. Then, of course, 5.85% tax will be applied to the wages earned this period.

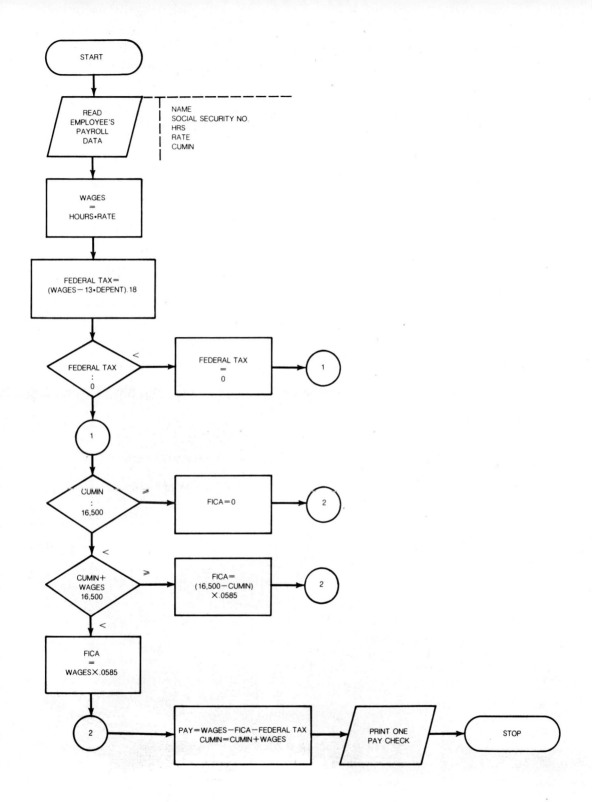

START

READ
EMPLOYEE'S
PAYROLL
DATA

NAME
SOCIAL SECURITY NO.
HRS
RATE
CUMIN

WAGES
=
HOURS•RATE

FEDERAL TAX=
(WAGES− 13•DEPENT).18

FEDERAL TAX
:
0

<   FEDERAL TAX
=
0   →   1

1

CUMIN
:
16,500

⩾   FICA=0   →   2

<

CUMIN+
WAGES
16,500

⩾   FICA=
(16,500−CUMIN)
×.0585   →   2

<

FICA
=
WAGES×.0585

2   →   PAY=WAGES−FICA−FEDERAL TAX
CUMIN=CUMIN+WAGES   →   PRINT ONE
PAY CHECK   →   STOP

EX. [2] COMPUTING THE TUITION FOR ONE STUDENT

A university controller wishes to establish a flowchart for computing the tuition any given student owes. The following procedure is used to calculate the tuition.

If the student is enrolled for less than ten credit hours, he pays $80.00 for each credit hour he takes.

If he enrolls for more than ten credits, a tuition of $800.00 is charged.

The controller has a set of cards for each student—one card for each subject the student takes. On each card appears the student's name and number, the subject number, and the subject credit hours.

The controller goes through the following basic steps when calculating the tuition.

1. Before reading the credit information from the cards, the controller clears a "counter" for calculating the number of credit hours the student takes by assigning "zero" to that counter.
2. Now the controller is ready to read the student's credit information.
3. After reading the number of credits, he will add that number to the counter.
4. The controller will continue reading in credit hours, adding them to the counter until there are no more cards left.
5. When all credits are read and added by the controller, he is ready to check whether the total number of credits is less than ten or not. If less than ten credits are taken, then the controller multiplies the total number of credits by 80 to calculate the student's tuition. However, if the total number of credits taken by the student exceeds or equals ten, a maximum fee of $800 is imposed.
6. Finally, the student's name and number is printed, together with the fee he owes the university.

These six basic steps are represented in the next flowchart.

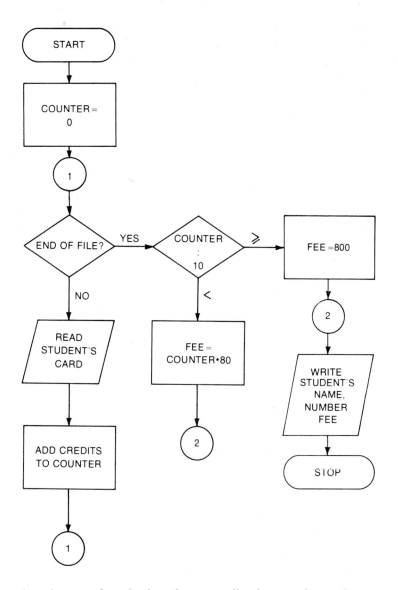

Assume that the set of cards that the controller has on the student are 80-column-cards on which the information is keypunched. Any person, even a competent keypuncher, can make errors. For example, she may forget to keypunch the number of credit hours or may keypunch the wrong number of credit hours. It is wise to build into a flowchart the opportunity for checking such contingencies, if possible. If no credit hours are indicated, or if the number of credit hours is too large (for example, it exceeds the maximum number of assigned credit hours—5), then the flowchart check can take care of this error:

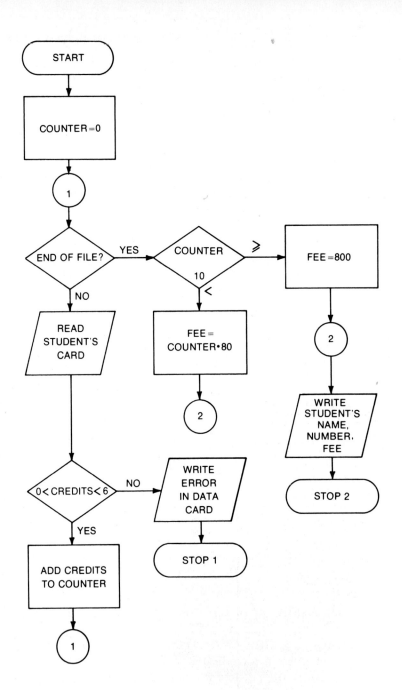

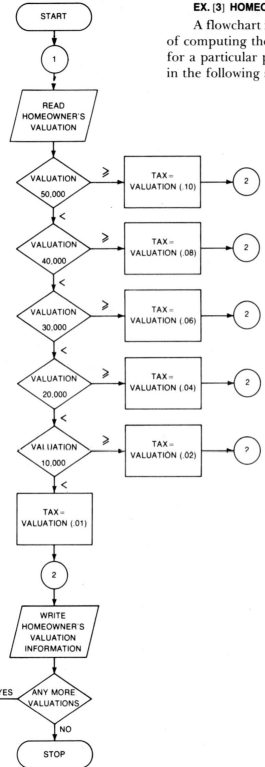

A flowchart is constructed for the purpose of computing the homeowner's real estate tax for a particular period. The valuation can fall in the following six classes:

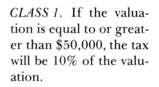

CLASS 1. If the valuation is equal to or greater than $50,000, the tax will be 10% of the valuation.

CLASS 2. If the valuation is equal to or greater than $40,000, but less than $50,000, the tax will be 8% of the valuation.

CLASS 3. If the valuation is equal to or greater than $30,000, but less than $40,000, the tax will be 6% of the valuation.

CLASS 4. If the valuation is equal to or greater than $20,000, but less than $30,000, the tax will be 4% of the valuation.

CLASS 5. If the valuation is equal to or greater than $10,000, but less than $20,000, the tax will be 2% of the valuation.

CLASS 6. If the valuation is greater than $00.00, but less than $10,000, the tax will be 1% of the valuation.

A set of cards is available on each homeowner in the community. Each of these cards contains the homeowner's name, address, and valuation. The steps taken to compute the tax are as follows:

1. Read in 1 homeowner's valuation information.
2. Check the valuation amount against the previous 6 valuation classes in order to calculate the appropriate tax.
3. Calculate the real estate tax.
4. Print out all appropriate information: homeowner's name, valuation, tax percentage, and real estate tax.

The above procedure can be applied to any similar tax calculation procedure, and as many cards can be used as there are homeowners. The valuation classes and the tax base may have to be changed.

EX. [4] MONTHLY PAYMENTS FOR A CAR LOAN

The monthly payments of a car loan equal the sum of the principal value of the loan and the monthly interest. If the loan is for financing a new car, the monthly interest is based on the total amount borrowed and therefore does not change from month to month.

The data used as input to calculate the monthly payment of the loan are:

- the customer's name
- the number of the loan
- the amount of the loan
- the interest rate
- the term of the loan

The interest rate is the yearly interest for a loan of $100. The term of the loan defines the number of equal monthly payments to be made to pay off the loan. It is assumed that any number of monthly payments can be made to pay off the loan.

The procedure used to calculate the monthly payment of the loan is as follows:

1. Read in customer's name, loan number, amount borrowed, interest rate, and term of the loan.
2. Calculate the interest for $1, borrowed during 1 year.
3. Calculate the total interest to be paid on the loan.
4. Calculate the monthly interest.
5. Calculate the principal value of the loan.
6. Add 4 and 5 for the monthly payment.
7. Write in the customer's name, loan number, amount borrowed, unit interest, term of the loan, and the monthly payment.

This procedure is executed for several loans and is represented in the flowchart.

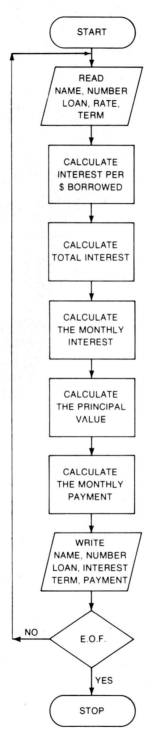

Checking the Logical Flow

A programmer uses flowcharting to establish the logical solution procedure for the problem he is about to code. Flowcharting facilitates the coding and the code will follow the flowcharting steps exactly. It is imperative for the flowcharting to establish the correct logical solution procedure for the problem; for, if the flowchart is incorrect, so will be the coded program. In this section one method for testing the flowchart is discussed.

By the use of some test data, the programmer is able to check whether the flowchart generates the correct anticipated results. If the anticipated results are obtained by manipulating the test data through the flowchart, then there is good reason to believe that the flowchart is correct.

This method is illustrated by the use of the following flowchart, which is supposed to represent the solution flow of the following problem.

Employees at several divisions of Ford Motor Company took a test. The following data has been prepared:

Data Card	*Content of Data Card*
First Card	1. Control value giving the number of employees who took the exam (N)
	2. One of the several division numbers (D)
Remaining Cards	1. Employee's number (S)
	2. Division number where he works (D1)

This data has to be processed in order to compute and output the average score obtained by the employees whose division number appears on the first data card. The following steps are represented in the flowchart:

1. Read the number of the people taking the exam (N) and the division number of interest (D).
2. Initialize the following counters to zero:
   —Counter T, for totaling the scores obtained by employees of division D;
   —Counter K, for the total number of people belonging to division D, and who took the exam;
   —Counter J, for counting the number of people considered in this process.
3. Read the identification number (S), division number (D1), and score (P) of one of the employees who took the exam.
4. If the employee belongs to division D (D = D1), then update counter T and K.
5. If all employees have not been considered (J < N) go to Step 3, otherwise go to Step 6.
6. After all employees have been considered, calculate the average score.

7. Write out the division number of interest (D), the total number of employees in division D who took the exam (K), and their average obtained on the exam (A).

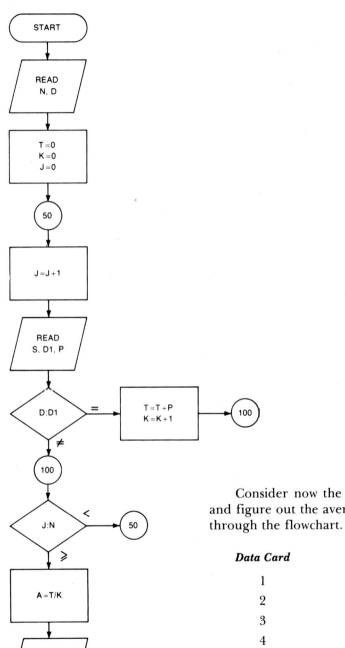

Consider now the following test data and figure out the average, without going through the flowchart.

Data Card	Data
1	5,143
2	47,118,525
3	58,143,612
4	111,148,490
5	143,143,597
6	90,163,720

According to the above data, division #143 is the division of interest. Only two people out of the five who took the exam belong to that division (data card #3 and #5). The average score for division #143 is therefore (612 + 597)/2 = 604.5.

The flowchart can now be checked for errors, by processing the above test data through the flowchart in the form of a **procedure**. This is: consider above data and record all the changes which occur in the variable names in a grid as shown below:

Change \ Variables	N	D	T	K	J	S	D1	P	A
1	5	(143)							
2			0	0	0				
3					1				
4						47	118	525	
5					2				
6						58	143	612	
7			612	1					
8					3				
9						111	148	490	
10					4				
11						143	143	597	
12			1209	(2)					
13					5				
14						90	163	720	
15									(604.5)

The final results therefore are: D = 143

K = 2

A = 604.5

These results coincide with the previously calculated ones, so there is good reason to believe that the flowchart is correct.

Exercises

PROBLEM #1

Draw a flowchart for computing the weekly pay for several employees. The data that should be read in for each employee are:

1. The employee's name.
2. The employee's base pay rate.
3. The employee's number of hours worked.

The flowchart should compute for each employee:

1. The employee's regular 40-hour gross pay.
2. The employee's overtime gross pay (assume that the overtime pay equals 1½ times the base pay).
3. The employee's total gross pay.

Write out the following information for each employee:

1. The employee's name and base pay rate.
2. The total number of hours worked.
3. The regular 40-hour gross pay.
4. The overtime gross pay.
5. The employee's total gross pay.

PROBLEM #2

Draw a flowchart to evaluate capital budgeting proposals. A firm will accept a proposal that has a positive Net Present Value. The Net Present Value is equal to the present value of future cash inflows, resulting from the proposal, minus the initial cash outlay for the proposal.

NPV = Present value of future cash inflows − Original cash outlay

The present value of future cash inflows is computed by multiplying the future yearly inflow by a previously calculated discount factor. (The discount factor is a function of the required rate of return and the number of years of cash inflows. Assume that the discount factor is obtained from tables.)

The input data consists of the initial cash outlay, the yearly cash inflows, and the obtained discount factor.

Generate a listing of the accepted proposals only.

PROBLEM #3

Construct a flowchart that will input ten sets of three numbers (N1, N2, N3). For each set of three numbers output the three numbers and the value of K, where K equals 0 (zero) if the three numbers are unique and K equals 1 (one) otherwise. Check your flowchart for errors by processing the following data through the flowchart in the form of a procedure:

N1	N2	N3
17	18	18
17	14	15
17	19	17
17	0	0
0	17	17
4	5	9
12	12	11
5	3	4
12	12	12
11	22	33

PROBLEM #4

The ABC Computer Center compiles statistics each day on the usage of its system. At the end of each work day a card is punched with the following information:

1. The number of batch jobs run during that day.
2. The number of teletype signons during that day.
3. The total downtime (in minutes) during that day.

For the month of April you are given 30 cards with that data (one for each work day).

Give the flowchart that will input this data and calculate and print the following:

1. Total number of batch jobs run during the month.
2. Total number of teletype signons during the month.
3. Number of days on which there were more teletype signons than batch jobs.
4. Average number of teletype signons on days that had no more than 30 minutes of downtime.
5. The day on which the most batch jobs were run (a number between 1 and 30, inclusive; you may assume that there are no ties).

PROBLEM #5

Consider the following flowchart and data and answer the questions.

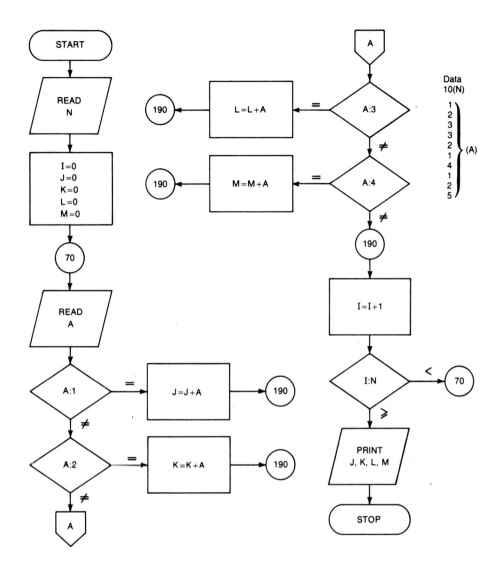

Question 1: At the time that I goes from 6 (six) to 7 (seven) what are the values of:

J _____ K _____ L _____ M _____?

Question 2: What values are printed:

J _____ K _____ L _____ M _____?

3
Introduction to BASIC Programming

BASIC is a high level programming language which closely resembles the ordinary language of mathematics. Each BASIC statement must be broken down and translated into a series of instructions in machine language which can be understood and/or executed by the specific computer in use.

The original BASIC program written by the programmer is known as the "Source Program." The machine program which consists of the machine-coded instructions and which is actually used by the computer is called the "Object Program." The conversion of source programs written in BASIC to a machine language is carried out by a translator. This translator can either be a compiler, or, more likely, an interpreter. The chief difference between a compiler and an interpreter is that the compiler reads the entire source program and translates that in machine instructions before executing them, whereas an interpreter translates and executes each source statement as it reads it. Besides translating the source program in machine language, storage assignments are made, programming errors are checked and messages and diagnoses are printed out.

Due to the general acceptance of the BASIC language, BASIC interpreters are available for most of the computers manufactured in the United States. Each BASIC interpreter is programmed for a specific machine, and that programming must take the actual characteristics of the machine into consideration.

The BASIC language, as discussed here, is relatively independent of the computer in use. Therefore, the BASIC programmer need have no special comprehensive knowledge of the computer, except for a general knowledge of computer operating principles and the types of input and output devices available.

The BASIC Program

The BASIC program is an ordered list of statements or "sentences." Figure 3.1 shows a sample BASIC program.

```
10    READ H, R, D
20    LET W = H*R
30    LET F = (W − 13*D)*.18
40    IF F < 0 THEN: F = 0
50    LET P = W − F
60    PRINT H, R, W, F, P
70    DATA 35, 4.5, 4
80    STOP
90    END
```

Figure 3.1.   A Sample BASIC Program

There are two classes of statements, the **executable statements** and the **nonexecutable statements.** In Figure 3.1, **executable statements** (lines 10 through 60, and 80) are the Input/Output statements (lines 10 and 60), the Assignment statements (lines 20, 30, and 50), and the Control statements (lines 40 and 80). The **nonexecutable statements** are the Specifications, Subprograms and DATA statements (line 70 in Fig. 3.1). The syntax of the different types of statements is explained and discussed in the following chapters. The Input/Output statements direct the computer in transmitting information between the computer's memory and the Input/Output devices. Arithmetic computations and assignments are directed by assignment statements. The logical order in which statements are executed is controlled by the Control statements. The nonexecutable specification statements are descriptive in nature and inform the compiler of the nature and arrangement of Input/Output data, and the allocation of storage. DATA statements provide input values and Subprograms are defined, called for, and used through subprogram statements.

A sequence of statements make up a BASIC program. All statements are preceded by unique ordered statement numbers. This physical ordering of statement numbers is done by the use of integer constants such that the first statement carries a smaller number than the second statement. It is not necessary to give consecutive integer numbers to consecutive statements. In order to facilitate the insertion of statements later it is good practice to number the statements by tens. Some systems will assign statement numbers to statements when asked for; most of these systems will allow for inserting by assigning numbers by tens.

Since the BASIC language is suited for moderately sized scientific and business-oriented problems there are limitations on program size, statement number, statement size, and other details. These limitations vary from system to system. One typical such limitation is:

—program size: no more than 500 statements.

—statement numbers: in the range of 1 through 99999.

—statement size: 255 characters (with an appropriate continuation character, "—", as last character of the physical line).

A BASIC program consists of the following components:

1. Program name
2. Numbered BASIC statements
3. Comments

Program name. BASIC programs are temporarily or permanently stored in files through the teletype or batch input for immediate or later execution. They are filed and retrieved by their name. Depending on the system the file name can consist of any number of characters.

Numbered BASIC statements. Each BASIC statement starts with a unique statement number, generally followed by a BASIC key word.

The key word indicates the function that the statement performs. Here are some of the BASIC key words which are discussed in later chapters:

Key Word	Function
REMARK	Comments
LET (optional)	Assignment
READ	Batch Input
DATA	For Supplying Input
INPUT	Terminal Input
PRINT	Output
STOP	Terminating
END	Terminating
GOTO	Unconditional Transfer
IF (ON GOTO)	Conditional Transfers
FOR-NEXT	Looping
DIMENSION	Dimensioning Arrays
MAT	Matrix Functions
DEF-DEFEND	Function Definition
GOSUB	Transfer to Subroutine
RETURN	Return from Subroutine
RESTORE	Restore the Original Data Stream

Some of the key words may be abbreviated, such as:

REM for REMARK

DIM for DIMENSION

Comments. It is often handy for the programmer to be able to inject notes and general comments into the program to improve readability of the program. These comments are made possible by the use of REMARK. A remark card has to be properly identified by the key word "REM" followed by the comments one wishes to make. Such comment cards are used solely to serve as aids for the program writer or reader in keeping track of the program parts and logic, especially when the program is very lengthy. In the execution of the BASIC program, the comments are ignored and therefore do not affect the operation of the program.

Some BASIC systems allow appending remarks to BASIC statements by having the BASIC statement followed by /*"comment."

EX. [1]

      10   REM INTEREST CALCULATION
      20   LET I=CAP*(1+R)**N−CAP

EX. [2]

      10   LET I=CAP*(1+R)**N−CAP   /*I=INTEREST

The following chapters discuss the BASIC language in detail.

Processing a BASIC Program

The main steps in executing a BASIC job are:

1. Connect and sign into or log into the computing system.
2. Load the BASIC translator into storage (not required on all systems).
3. Input the BASIC program (source program) into the computer through one of several input devices. The input device might be a terminal or a card-reader, which is connected with the computer system.
4. Translate the BASIC program in machine language (or create the object program) by the use of the BASIC compiler or interpreter.
5. Execute the object program and provide data when necessary.
6. Print out the results (if any).

   (Steps 4, 5 and 6 are performed repeatedly for each BASIC statement if an interpreter is used.)

This procedure is represented in the Figure 3.2 schematic diagram.

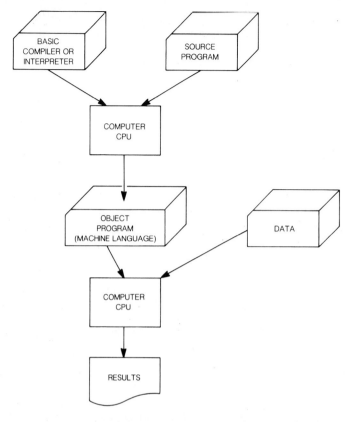

Figure 3.2. *Typical BASIC Program Compiling and Executing Procedure*

The BASIC program is the source program and is written and prepared in machine-readable form (punched cards, paper tapes, teleinput, etc.). This source program is an ordered list of executable and nonexecutable statements. Whereas the executable statements are closely related to the original algorithm or solution procedure as established in the flowchart, the nonexecutable statements describe certain variables and other elements of the program. The source program (BASIC program) is the data for the BASIC compiler, which transforms it into an object program. Any error (referred to as syntax error) that the compiler detects in the source program during compilation is described in the form of a statement reference and a more or less understandable message. If no syntactical or grammatical errors are found during compilation, then the object program is loaded into the computer, which executes the program. The debugging process continues during execution of the program; therefore, more error messages can be generated. Beware of a diagnostic-free program; such a program may produce undesired answers as a consequence of faulty translation of the solution procedure into the BASIC language.

Let us now look at the specific commands and procedure in order to execute the following BASIC program via a terminal.

```
10    PRINT "READ IN TWO CONSTANTS FOR A AND B"
20    INPUT A, B
30    LET C = A + B
40    PRINT "THE SUM OF A AND B EQUALS"; C
50    STOP
60    END
```

Try to figure out what this program does! It is rather straightforward. Statement 10 prints what is in the quotation marks. Statement 20 inputs two values, one for A and one for B. At this time data for A and B must be provided, as will be explained later. In statement 30 the value for A is added to the value of B and the result is assigned to C. Finally, the system will write out the value stored under C when statement 40 is executed. After this the execution of the program will stop.

When executing a BASIC program via the terminal (or in batch mode) we must be familiar with the job control language (JCL) and other control statements of the system that is being used. Therefore, at this point it is necessary that your instructor identifies the appropriate JCL of your system. The JCL used in what follows is standard for the DEC10 system (Digital Equipment Corporation System 10, TOPS Operating System). For your convenience, space is provided so that you can fill in the appropriate JCL for your system while you go through the following steps:

1. Sit down at the teletypewriter (TTY) and set the "DUPLEX" switch to HDX (half duplex) or FDX (full duplex), depending upon the type of system you use.

   Note 1: Most TTY units have such a switch. If you do not find it, you are probably working with a full duplex machine. The "duplex" switch is a toggle switch located at the right hand side of your terminal.

2. Switch the power switch of the acoustic coupler in the ON position. Also, make sure that the switch on the right hand bottom of your keyboard is on LINE. (If you do not have this switch, you must have an ORIGinate switch, which you must depress.)

   Note 2: The coupler is a tan box with two black "ears." If you do not have this box, then your telephone is hard wired with your teletype unit.

3. Dial your computer center.

   Note 3: The phone will ring. If you hear a busy sign, try again later. If you hear a steady, high-pitched tone, then you have successfully reached the computer.

4. As soon as you hear the high-pitched tone, place the phone receiver down on the coupler's ears, where it fits snugly. If you do not have a coupler, then omit this step.

5. Now you are ready to make contact with your system. At this point you should check with your system to find out how you contact the MONITOR.

   On the DEC10 system:
   > Simultaneously press the following two keys, CTRL and C, and follow this by pressing the RETURN key.

   On your system: _____

   _____

   Note 4: The RETURN key is located at the right hand side of the central keyboard. From now on the expression "send the line" will be used to mean "press the RETURN key." Sending a line has the following effects:
   1. The line information you have typed in is sent to the computer.
   2. The typing element returns to its leftmost position and the paper in the teletype is automatically advanced.

6. Wait now until the system types out an acknowledgment. On the DEC10 system a period (.) appears. At this point check your system's manual for the appropriate acknowledgment sign

   which is: _____ .

   Note 5: The acknowledgment sign is a prompting sign. The time-sharing system is now waiting for you to issue a system's command. At this point it must be the login command.

7. Now signon or login by typing

   LOGIN your user number   (send the line)
                                             for the DEC10 system

   or

   _____   (send the line) for your system

   Note 6: If you make an error in typing a character of information, you can delete the character by using the RUBOUT key for the DEC10 system; or by _____ for your system. If you repeat the above procedure "k" consecutive times, then you delete the rightmost "k" characters from the line you are currently typing on. Note that if you have already sent the line by pressing the RETURN key, then it is too late to alter the content of that line by the use of the above procedure.

8. To secure your account you may have a password. The system is ready to receive this now. The DEC10 system prompts you by displaying PASSWORD: Follow this by your password and send the line. Your system: _____

_____ and send the line.

Note 7: If your password is correct, the system may respond with: the time, date, and day of the week. An error message will occur if your user ID and password do not match. The system will let you TRY AGAIN.

9. You will now receive a prompting sign from your system, indicating that it is ready for a system's command. If you want to run a BASIC program, then you must give the following command:

    R BASIC   (send the line) for the DEC10 system

or

_____ for your system

Note 8: Issuing one of the above commands activates the BASIC compiler or translator and the system is ready to receive a BASIC program or ready to run an old BASIC program.

10. Assume you wish to create a new file in which you want to store a BASIC program to run.

—The DEC10 BASIC system will ask you whether you need help. If you wish to create a new BASIC file, then you respond by typing NEW.

                             (send the line)

Then the DEC10 BASIC system will ask for a new file name
    NEW FILE NAME—filename   (send the line)
          (1 to 6 letters)

Finally the DEC10 BASIC system will wait to receive BASIC statements.
—Your system will _____

_____

_____

11. Now you are ready to type your BASIC program line by line. Make sure that each line is numbered and that each line number contains no more than five digits.

Note 9: Some systems automatically number the lines, starting with 10 and incrementing each line count by 10.

Note 10: If you make errors while you type in the program and if you have not sent the line yet, then you can correct these by following the instructions in Note 6 (above).

12. Now type in

    LIST   (send the line) for the DEC10 systems

    or

    _____   (send the line) for your system

Note 11: The command LIST causes a listing of the contents of your file (this is your BASIC source program) at the TTY. Note that file line numbers are shown, together with the content of those lines. Examine this copy for possible typing errors on your part. If you spot a typing error in a BASIC statement, correct the error this way:

1. Type the number of the statement which contains the offending statement, then
2. Retype the entire BASIC statement (including the statement number) and send the line.

This has the effect of replacing the old (incorrect) line in the file with the newly-typed (correct) line of information.

13. Now type in

    RUN   (send the line) for the DEC10 system

    or

    _____   (send the line) for your system

Note 12: Issuing the RUN command causes the BASIC compiler to process your BASIC source program. The compiler may or may not find violations of the BASIC grammar in the source program.

Grammatical Errors Detected

If and when the compiler encounters grammatical errors, it will list the offending BASIC statement at the TTY. Correct the offending statement via the instructions in Note 11 (above).

                                              (send the line)

Now return to step 13.

No Grammatical Errors Found

If no errors are found in the grammar of your BASIC source program, execution of the machine-language equivalent will automatically begin. Go on to step 14.

14. Now type in the data for the program.

Note 13: The program will now come to you at the TTY to get the data via execution of the one or more INPUT statements in your program. Suppose, for example, that the INPUT statement in your program is being executed (statement 20). Then there will be no apparent action at the TTY (because the program will be waiting for you to type in the data and "send the line"). Note carefully that the program *will not tell you* that it is waiting for data unless you "tell it to tell you," that is, unless you have provided in your program, ahead of each INPUT statement, a PRINT statement which outputs a message to the effect "NOW ENTER THE DATA," or "NOW ENTER THE VALUES FOR ALPHA, BETA, AND GAMMA," or whatever. In our example it is the PRINT statement and the "READ IN TWO CONSTANTS FOR A AND B". It is your responsibility as programmer to know *which* INPUT statement the computer has reached in execution of your program. (This can be determined on logical grounds alone, but it can be a tedious determination if there are many different INPUT statements in the program.) In general, for runs in time-shared mode, it is probably best to include a PRINT statement ahead of each INPUT statement, thereby producing messages such as "READ IN TWO CONSTANTS FOR . . .", and listing the variables whose values the user is to supply: "A AND B". Knowing which INPUT statement is being executed, you then type on one line at the TTY the list of values which are to be assigned to the corresponding list of variables in the INPUT statement, as follows:

8,23

When the list of numbers has been typed in, "send the line." The computer then continues with the next step in the execution of your program.

15. Now terminate the Run.

Note 14: If, after a complete data set has been processed, your program executes a STOP statement, this automatically causes the run to terminate. The computer will type a message that it is READY for another command.

16. Now type in

    SAVE   (send the line) for the DEC10 system

or

    _____   (send the line) for your system

Note 15: If you wish to save the BASIC file for a future run, then you must give the above command before you get out of BASIC.

17. Now type in the following to leave the system

    BYE   (send the line) for the DEC10 system

or

    _____   (send the line) for your system

Note 16: Now wait for the system to print out statistics for your run. After producing these statistics, turn OFF your teletype switch, turn OFF your coupler switch, and hang up the telephone.

```
.LOG 57000,274
JOB 45 E.M.U. KL10B V.10B TTY42
PASSWORD:
1501    07-JUN-79        THUR

.R BASIC


READY, FOR HELP TYPE HELP.
NEW
NEW FILE NAME----ABLE

READY
10 PRINT "READ IN TWO CONSTANTS FOR A AND B"
20 INPUT A,B
30 LET C=A+B
40 PRINT "THE SUM OF A AND B EQUALS";C
50 STOP
60 END
LIST


ABLE            15:03           07-JUN-79



10 PRINT "READ IN TWO CONSTANTS FOR A AND B"
20 INPUT A,B
30 LET C=A+B
40 PRINT "THE SUM OF A AND B EQUALS";C
50 STOP
60 END

READY
RUN

ABLE            15:03           07-JUN-79



READ IN TWO CONSTANTS FOR A AND B
?8,23
THE SUM OF A AND B EQUALS 31



TIME:  0.02 SECS.

READY
BYE
JOB 45  USER WU,NESA [57000,274]
LOGGED-OFF TTY42 AT 15:04:11 ON 7-JUN-79
RUNTIME: 0:00:00, KCS:4, CONNECT TIME: 0:02:57
DISK READS:90, WRITES:16, BLOCKS SAVED:200
```

Figure 3.3. *Sample BASIC Run*

Final Note

Some systems allow you to create, to list, to delete, and to execute BASIC files while you communicate with the MONITOR. For the DEC10 system these commands are:

CREATE filename.BAS
TYPE filename.BAS
DELETE filename.BAS
EXECUTE filename.BAS

For your system these commands are:

_____

_____

_____

_____

A complete execution listing for the sample BASIC program is shown on pg. 46. The underlined portion is generated as response by the computing system. The portion of the listing that is entered by the terminal operator (you or me) is not underlined.

Exercises

PROBLEM #1

Read the instructions in this chapter and get acquainted with your terminal and computing system. Adjust the instructions according to your system by filling in the blanks.

PROBLEM #2

Redo the sample run as shown in figure 3.3 on your system.

PROBLEM #3

The following is a complete BASIC program that calculates the wages, the federal tax, and the pay as exhibited in the flowchart on page 21.

```
10    PRINT "INPUT THE NUMBER OF HOURS WORKED"
20    INPUT H
30    PRINT "INPUT THE RATE PER HOUR WORKED"
40    INPUT R
50    PRINT "INPUT THE NUMBER OF DEPENDENTS"
60    INPUT D
70    LET W = H*R
80    LET F = (W − 13*D)*. 18
90    IF F < 0 THEN: F = 0
100   LET P = W − F
```

```
110   PRINT "WAGES = "; W, "FEDERAL TAX ="; F
120   PRINT "PAY ="; P
130   END
```

Use the information from this chapter and run this BASIC program from a terminal. As soon as you execute the above program you are asked to input the number of hours worked, the rate per hour worked and the number of dependents. When you get prompted for this information, give the following values:

35 for HOURS

4.5 for RATE

4 for DEPENDENTS

4

Assignment Statements

An arithmetic assignment statement is a defined operation that causes a change in form, value, and/or location. The processing symbol is, therefore, used to represent the arithmetic statement in a flowchart.

In BASIC the arithmetic statements appear as follows:

$$10 \quad \text{LET D} = \text{C*.045}$$
$$20 \quad \text{LET W} = \text{R*H}$$
$$30 \quad \text{LET A} = \text{S/Q}$$
$$4 \quad \text{A} = \text{B}$$
$$2 \quad \text{P} = 10$$

The arithmetic or numeric assignment statement consists of:

1. The key word **LET** is optional for large systems, however, it must be used for most microcomputers.

2. A variable name to the left of the equal sign.

3. The equal sign.

4. The arithmetic expression to the right of the equal sign.

```
        (LET)
    VARIABLE NAME
         =
ARITHMETIC EXPRESSION
```

Variable Name

A variable is a quantity whose values can be changed. It represents a single storage cell or location into which a constant or number can be stored. The variable name can consist only of either a single letter (**A** through **Z**) or a letter followed by one or two decimal digits. (Most systems allow for only one decimal digit resulting in a total of 286 possible names.) This allows for a maximum of 2,886 different variables in any one BASIC program: 26 single letters; 260 letters followed by one single number including 0; and 2,600 letters followed by a string of two numbers including 00.

The following variables are, therefore, too long:

INTEREST, CAP, LOVE, DUMMY.

Correct variable names are:

A, B, C, C1, C12.

Due to the restriction in the length and combination of letter/number organization of variable names it is almost impossible to construct meaningful variable names. To improve the readability of a BASIC program it is therefore recommended to enter comment statements, explaining the variables used in the program.

Arithmetic Expression

An arithmetic expression is an orderly arrangement of constants and/or variables joined by operators. It is used for computations with numbers.

Examples of arithmetic expressions follow:

C*4.5E−2	[1]
R1*H	[2]
S/Q	[3]
B	[4]
−10	[5]
(W−13.*D)*18E−2	[6]
N+1	[7]
100	[8]

Note that a single constant (expression [8]) and a single variable (expression [4]) can be an expression. As will be explained later, the * is used to indicate a multiplication.

CONSTANTS

Constants are quantities which cannot change. They are fixed numbers, with or without a decimal point.

On the IBM System/360 and on other systems, the magnitude of a constant ranges from 10^{-78} to 10^{75}, with a precision of 7 decimal digits (single precision) up to 17 decimal digits (double precision). If only single precision constants are allowed, then all numbers containing more than seven digits are usually rounded off.

For example:

$$123456789 \text{ is rounded off to } 123456700$$
$$1234.56789 \text{ is rounded off to } 1234.567$$

Note that only significant digits are counted, not leading zeroes.

For example:

$$0.001234567 \text{ is not rounded off}$$

In the previous examples, expressions [1], [5], [6], [7], and [8] contain BASIC constants of various types. There are various ways in which a constant can be written:

1. With a positive or negative sign. A positive sign is optional (Example: -10 in expression [5])
2. With a decimal point (Example: 13. in expression [6]) or without a decimal point (Example: 100 in expression [8].)
3. With the conventional decimal exponent (Example: 4.5E-2 in expression [1] and 18E-2 in expression [6].)

When a BASIC constant is represented with a decimal exponent, then the exponent part E is always followed by a positive or a negative integer exponent constant. The plus ($+$) sign is optional if the exponent is positive. The E stands for the decimal base (10). In the above example, 4.5E-2 stands for 4.5×10^{-2} or equals .045.

When the E format is used, it is necessary to have a BASIC constant of type 1. or 2. preceding the E and the exponent part cannot contain more than two digits.

Other examples of constants are:

+7.1, -2, 999.92, 33.5E10, 7.2E-13, 12345E7

OPERATORS

Variables and constants are connected in an arithmetic expression by operators. The arithmetic operators are:

Addition ($+$)

Subtraction ($-$)

Negation or Unary Minus ($-$)

Multiplication (*)

Division (/)

Exponentiation ($\uparrow$ or **) ($\wedge$ sign is used for some small systems)

Not all systems recognize the "**" operator.

The following examples illustrate how arithmetic expressions are interpreted by the computer:

R1*H1 → multiply the value stored for R1 by the value stored for H1

C2*.045 → multiply the value stored for C2 by 4.5%

C*(1.+.045)10** → multiply the value stored for C by $(1.+.045)^{10}$ to calculate the accumulated savings.

G1−F1 → take whatever value is found in the storage location F1 and subtract it from the value found in the place called G1.

W9*.02 → go to the place called W9 and multiply whatever value is stored therein by .02.

S/X → divide the value stored for S by the value stored for X.

Arithmetic Rules

RULE 1

Basic operations are performed in a specific order or hierarchy, summarized as follows:

1. Expressions are evaluated from left to right.
2. All exponentiations are done first.
3. All multiplications and divisions are done next.
4. Finally, all additions, subtractions and unary minuses are done.

This hierarchy is used to define which of two consecutive operations is performed first.[1] If the first operator is of higher hierarchy than or equal hierarchy to the second one, then the first operation is performed. If not, the second operator is compared to the third, etc. When the end of the expression is encountered, all of the remaining operations are performed from right to left (reverse order).

Examples:

$$2.0*4.0 + 6.0**2/2.0 \qquad [1]$$

In example [1] the operations are performed in the following order:

first **2.0*4.0** with a result equal to 8.0 [8.0 + 6.0**2/2.0]

second **6.0**2** with a result equal to 36.0 [8.0 + 36.0/2.0]

third **36.0/2.0** with a result equal to 18.0 [8.0 + 18.0]

---

1. There are several interpretations to the rule of the hierarchy; all lead to the same result. Above is the IBM interpretation.

fourth **8.0 + 18.0** with a result equal to 26.0

$$-5.0\uparrow2 + 2.0/5.0*10 \qquad [2]$$

In example [2] the operations are performed in the following order:

first **5.0↑2** with a result equal to 25.0 [−25.0 + 2.0/5.0*10]
second **−25.0** with a result equal to (−25.0) [(−25.0) + 2.0/5.0*10]
third **2.0/5.0** with a result equal to .4 [(−25.0) + .4*10]
fourth **.4*10** with a result equal to 4.0 [(−25.0) + 4.0]
fifth **(−25.0) + 4.0** with a result equal to (−21.0)

$$2.\uparrow2.\uparrow3. + 7./2. \qquad [3]$$

In example [3] the operations are performed in the following order:

first **2.↑2.** with a result of 4.0 [4.↑3. + 7./2.]
second **4.↑3** with a result of 64.0 [64.0 + 7./2.]
third **7./2.** with a result of 3.5 [64.0 + 3.5]
fourth **64.0 + 3.5** with a result of 67.5

RULE 2

Parentheses may be used freely to indicate the desired order of operations to be followed by the computer. When there are nested parentheses, the calculations proceed from the inner to the outer parentheses. Within each set of parentheses the rule of the hierarchy is followed in the evaluation of the expression within these parentheses. Necessary parentheses should never be left out, and each left parenthesis should have a matching right parenthesis. There is no limit on the number of paired parentheses used in any BASIC expression.

The following algebraic expression $\dfrac{A + B}{C + D}$ can be written in BASIC correctly as follows: **(A + B) / (C + D).** Omitting any of the parentheses would be an error.

Examples:

$$(2.\uparrow(2.\uparrow3.) + 7)/2. \qquad [4]$$

In example [4] the operations are performed in the following order:

first **2.↑3.** with a result equal to 8. [(2.↑8. + 7)/2.]
second **2.↑8** with a result equal to 256. [(256. + 7)/2.]
third **256 + 7** with a result equal to 263. [263./2.]
fourth **263./2.** with a result equal to 131.5

$$(-5.0)\uparrow2 + 2.0/(5.0*10) \qquad [5]$$

In example [5] the operations are performed in the following order:

first −**5.0** with a result equal to (−5.0) [(−5.0)↑2 + 2.0/5.0*10)]

second (−**5.0**)↑**2** with a result equal to 25. [25 + 2.0/(5.0*10)]

third **5.0*10** with a result equal to 50. [25 + 2.0/50.]

fourth **2.0/50** with a result equal to .04 [25 + .04]

fifth **25 + .04** with a result equal to 25.04

RULE 3

Caution has to be taken in performing exponentiation. Negative numbers can only be raised to integer powers. Positive numbers can either be raised to integer or real powers. If an exponent is not an integer, then the log functions are used during the evaluation.

$$A**B = antilog_{10} (B \cdot log_{10} A)$$

Since the log_{10} of a negative number does not exist, this explains why negative numbers must be raised to an integer number, resulting in repeated multiplication of the number by itself:

$$(-2)**4 = (-2) (-2) (-2) (-2)$$

RULE 4

Two arithmetic operations can never be next to each other.

For example, the correct way for indicating that A is to be multiplied with unary minus B is as follows:

$$A*(-B) \qquad [6]$$

Two constants and/or symbolic names may never appear next to each other. An acceptable way of indicating the multiplication between A and B in algebra is AB. In BASIC, the multiplication has to be indicated explicitly as follows:

A*B

Examples:

Algebra	Correct BASIC	Incorrect BASIC	
A.B	**A*B**	AB	[7]
(A+B)C	**(A+B)*C**	(A+B)C	[8]
$\frac{A+B}{-C}$	**(A+B)/(−C)**	(A+B)/−C	[9]

RULE 5

When a symbolic name is used in an arithmetic expression of a BASIC program, then a constant must have been assigned to that symbolic name in a previous BASIC statement of the same program. Initially, all BASIC variables are undefined. Through LET or a READ statement constants can be assigned to the variables.

Example:

$$10 \qquad D = (A+B)**C \qquad [10]$$

Statement [10] is a legitimate BASIC statement if the values of A, B, and C have been defined in a BASIC statement prior to statement [10]. Some BASIC compilers however preset all of the program's numeric variables to zero. This is however a rare exception to the above rule.

RULE 6

BASIC arithmetic is real arithmetic. Unlike the FORTRAN language, BASIC contains no implicit integer arithmetic by using integer constants.

For example, in the expression:

$$7 + 8/10 \qquad [11]$$

The result equals 7.8.

In order to truncate or drop the decimal part of the result in expression [11] the **INT** function should be used:

$$INT \ (7 + 8/10) \qquad [12]$$

Now expression [12] results in 7.

With a minor modification the **INT** function can be used for rounding to the nearest integer. In [13] the rounding is accomplished by the use of the INT function and by adding .5 to the expression in example [11].

$$INT \ (7 + 8/10 + .5) \qquad [13]$$

Other useful BASIC functions are discussed in a later chapter.

Examples of Arithmetic Assignment Statements

THE ONE-YEAR-INVESTMENT

In calculating the investment of a capital sum at the end of one year, the following formula can be used:

SAVINGS = CAPITAL (1 + INTEREST RATE)

If we chose the following variable names in BASIC;

> **S** for SAVINGS
> **C** for CAPITAL
> **R** for INTEREST RATE

Then the appropriate BASIC arithmetic statement is:

$$\text{or} \quad \begin{array}{lll} 20 & S = C*(1 + R) & [1] \\ 20 & \text{LET } S = C*(1 + R) & [2] \end{array}$$

Note the need for the multiplication sign!

The statements [1] or [2] are valid in a BASIC program, if the variables C and R are previously defined within the BASIC program that contains [1] or [2].

```
 1   LET C = 10000
 2   LET R = .05
20   LET S = C*(1 + R)
```

THE COMPOUNDED INTEREST PROBLEM

The one-year-investment problem can easily be extended to compute the compounded interest after N years, by the use of the following algebraic expressions:

$$\textbf{SAVINGS} = \textbf{CAPITAL} \ (1 + \textbf{RATE})^{\textbf{YEARS}}$$
$$\textbf{INTEREST} = \textbf{SAVINGS} - \textbf{CAPITAL}$$

A complete set of BASIC statements are:

```
10   LET C = 10000
20   LET R = .05
30   LET N = 12
40   LET S = C*(1 + R)↑N
50   LET I = S - C
```

where **C** stands for capital
      R stands for rate
      N stands for years
      S stands for savings
      I stands for interest

THE ECONOMICAL BORROWING AMOUNT

The following algebraic expression is the EOQ (Economic Order Quantity) interpretation to the economic borrowing amount problem:

$$\textbf{EBA} = \sqrt{\frac{2 \cdot \textbf{FC} \cdot \textbf{CASH}}{\textbf{COST}}}$$

Where **FC** is the incremental fixed cost of obtaining money on a loan basis.

CASH is the total amount of cash to be used in next time period.

COST the cost of keeping $1 on hand.

The above expression can be rewritten as follows:

$$\textbf{EBA} = \left(\frac{2 \cdot \textbf{FC} \cdot \textbf{CASH}}{\textbf{COST}} \right)^{.5}$$

A suitable BASIC statement is

$$40 \quad \textbf{LET E1} = \textbf{(2*F*C1/C2)} \uparrow \textbf{.5}$$

where **E1** stands for EBA

F stands for FC

C1 stands for CASH

C2 stands for COST

Again **F, C1,** and **C2** must be defined.

THE ROOT PROBLEM

In computing the roots of

$$\textbf{AX}^2 + \textbf{BX} + \textbf{C} = \text{O},$$

the discriminant must be calculated as follows:

$$\textbf{D} = \textbf{B}^2 - \textbf{4AC}$$

Under the assumption that the discriminant is positive the two roots for the above algebraic statement can be calculated as follows:

$$X1 = \frac{-B + \sqrt{D}}{2A} \qquad \text{or} \qquad X1 = \frac{-B + D^{.5}}{2A}$$

$$X2 = \frac{-B - \sqrt{D}}{2A} \qquad \text{or} \qquad X2 = \frac{-B - D^{.5}}{2A}$$

Under the assumption that A, B, and C are known to BASIC the following three BASIC statements accomplish the task of root finding:

$$10 \quad \textbf{LET D} = \textbf{B**2} - \textbf{4*A*C}$$
$$20 \quad \textbf{LET X1} = \textbf{(-B + D**.5)/(2*A)}$$
$$30 \quad \textbf{LET X2} = \textbf{(-B - D**.5)/(2*A)}$$

String Variables, Constants and Assignment

A string variable handles alphanumeric data. Nonsubscripted string variables can be distinguished from other nonsubscripted variables by their name. Some systems require the use of a single letter, followed by the $ character.

Examples:

A$, B$, Z$

String variables are used to store string constants. For most systems the maximum number of digits that any string may contain is fifteen. A string may contain letters, decimal digits, special characters, and even punctuations. A string constant is always packed in between two quotation marks. For example:

String Constant	String Content	Length
"HELLO"	HELLO	5 characters
""KEEP OUT""	"KEEP OUT"	10 characters
""	empty string	zero characters

Note in the above example the representation of a Null string or empty string. Two adjacent quotes are used if the string represents a quote. One set of the quotes belongs to the string content. A blank in a string constant is counted as a character.

String or alphanumeric variables may appear in assignment statements in two different ways. Firstly, one can assign string constants to string variables through the LET statement as follows:

10 LET A$ = "END OF CHAPTER"

Secondly, one can equate two string variables as follows:

20 LET Z$ = A$

In this example a string constant must previously have been assigned in the program to the string variable A$.

Summary of Rules

1. Basic operations are performed in a specific order ($\uparrow, *, /, -, +$).
2. Parentheses may be used to indicate the desired order of operations.
3. Negative numbers can only be raised to integer powers.
4. Two arithmetic operations can never be next to each other.
   Two constants and/or symbolic names may never appear next to each other.
5. When a symbolic name is used in an arithmetic expression of a BASIC program, then a constant must have been assigned to that symbolic name in a previous BASIC statement of the same program.
6. BASIC arithmetic is real arithmetic. INT function can be used to truncate the result.

Exercises

PROBLEM #1

Write a single BASIC expression for each of the following algebraic expressions:

(a) $x + y^3$

(b) $(x + y)^3$

(c) x^4

(d) $a + \dfrac{b}{c}$

(e)   a[x + b(x + c)]

(g) $a + \dfrac{b}{c + d}$

(f) $\dfrac{a + b}{c}$

(h) $\dfrac{a + b}{c + d}$

PROBLEM #2

Consider the symbolic name I to which an integer constant is assigned that is larger than 10,000. Write one single assignment statement in line 100 that assigns to J the third digit of I (third digit from the right) (ex. 246891, J = 8).

PROBLEM #3

Find the value of X or I after each of the following expressions is executed, and indicate the order of operations.

(a)   10   LET I = INT(25/3**3) + 7/10*(2*(7−3))
(b)   20   LET X = 4/5*(4**2−6)
(c)   30   LET X = 5.0 + 2.0/5.0*25.0**0.5
(d)   40   LET I = INT(7/8**2) + 10/2**3
(e)   50   LET I = 5/2*2**2
(f)   60   LET X = 5.0 + 5.0/5.0**2
(g)   70   LET X = 10.0 − 3.0/5.0*25.00**0.5
(h)   80   LET I = 5.0 + 9.0**0.5/2.0
(i)   90   LET X = 5/6*3/4
(j)   100 LET I = (6/2*5/6) + 2**3

PROBLEM #4

Are the following identical pairs (Yes or No)? Show why they are or are not identical pairs.

(a)   3.167 and 03.167
(b)   87.21E+02 and .008721E+05
(c)   31. and 31
(d)   .0057 and 57.0E-04

PROBLEM #5

Which of the following arithmetic expressions are invalid and why?

(a)   −B − B*B
(b)   E**M + M**E
(c)   AB + C/E
(d)   D − E/1.5 + 6.7/A/X

(e) M**I + E**M

(f) −B − B* − B

PROBLEM #6

Write a correct algebraic expression for each of the following BASIC statements.

(a) 10   LET A = 10 − B/5*25*5

(b) 20   LET I = (A/B*C/D)

(c) 30   LET I = 25/3**3 + 7/10*(2*(7 − 4))

(d) 40   LET K = A/(1.0 + B/(2.7 + C))

(e) 50   LET Y = (10.E − 6 + A*X**3)**(2/3)

PROBLEM #7

Write complete BASIC statements for each of the following:

(a) $k = \dfrac{a}{b} + \dfrac{c \cdot d}{f \cdot h \cdot g}$

(b) $d = \dfrac{\dfrac{a}{b} - 1}{g\left(\dfrac{g}{d} - 1\right)}$

(c) $Q = \dfrac{(10A)^{30}}{B - C}$

(d) $F = \left(\dfrac{A + B}{3}\right)^{c} + D$

(e) $Q = (I + K)^{2^{2}} + 2J^{K} + J$

(f) $y = \sqrt[c]{\dfrac{\left(\dfrac{a}{b}\right)^{2} - 3a}{g\left(\dfrac{g}{d} - 1\right)}}$

5

Input/Output Statements

The purpose of the **INPUT/OUTPUT** statements, to be discussed in this chapter, is to be able to read or to obtain data during the execution of the BASIC program, or to print results which have been obtained during the execution of the program. **INPUT** statements are used to assign constants to variables. The combination of the **READ/DATA** statements is used for batch input (nonterminal programs) and the **INPUT** statement is used for terminal input. The **PRINT** statement is used for batch or terminal output.

The general INPUT/OUTPUT symbol is used to represent a READ, INPUT or PRINT operation in a flowchart.

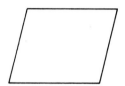

READ, DATA Statement

The general form of the READ statement is

READ ⟨list⟩

where: **READ** is the BASIC keyword that references the read function
⟨**list**⟩ contains an ordered list of variable names and/or input controls, separated by commas.

The READ statement is used for batch input and needs a DATA statement(s), from which it obtains its input values. The general form of the DATA statement is

DATA ⟨list⟩

where: **DATA** is the BASIC key word that references the data function of this statement
⟨**list**⟩ contains an ordered set of constants, separated by commas.

VARIABLES AND CONSTANTS

The variables in the READ statements correspond to the constants in the DATA statements in an ordered fashion:

—the first variable refers to the first constant
—the second variable refers to the second constant
—and so on

During the execution of a BASIC program, the DATA statements are considered to be a large data block that contains the first value of the first DATA statement in its first cell and the last value of the last DATA statement in its last cell.

There should be at least as many constants in DATA statements as there are variables to be assigned through READ statements.

EX. [1]

```
10    READ A,B,C
20    DATA 10,20,30
```

Since the READ statement results in assigning constants to the variables in its list and since the DATA statement provides these constants, the end result of the two BASIC statements in example [1] is the assignment of the constant 10 to the variable name **A,** the assignment of the constant 20 to the variable name **B,** and the assignment of the constant 30 to the variable name **C.** Note that the variable names **A, B,** and **C** are separated by commas. There is no comma at the end of the list in the **READ** statement. A similar observation can be made for the **DATA** statement.

EX. [2]

```
10    READ C,I,N   /*read capital, interest rate and years
20    LET S=C*(1+I)**N   /*calculate the compounded interest
30    DATA 10000, .05, 10
```

The three BASIC statements in example [2] are part of a BASIC program that calculates the savings on a capital investment, where the interest is compounded over **N** years. The READ statement contains three variable names: **C, I,** and **N,** which are separated by commas. At least three pieces of data are necessary. The first variable in the list of the **READ** statement (**C**) gets assigned the first constant in the list of the **DATA** statement (10000). The second constant in the **DATA** statement (.05) is assigned to **I** and the constant 10 is assigned to the third and last variable (**C**) in the list of the **READ** statement.

EX. [3]

```
10    READ C,I,Y$   /*read capital, interest rate and year
20    LET S=C*(1+I)   /*calculate savings at end of year Y$
30    DATA 10000, .05, "1979"
```

Example 3 illustrates how the string constant 1979 is assigned to the string or alphanumeric variable **Y$**. It is good practice to put the string constant in double quotes. Double quotes are necessary when the string contains blanks or commas.

INPUT CONTROLS

A commonly used input control is the SKP (the input data skipping) control.
Its format is:

$$SKP \text{ (exp)}$$

where: **SKP** is the skip control specification
exp is an arithmetic expression

When a **SKP** control is given in the list of the **READ,** then the expression in parenthesis is evaluated. The absolute value, truncated to the integer refers to the number of input constants to be skipped during input. All systems allow for a maximum number of items to be skipped. On some systems one may skip as many as one thousand items.
The **SKP** function is restricted to nonmatrix reading.

EX. [4]

```
10    READ A,B,SKP (2),C
20    DATA 10,20,30,40,50
```

The **READ/DATA** combination in example [4] skips over the constants 30 and 40 and reads 10 for **A,** assigns 20 to **B,** and 50 to **C.**
The SKP control is separated from the other list items by commas.

A similar result is obtained by the following **READ/DATA** arrangement.

```
10    READ A,B,SKP (−1.4*2),C
20    DATA 10,20,30,40,50
```

Note that (−1.4*2) equals −2.8. The truncated absolute value of −2.8 equals 2.

Some systems, however, do not allow the skip control.

Rules

RULE 1

Multiple DATA statements can be used for one READ statement and several READ statements can share one DATA statement.

EX. [5]

    10   READ A,B,C
    20   DATA 10
    30   DATA 20,30

In Example [5] the constant 10 is equated to **A,** the constant 20 to **B,** and the constant 30 is equated to **C.**

EX. [6]

    10   READ A
    20   READ B,C
    30   DATA 10,20
    40   DATA 30

Example [6] is quite legitimate. The variable in the list of the first **READ** statement obtains its constant out of the same **DATA** statement as does the first variable in the list of the second **READ** statement. The second variable in the list of the second **READ** statement obtains its constant assignment from a second **DATA** statement.

RULE 2

DATA statements are nonexecutable statements. Therefore, they may appear anywhere in the program. However, it is good practice to place them at the very end, just before the **END** statement.

The advantage of locating the **DATA** statement at the very end of the program should be obvious! One may wish to change the **DATA** at a later time, which might result in more data than originally planned for and consequently more **DATA** statements will have to be constructed. If the **DATA** statements were at the end, then the renumbering of statements is minimized.

RULE 3

A **DATA** block can contain more constants than required by the **READ** statements. The **READ** statement, however, cannot contain more variables than there are constants in **DATA** statements.

If a **DATA** block contains more constants than required by the **READ** statements, the extra constants are ignored. An "out of data," "end of file," or a similar message is given by the system if the read statement attempts to read in data that does not exist. Since this is a grave error, execution of the BASIC program is terminated.

The INPUT Statement

The general form of the **INPUT** statement is:

INPUT ⟨list⟩

where: **INPUT** is the BASIC keyword that references the terminal input function

    ⟨**list**⟩ contains an ordered list of variable names and/or input controls, separated by commas.

The **INPUT** statement is used for reading data from a terminal. During the execution of the basic **INPUT** statement the system prompts the programmer or the tele-user for the input constants or strings, by printing a question mark(**?**).

When this prefix character (**?**) appears on the teletype the user must input the data items in the correct order and separated by commas.

    Just like for the **READ/DATA** statements, the variables in the **INPUT** statement correspond to the constants the user types behind the prompting prefix character (**?**).

There should be at least as many constants printed as there are variables in the list of the **INPUT** statement. String constants can also be inputed through the **INPUT** statement. These string constants must be enclosed in quotation marks (**"**) and can only be assigned to string variables in the list of the **INPUT** statement.

Example [1] of this chapter looks on the teletype as follows:

10   INPUT A,B,C

During the execution of the above statement the system will prompt for input by printing the prefix character (**?**). The user must then input the correct constants, separated by commas, as follows:

? 10,20,30

Example [2] of this chapter looks on the teletype as follows:

10   INPUT C,I,N   /*input capital, interest rate and years
20   LET S=C*(1+I)**N   /*calculate the compound interest

During the execution of the BASIC program which contains the above statements, the system will prompt the user to input data to execute statement number 10, the **INPUT** statement. As soon as the prefix character (**?**) appears on the terminal, the user must supply the input, as follows:

? 10000,.05,10

Now 10000 is assigned to C, .05 is assigned to **I,** and **N** equals 10. The next statement, statement 20, can now be evaluated.

    If a string has to be inputted, the string must be embedded in quotation marks. Correct string variables must be used in the list of the **INPUT** statement. The skip control (**SKP**) causes a number of items to be skipped. Example [4] of this chapter looks on the teletype as follows:

10   INPUT A,B,SKP(2),C

When the prompting prefix character (?) is given, the data must be supplied as follows:

? 10,20,30,40,50

The PRINT Statement

The general form of the PRINT statement is:

PRINT ⟨list⟩

where: **PRINT** is the BASIC keyword that references the terminal and batch output function.

⟨**list**⟩ contains an ordered list of carriage controls, variable names, arithmetic expressions, messages, and/or output controls.

The **PRINT** function is used for batch and terminal output. The output line is split up into fields of 15 spaces (width). For a 75-column-wide teletype output, there are five fields of 15 spaces each. The data items in the list of the **PRINT** statement are printed, left adjusted in the next available printing zone. If more than five items need to be printed, the output cannot fit on one line. Then, the remainder is printed on the next line, and so on. There exists a way to pack data, as will be explained shortly.

CARRIAGE CONTROL, COMMAS, AND SEMICOLONS

Carriage control characters occur as first items in the list of **PRINT** statements. Carriage control characters control the positioning of the printing paper. They are embedded in quotation marks ("), just like string constants and messsages. Some commonly used carriage controls are:

" "   (one blank embedded in quotes): for single spacing

"**0**"   (one zero embedded in quotes): for double spacing

"**−**"   (one minus embedded in quotes): for triple spacing

"**1**"   (one embedded in quotes): for skipping to the top of a new page (batch) or for skipping 6 lines on the terminal

Double spacing can be obtained through a **PRINT** statement without a list.

If the first item of a **PRINT** statement is a string that contains one of these carriage controls, then the control is executed and is not printed with the other string characters. If the list of a **PRINT** statement does not contain a carriage control character, then single spacing is assumed. The use and effect of certain carriage controls will be illustrated in some examples.

The comma is the normal separator between items in the list. It causes the movement of the printer to the next printing zone. It is legal to put a comma behind the last list item in the **PRINT** statement. This deletes the carriage return.

```
10    PRINT "1***YEAR END SAVINGS***", "1979"
20    PRINT
30    PRINT "CAPITAL", "INTEREST RATE",
40    PRINT "SAVINGS"
```

Above four BASIC PRINT statements are part of a BASIC program. The first **PRINT** statement (10) causes the carriage to skip 6 lines before it prints ***YEAR END SAVINGS***. This takes up the first 22 spaces. The next string is put in the third printing zone, starting in column 31.

The second **PRINT** statement causes the next line to be skipped. The third PRINT statement does not contain any carriage control character; single spacing therefore is in effect. It prints **CAPITAL** in the first printing zone and **INTEREST RATE** in the second printing zone. Since a comma appears behind the last list item of this **PRINT** statement, the printing carriage is not returned. The last **PRINT** statement (40) prints **SAVINGS** on the same line as **CAPITAL** and **INTEREST RATE,** in the third printing zone of that line.

Shorter zones (shorter than 15 columns) can be obtained through the use of **semicolons.** The user should experiment to find the zone length, since this depends largely upon the system. Not all systems support carriage control for terminal output.

VARIABLE NAMES AND ARITHMETIC EXPRESSIONS

Assigned variables in a BASIC program can be printed through calling on them in the list of the **PRINT** statement. Remember that constants can be written in several ways, either in exponential form or not. Some constants will be printed in exponential form, others not. If the constants are exact whole numbers, the nonexponential form is used, otherwise up to six significant digits are printed in E format. The exponential form is used if the constant is smaller than .1 and if the entire significant part of the constant cannot be expressed as a decimal number. The **E** format is also used if the integer number consists of more than nine digits. The user should experiment with constants since not all systems follow the above printing conventions. All systems, however, print constants left adjusted in the printing zones of the output medium. The positive numbers are preceded by a blank space, whereas negative numbers are preceded by the minus sign.

EX. [2]

```
10    LET A=7.23
20    LET B=A*2
30    LET C=-B
40    PRINT A,B,C
```

The four BASIC statements of Example [2] result in the printing of three constants: 7.23, 14.46, and -14.46 as follows: The first constant, 7.23, is printed in the first printing zone and starts in column 2, since it will be preceded by a blank. The second constant, 14.46, is printed in the second printing zone as follows: a blank column 16, the digit 1 in column 17, 4 in column 18, the decimal point in column 19, 4 in column 20, and 6, the last digit, in column 21. The last constant appears in the third printing zone with the minus sign in column 31, followed by 14.46.

The **PRINT** statement can also be used to print results of expressions which are contained in its list.

EX. [3]

        10   LET A=7.23
        20   PRINT A, (A*2), (−A*2)

Example [3] results in the exact same output as Example [2]. Note that constants and expressions can appear together in the list of the **PRINT** statement.

STRINGS OF MESSAGES

Strings of characters can also appear in the list of a **PRINT** statement. Strings of characters are used to label output constants, to put headings for tables and to convey messages with respect to the request of input. Messages should be placed within quotations. These messages are printed exactly as are.

EX. [4]

        10   LET N=2
        20   LET I=.05
        30   LET C=10000
        40   LET S=C*(1+I)**N
        50   PRINT "THE ACCUMULATED SAVING=$";S

The **PRINT** statement in Example [4] results in the following output that starts in column 1:

THE ACCUMULATED SAVING=$ 11025

Since no comma appears between the string characters and the variable name S, the constant associated with S is put immediately behind the string output. If the string and the variable were separated by a comma, then the constant associated with S would have been printed in the next printing zone. This output might not look quite satisfactory.

The production of headings is illustrated in the next example:

EX. [5]

        10   LET N=2
        20   LET I=.05
        30   LET C=10000
        40   PRINT "CAPITAL", "INTEREST", "YEARS", "SAVINGS"
        50   PRINT C,I,N,(C*(1+I)**N)

The first **PRINT** statement prints, left adjusted, the heading of **CAPITAL** in the first printing zone, the heading **INTEREST** in the second printing zone, **YEARS** in the third printing zone, and **SAVINGS** in the fourth printing zone. On the next line statement number 50 prints, left adjusted, 10000 in the first printing zone, .05 in the second printing zone, 2 in the third printing zone, and finally the constant 11025 in the fourth printing zone.

When a BASIC program becomes complex and contains several **INPUT** statements, then it might be wise to prompt the user for **INPUT** by printing some kind of a message. Example [6] illustrates this

EX. [6]

```
10    PRINT "INPUT CAPITAL, INTEREST RATE AND YEARS"
20    INPUT C,I,N
30    LET S=C*(1+N)**N
```

During the execution of the above statements in a BASIC program the first **PRINT** statement prompts the user that it needs data. This reminds the teletypewriter user that the **INPUT** statement will be executed next, and that he should be ready to give the system the capital value, interest rate, and years, as soon as the system prompts him to do so.

The use of these types of **PRINT** statements makes the BASIC program very interactive. They offer the user the advantage of being able to tell what is going on and what input has to be given.

OUTPUT CONTROL FORMATS

The most frequently used output controls are:

TAB	(the output tab function)
;	(list item separator to produce packed output)
,	(normal list item separator)
:	(the output carriage return)

Only the first and last of these need further explanation.

The general form of the **TAB** format is

TAB (exp)

where: **TAB** is the output control to indicate the positioning of the printing head.

exp is an arithmetic expression whose absolute truncated value indicates the column to tab to

EX. [7]

10   PRINT A,B,TAB(40);C

In this example the value of **A** is printed in the first printing zone, the value of **B** is printed in the second printing zone, whereas the value of **C** is printed in the third printing zone, but starting in column 40.

The colon (:) between two list items in the **PRINT** list is used to give a carriage return. It may also occur at the end of a **PRINT** list.

EX. [8]

$$10 \quad \textbf{PRINT A,B,:TAB(20);C}$$

In this example the value of **A** is printed in the first printing zone, and the value of **B** is printed in the second printing zone. The value of **C** is printed on the next line, but starting in column 20.

Summary of ⟨list⟩

READ ⟨list⟩
DATA ⟨list⟩

    variable names and constants
    input controls: **SKP** (skip input data)

INPUT ⟨list⟩

    variable names
    input controls: **SKP** (skip input data)

PRINT ⟨list⟩

    carriage controls: " "   (single spacing)
                   "0"   (double spacing)
                    "–"   (triple spacing)
                    "1"   (skip to top of next page on batch)
                         (skip 6 lines of terminal)
    variable names
    arithmetic expressions
    strings of messages
    output controls: **TAB** (output tab function)
                      ; (list item separator for packed output)
                      , (normal list item separator for zoned output)
                      : (output carriage return)

Exercises

PROBLEM #1

Write a set of PRINT statements that prints the heading: INVESTMENT ACCUMULATION centered on a line of 75 print positions.

This should be followed by the following sentence: THE ACCUMU-LATED SAVINGS OF $100 INVESTED OVER 12 YEARS AT A 5% IN-

TEREST RATE EQUALS $————. Note that the accumulated savings is calculated with the following formula:

$$100 (1 + .05)^{12}$$

PROBLEM #2
Write one BASIC PRINT statement that prints the constants for C, R, Y, and A on one printing line.

PROBLEM #3
Write one BASIC PRINT statement that prints each of the constants for C, R, Y, and A on a separate line. Provide for labeling these constants: C stands for capital; R stands for rate; Y stands for years; A stands for accumulated savings.

PROBLEM #4
Write all BASIC statements for the following: Read from a DATA statement the constant S1, representing the side of a square, two constants representing the smallest side of a rectangle (R1) and the largest side of the rectangle (R2), and two constants, one representing the height of a triangle (T1), the other one representing the base of the triangle (T2). Then calculate the areas of the square (S), the rectangle (R), and the triangle (T). Output and label all pertinent information.

PROBLEM #5
At the Good Samaritan Hospital patients call in to obtain emergency services. Nurses often request the temperature reading of the sick patient before allowing admittance to the emergency pediatric clinic. Since the Good Samaritan Hospital serves the University community, some callers are European and measure the temperature in centigrade.

Write all BASIC statements to INPUT from a terminal the temperature in centigrade and to convert it into fahrenheit equivalence.

Centigrade temperatures are converted to Fahrenheit by multiplying the centigrade temperature by 9/5 and adding 32 degrees.

6
Running Some Elementary BASIC Programs

Stopping and Correcting a BASIC Program

The normal procedure for stopping the execution of a BASIC program is through the **END** or the **STOP** statement. If the **END** statement is used, then it must be the final statement in the program, having the largest line number. The **STOP** statement does not work on all systems.

Some systems allow for the use of a **PAUSE** or a **WAIT** statement. These statements stop the execution of the BASIC program temporarily.

There are other ways to stop the execution of a BASIC program. Some of these are discussed here; their usage, however, is not always recommended! If one tries to go beyond the physical last statement in the BASIC program, then the system tells the user that he is running off the end of the program. This, of course, causes the execution to terminate. When the system wishes to obtain input as a result of the execution of an INPUT statement and no data is available, then type **ENDFILE.** This causes stoppage of the execution of your program. The system will then indicate at which point in the program the execution is terminated and the statement number of the "unsatisfied" INPUT statement is printed. Just like for the **STOP, PAUSE** and **WAIT** statements the **ENDFILE** statement does not work on all systems.

During compilation of a BASIC program syntactical errors are communicated to the programmer. You can follow this by a **STOP,** which will stop the execution of your program. Hitting the Attention or Break key followed by the typing of **STOP** also terminates whatever is going on.

Most time-sharing systems allow for correcting or expanding on a BASIC program. This can be accomplished by simply referencing the correct line number and by retyping the line. That corrected or new line will replace the previous line or will be inserted in the currently active program. A line can be deleted by typing the appropriate line number and by leaving the rest of the line blank. Before running (**RUN** command), listing (**LIST** command), or saving (**SAVE** command), the new program statements are sorted by their line numbers and are rearranged if necessary. The systems editing package, if available, should be used if more complicated corrections must be made.

Examples of Elementary BASIC Programs

In the development of a BASIC program to solve a problem, a major effort should go into constructing the flowchart. When developing the flowchart, keep the BASIC programming language in mind, to the effect that writing the BASIC program will just be a matter of coding. When writing the BASIC program to be run on the computer from a teletype, make the program interactive or conversational. That is, whenever input is required, program the input request into the program by the use of a PRINT statement ahead of the INPUT statement. This is illustrated within the various examples exhibited in this chapter.

COMPUTATION OF GROSS AND NET PROFITS (EX. [1])

Calculation of the Gross Profit and the Net Profit is very straight forward, as exhibited in the flowchart. The Gross Sales Cost, the Cost of Goods Sold, and the Operating Expenses in dollars, after being prompted for, are read into the system. The two PRINT blocks include the calculation of the Gross and Net Profit, since BASIC allows this. Next follows the BASIC program and output.

EX. [1] COMPUTATION OF GROSS AND NET PROFITS

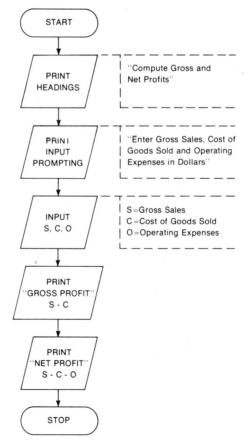

```
10 PRINT "1COMPUTE GROSS AND NET PROFITS"
 20 PRINT " ENTER SALES, COST OF GOODS SOLD, AND OPERATING EXPENSES IN
*S"
 30 INPUT S,C,O
 40 PRINT " GROSS PROFIT", S-C
 50 PRINT " NET PROFIT", S-C-O
 60 STOP




COMPUTE GROSS AND NET PROFITS
ENTER SALES, COST OF GOODS SOLD, AND OPERATING EXPENSES IN $
?100000,89000,10000
 GROSS PROFIT     11000
 NET PROFIT       1000
```

The above BASIC program features the following:

1. The BASIC statements are numbered from 10 to 60, in steps of 10.
2. The first PRINT statement results in typing the headings "COMPUTE GROSS AND NET PROFITS". Note that the first character behind the opening quotation mark, is a carriage control that results in the skipping of six lines on the terminal.
3. The second PRINT statement prompts for the desired input, which gets requested during the execution of the INPUT statement in Line 30.
4. Gross and Net Profit are calculated and printed during the execution of the last two PRINT statements.

EX. [2] REAL ROOTS OF A QUADRATIC EQUATION

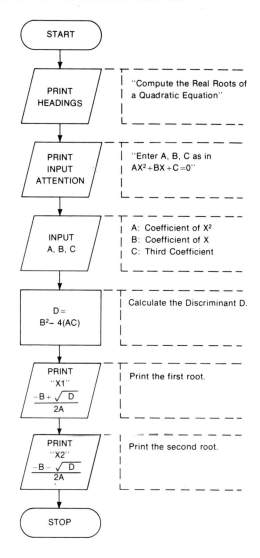

Consider a quadratic equation of the following form:

$$AX^2 + BX + C = 0$$

where **A, B,** and **C** are coefficients. If the discriminant is positive, then this quadratic equation has two real roots.

The discriminant is calculated as follows:

$$D = B^2 - 4AC$$

The real roots **X1** and **X2** are then:

$$X1 = \frac{-B + \sqrt{D}}{2A}$$

$$X2 = \frac{-B - \sqrt{D}}{2A}$$

Under the assumption that the discriminant is positive, the flowchart on the previous page represents this rootfinding procedure. The resulting BASIC program and its output are as follows:

PROGRAM AND OUTPUT

```
10 PRINT "1COMPUTE THE REAL ROOTS OF A QUADRATIC EQUATION"
20 PRINT "ENTER A,B,C AS IN A*X**2+B*X+C=0"
30 INPUT A,B,C
40 D=B**2-(4*A*C)
50 PRINT " X1=",(-B+(D)**.5)/(2*A)
60 PRINT " X2=",(-B-(D)**.5)/(2*A)
70 STOP




COMPUTE THE REAL ROOTS OF A QUADRATIC EQUATION
ENTER A,B,C AS IN A*X**2+B*X+C=0
?1,-2,1
 X1=             1
 X2=             1
```

EX. [3] STRAIGHT LINE DEPRECIATION

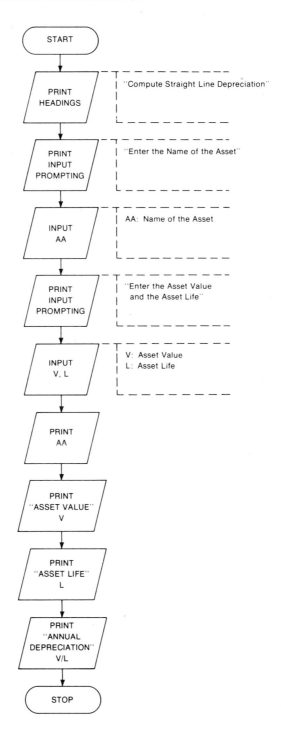

Huron-Plaza-Apartments **(AA)** represents a value of $1,250,000 **(V)** and will be depreciated over 22 years **(L)** (the estimated life of the asset). Using the straight line depreciation method, the annual depreciation equals

$$\mathbf{V/L} = \$1,250,000/22 = \$56,818.18$$

as illustrated in the flowchart and the following BASIC program.

PROGRAM AND OUTPUT

```
10 PRINT "1CØMPUTE STRAIGHT LINE DEPRECIATIØN"
20 PRINT " ENTER THE NAME ØF THE ASSET"
30 INPUT AA
40 PRINT " ENTER THE ASSET VALUE AND ASSET LIFE"
50 INPUT V,L
60 PRINT AA;
70 PRINT " ASSET VALUE",V
80 PRINT " ASSET LIFE",L
90 PRINT " ANNUAL DEPRECIATIØN",V/L
100 STØP




 CØMPUTE STRAIGHT LINE DEPRECIATIØN
 ENTER THE NAME ØF THE ASSET
?HURØN-PLAZA-APARTMENTS
 ENTER THE ASSET VALUE AND ASSET LIFE
?1250000,22
 HURØN-PLAZA-APARTMENTS
 ASSET VALUE     1250000
 ASSET LIFE      22
 ANNUAL DEPRECIATIØN            56818.18
```

As indicated in Chapter 4 (string variables, etc.), some systems require the use of a single letter, followed by the $ character to represent a string variable. The BASIC compiler for the IBM 360/67 at UM does not follow this convention. This compiler accepts names consisting of two identical letters, or two identical letters followed by a single decimal digit. Since most programs in the BASIC book are run on the IBM 360/67 at UM, these string conventions are used. The string variable used in this program is **AA** (Lines 30 and 60). On other systems these statements might look as follows:

30   INPUT A$
60   PRINT A$

```
START
↓
PRINT
"INPUT
INTEGER
PLEASE"
↓
INPUT
C
↓
R5 =
C−INT (C/5)*5
↓
R7 =
C−INT(C/7)*7
↓
R9 =
C−INT(C/9)*9
↓
PRINT
R5
↓
PRINT
R7
↓
PRINT
R9
↓
STOP
```

EX. [4] THE REMAINDER OF A DIVISION

Consider dividing the integer constant 9999 by the integer constant 5. The truncated integer result is 1999 and the remainder is 4. This remainder can be obtained by subtracting from the original integer constant 9999 the product of the truncated integer quotient with the divisor 5. In BASIC, the truncated integer quotient is obtained by the use of the **INT** function, as explained in Chapter 4. The above procedure can be used to calculate the remainders which result when a constant **C** is divided by 5, 7, and 9 and is illustrated in this flowchart and in the following BASIC program.

PROGRAM AND OUTPUT

```
10 PRINT "INPUT INTEGER CONSTANT PLEASE"
20 INPUT C
30 LET R5 = C-INT(C/5)*5
40 LET R7 = C-INT(C/7)*7
50 LET R9 = C-INT(C/9)*9
60 PRINT "REMAINDER WHEN ";C;" IS DIVIDED BY 5 = ";R5
70 PRINT "REMAINDER WHEN ";C;" IS DIVIDED BY 7 = ";R7
80 PRINT "REMAINDER WHEN ";C;" IS DIVIDED BY 9 = ";R9
90 STOP


 INPUT INTEGER CONSTANT PLEASE
?9999
 REMAINDER WHEN  9999 IS DIVIDED BY 5 =  4
 REMAINDER WHEN  9999 IS DIVIDED BY 7 =  3
 REMAINDER WHEN  9999 IS DIVIDED BY 9 =  0
```

Exercises

PROBLEM #1

You are required to draw a flowchart and to write a program that will calculate the yearly compounded interest (to be earned at the end of 1979) for an investment of $75 made by your parents at the end of the year of your birth. Assume that the interest rate was always constant and is 4¾% yearly.

Assume that you run your program from the terminal and INPUT the investment ($75), your name, and date of birth.

Besides your name and a reasonable title, you are expected to PRINT your date of birth and the compounded interest, which should be labeled as follows: "Accumulated interest earned at the end of 1979 on the $75 invested the last day of 19__ equals_____".

PROBLEM #2

Write a BASIC program that INPUTS two sets of data from a terminal:

Set #1: Customer's name, quantity ordered, and discount ($) for each 100 dollars of merchandise he buys (no discount on units or tens of dollars).

Set #2: Rate per unit quantity.

Have the program calculate the amount the customer owes the company, given the above information and PRINT out with appropriate headings:

Customer's name, quantity bought, rate/unit, discount, and amount due. Before writing the program, flowchart the solution procedure.

PROBLEM #3

Here is CHARLIE BROWN!!!!! As a result of a BASIC program, a picture of Charlie Brown was printed as shown:

You are required to write a complete BASIC program that will result in this "piece of art" without the use of a READ or INPUT statement.

Note: The alphanumeric characters used in printing the picture are:

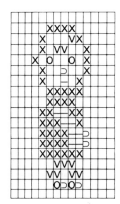

the letters X, V, O

the minus sign −

the sign for closing parenthesis)

PROBLEM #4

Write a program which INPUTS the name of an automobile and its price. Assume a 4% sales tax. Print out, with the appropriate headings, the name, price, sales tax, and the total cost of the automobile.

PROBLEM #5

Weighted Average Cost of Capital given the following input data:·

    1. total capitalization (T)
    2. amount of debt (D)
    3. amount of preferred stock (P)
    4. amount of net worth (W)
    5. the after-tax cost of a debt (C1)
    6. the after-tax cost of preferred stock (C2)
    7. the after-tax cost of net worth (C2)

Draw a detailed flowchart and write a BASIC program to be run from the terminal to calculate the weighted average cost of capital (W4).

The weighted average cost of capital is the sum of three weighted costs:

1. weighted cost of the debt (W1): $W1 = \left(\dfrac{D}{T}\right) C1$

2. weighted cost of preferred stock (W2): $W2 = \left(\dfrac{P}{T}\right) C2$

3. weighted cost of the net worth (W3): $W3 = \left(\dfrac{W}{T}\right) C3$

PROBLEM #6

Under the assumption that:

$$24 \text{ hours } = 1 \text{ day}$$
$$7 \text{ days } = 1 \text{ week}$$
$$4 \text{ weeks } = 1 \text{ month}$$
$$12 \text{ months} = 1 \text{ year}$$

design a flowchart and write a program that inputs a number of hours and breaks the hours down in years, months, weeks, days, and remaining hours. Output the original hours and the constituent years, months, weeks, days, and hours.

PROBLEM #7 THE ORIGINAL INVESTMENT PROBLEM

Assume you receive $3,000 from an investment you made ten years ago. For income tax purposes you must know what the amount of the original investment was. All you can determine, other than the already given information, is that the interest rate on the investment was 6%.

Draw a flowchart to determine the original investment, and then write a BASIC program and run it from the terminal.

7
Transfer Statements

In BASIC, as in all programming languages, statements are executed sequentially, in the sequence in which they are written. However, if one wishes to alter this logical flow of execution, one can use a large variety of transfers. The following transfer statements are discussed in this chapter.

1. The Unconditional GOTO statement
2. The Computed or Conditional GOTO statement
3. The IF-THEN statements

GOTO Statement

The **GOTO** statement is an unconditional transfer statement. It is the simplest transfer. The general form of the GOTO statement is:

GOTO n

where: **n** is a statement number or line number of an executable statement in the program to which control must be made

This transfer command offers the opportunity to transfer control to a statement, other than the next one in sequence. Control should not be transferred to a nonexecutable statement and the statement to which control is transferred must be labeled "n."

EX. [1] THE COMPOUNDED INTEREST PROBLEM

The following flowchart describes the flow of

1. inputting the interest rate per unit dollar (**R**)
2. calculating the quarterly interest rate per unit dollar (**Q**)
3. assigning one hundred to **A**, the capital value
4. calculating the year-end capital value due to quarterly compounding
5. calculating the effective interest (**B**), the simple interest (**R**), the quarterly interest (**Q**) in percentage
6. writing out the **R, Q,** and **B**

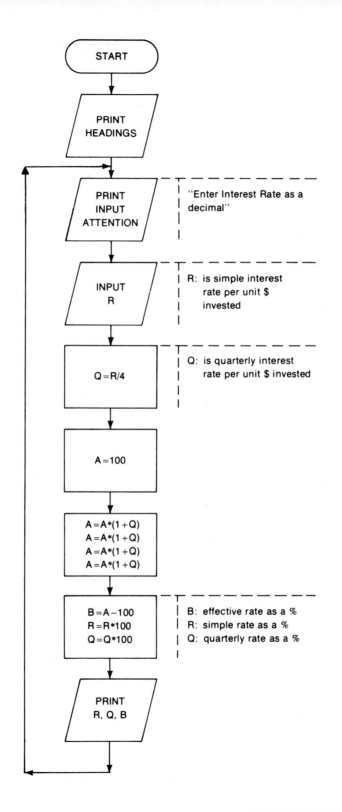

This flowchart is coded in BASIC as follows:

```
10 PRINT "1COMPUTE EFFECTIVE ANNUAL INTEREST DUE TO QUARTERLY"
20 PRINT " COMPOUNDING"
30 PRINT " ENTER INTEREST RATE AS A DECIMAL"
40 INPUT R
50 Q=R/4
60 A=100
70 A=A*(1+Q)
80 A=A*(1+Q)
90 A=A*(1+Q)
100 A=A*(1+Q)
110 B=A-100
120 R=R*100
130 Q=Q*100
140 PRINT " SIMPLE INTEREST    ",R,"%"
150 PRINT " QUARTERLY INTEREST   ",Q,"%"
160 PRINT " EFFECTIVE INTEREST   ",B,"%"
170 GOTO 30
```

The first two PRINT statements (lines 10 and 20) provide for printing the heading. The third PRINT statement:

30   PRINT "ENTER INTEREST RATE AS A DECIMAL"

prompts the user of this program for input, since the next statement:

40   INPUT R

results in a question mark (?). At that point the system is asking for input. Statements 70, 80, 90, and 100 can be pulled together as follows:

70   A=A*(1+Q)4**

The **GOTO 30** transfers control to line 30, the "input prompting" PRINT statement. If the user wishes to discontinue or stop the routine, then he can type **%ENDFILE,** which ends the program.

Note that the **GOTO** statement causes the computer to execute this BASIC program for several sets of data.

The output for the above program is as follows:

```
COMPUTE EFFECTIVE ANNUAL INTEREST DUE TO QUARTERLY
COMPOUNDING
ENTER INTEREST RATE AS A DECIMAL
?.06
   SIMPLE INTEREST                  6             %
   QUARTERLY INTEREST               1.5           %
   EFFECTIVE INTEREST               6.136355      %
ENTER INTEREST RATE AS A DECIMAL
?.25
   SIMPLE INTEREST                  25            %
   QUARTERLY INTEREST               6.25          %
   EFFECTIVE INTEREST               27.44293      %
ENTER INTEREST RATE AS A DECIMAL
?.50
   SIMPLE INTEREST                  50            %
   QUARTERLY INTEREST               12.5          %
   EFFECTIVE INTEREST               60.18066      %
ENTER INTEREST RATE AS A DECIMAL
?1.00
   SIMPLE INTEREST                  100           %
   QUARTERLY INTEREST               25            %
   EFFECTIVE INTEREST               144.1406      %
ENTER INTEREST RATE AS A DECIMAL
?%ENDFILE
```

Note the printed question marks (?) when the system desires input. The compounded interest problem is run for four sets of data:

$$R=.06 \qquad \text{or } 6\%$$
$$R=.25 \qquad \text{or } 25\%$$
$$R=.50 \qquad \text{or } 50\%$$
$$R=1.00 \qquad \text{or } 100\%$$

The **%ENDFILE** terminates the execution of this **BASIC** program. Some systems do not accept **%ENDFILE**; in this case a **CONTROL C** (simultaneously depressing the **CONTROL** and **C** keys) is used to discontinue processing.

EX. [2] COMPUTE THE ECONOMIC ORDER QUANTITY—EOQ

EOQ stands for the "economic order quantity," when stock replenishment is instantaneous.
The EOQ depends on:

the annual usage of stock, or number of units per period: **S**
the order cost per order: **O**
the carrying cost per item and per period: **C**

The EOQ, Q, can be calculated through the following formula:

$$Q = \sqrt{\frac{2 \times S \times O}{C}}$$

The flowchart is as follows:

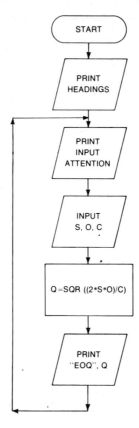

The flowchart is coded in BASIC as follows:

```
10 PRINT " CØMPUTE ECØNØMIC ØRDER QUANTITY"
20 PRINT " ENTER # UNITS PER PERIØD,ØRDER CØST PER ØRDER"
40 PRINT " & CARRYING CØST PER ITEM PER PERIØD"
50 INPUT S,Ø,C
60 Q=SQR((2*S*Ø)/C)
70 PRINT " EØQ",Q
80 GØ TØ 20
```

Again, the second and third PRINT statement (line 20 and 40) prompt the user for input.

Line 60 is an arithmetic assignment statement:

$$60 \quad Q=SQR(\ (2*S*O)/C)$$

It contains the square root (**SQR**) function. In a later chapter other BASIC functions will be discussed. The square root function takes the square root of the expression in the **SQR** argument: **(2*S*O)/C**. Same result can be obtained by rewriting line 60 as follows:

60   Q=((2*S*O)/C)**.5

The **GOTO** statement causes the program to be executed for more than one set of data. Two sets of data are used here! The **%ENDFILE** (or **CONTROL C**) terminates the execution of this program. The above program generates the following output:

```
CØMPUTE ECØNØMIC ØRDER QUANTITY
ENTER # UNITS PER PERIØD,ØRDER CØST PER ØRDER
& CARRYING CØST PER ITEM PER PERIØD
?100,500,25
  EØQ             63.24555
ENTER # UNITS PER PERIØD,ØRDER CØST PER ØRDER
& CARRYING CØST PER ITEM PER PERIØD
?5,10,100
  EØQ             1
ENTER # UNITS PER PERIØD,ØRDER CØST PER ØRDER
& CARRYING CØST PER ITEM PER PERIØD
?%ENDFILE
```

The Computed or Conditional GOTO Statement

The general form of the computed GOTO statement is:

GOTO (n_1, n_2, n_3, . . ., n_m), exp

where: n_1, n_2, n_3, . . ., n_m are line numbers
   exp is an arithmetic expression whose truncated numeric value is used to select a line number

Some systems use the following general form:

ON exp GOTO n_1, n_2, n_3, . . ., n_m

where: **exp** is an arithmetic expression whose truncated numeric value is used to select a line number

n_1, n_2, n_3, . . ., n_m are line numbers

The computed **GOTO** statement provides us with a m-way check and one single transfer, based upon the truncated value of the expression. The truncated value of the expression is computed and checked for being between one and the number of line numbers. The execution of the program terminates if that truncated value is not between one and the number of line numbers. Otherwise a transfer is made as follows:

if the truncated value of the expression equals **1**, then transfer is made to n_1

if the truncated value of the expression equals **2**, then the transfer is made to n_2

•

•

•

if the truncated value of the expression equals **m**, then the transfer is made to n_m

The following decision set-up can be used in a flowchart for a multiple check and a one-way transfer:

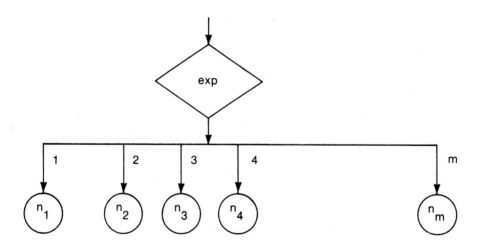

EX. [3] THE QUARTERLY COMPOUNDED INTEREST PROBLEM

This example is similar to example [1] at the beginning of this chapter. It calculates the compounded rate and interest according to the following flowchart.

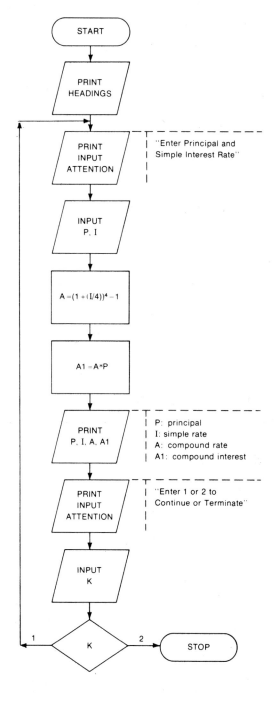

The flowchart is coded in BASIC as follows:

```
10 PRINT "1CØMPUTE CØMPØUND INTEREST (QUARTERLY CØMPØUNDING)"
20 PRINT " ENTER PRINCIPLE AND SIMPLE INTEREST RATE"
30 INPUT P,I
33 LET A=(1+(I/4))**4-1
36 LET A1=A*P
40 PRINT " PRINCIPLE",P
50 PRINT " SIMPLE RATE",I
60 PRINT " CØMPØUND RATE",A
70 PRINT " CØMPØUND INTEREST",A1
80 PRINT " ENTER 1 ØR 2 TØ CØNTINUE ØR TERMINATE"
90 INPUT K
100 GØTØ (10,110),K
110 STØP
```

Note the consequences of lines 90 and 100:

90   INPUT K

100   GOTO (10, 110), K

The computed **GOTO** enables the user of this program to stop its execution by reading in a value of 2 for **K**. If **K** equals **1**, the program will execute line 10 and therefore continue execution.

The above program generates the following output:

```
 CØMPUTE CØMPØUND INTEREST (QUARTERLY CØMPØUNDING)
 ENTER PRINCIPLE AND SIMPLE INTEREST RATE
?100,.06
 PRINCIPLE         100
 SIMPLE RATE       0.06
 CØMPØUND RATE    6.136355E-2
 CØMPØUND INTEREST               6.136355
 ENTER 1 ØR 2 TØ CØNTINUE ØR TERMINATE
?1


 CØMPUTE CØMPØUND INTEREST (QUARTERLY CØMPØUNDING)
 ENTER PRINCIPLE AND SIMPLE INTEREST RATE
?250,.10
 PRINCIPLE         250
 SIMPLE RATE       0.1
 CØMPØUND RATE    0.1038129
 CØMPØUND INTEREST               25.95322
 ENTER 1 ØR 2 TØ CØNTINUE ØR TERMINATE
?2
```

The IF-THEN Statements

IF-THEN statements are transfer statements which are suitable for a two-way branching. Three types of **IF-THEN** statements are discussed here. The **IF-THEN** statements are easier to read than the computed **GOTO** statements, since they are closer to the English language.

TYPE 1

The general form of the **type 1 IF-THEN** statement is:

$$\textbf{IF exp1 reln exp2 THEN n}$$

Some BASIC versions allow:

$$\textbf{IF exp1 reln exp2 THEN GOTO n}$$

where: **n** is a line number, just like in **GOTO n**

exp1 & exp2 are arithmetic expressions
reln is a relational operator
exp1 reln exp2 is a logical expression

Several relational operators are used in BASIC. The six relational operators are:

BASIC representation	Algebraic form	Meaning
=	=	equal to
>	>	greater than
<	<	less than
< >	≠	not equal to
< =	≤	less than or equal to
> =	≥	greater than or equal to

In the logical expression, arithmetic expression number 1 and arithmetic expression number 2 are evaluated and compared to see whether they satisfy the relational operator. If the relation does not hold (or is **FALSE**), then control passes to the next executable statement. If the relation holds (or is **TRUE**), then control is transferred to line number n.

EX. [4] FIND THE REAL ROOTS OF A QUADRATIC EQUATION

Consider a quadratic equation of the following form:

$$\textbf{AX}^2 + \textbf{BX} + \textbf{C} = \textbf{0,}$$

where **A, B,** and **C** are coefficients. This quadratic equation has two real roots, call them **X1** and **X2,** if the discriminant, **D**=**B**^{2}−**4AC,** is positive. If the discriminant is negative, then there is a real and imaginary part. This simple procedure as outlined by the following flowchart calculates and checks the discriminant. If the discriminant is positive, the two roots are calculated as follows:

$$X1 = \frac{-B + \sqrt{D}}{2A}$$

$$X2 = \frac{-B - \sqrt{D}}{2A}$$

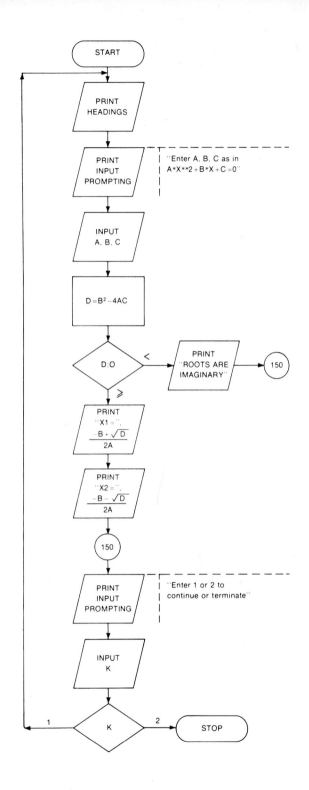

The flowchart is coded in BASIC as follows:

```
10 PRINT "1COMPUTE THE REAL ROOTS OF A QUADRATIC EQUATION"
20 PRINT " ENTER A,B,C AS IN A*X**2 + B*X + C = 0"
25 INPUT A,B,C
30 D=B**2-(4*A*C)
40 IF D>=0 THEN 70
50 PRINT " THE ROOTS ARE IMAGINARY"
60 GOTO 150
70 PRINT " X1=",(-B+SQR(D))/(2*A)
80 PRINT " X2=",(-B-SQR(D))/(2*A)
150 PRINT " ENTER 1 OR 2 TO CONTINUE OR TERMINATE"
160 INPUT K
170 GOTO (10,180),K
180 STOP
```

This program contains several transfer statements: an **IF-THEN** statement (line 40), a simple **GOTO** statement (line 60) and a computed **GOTO** statement (line 170). The **IF-THEN** statement in line 40:

$$40 \quad \text{IF } D >= 0 \text{ THEN } 70$$

checks on the value of **D** (the discriminant which is evaluated in line 30). If **D** is larger than or equal to 0, then control is passed to line 70; otherwise the next statement is executed, which results in the printing of **"THE ROOTS ARE IMAGINARY"**.

Line 70 and line 80 prints and calculates the two roots, which are labeled **X1** and **X2**.

The **INPUT** and the computed **GOTO** statements in line 160 and 170 respectively are used to stop or to continue execution with another set of data.

This program generates the following output:

```
 COMPUTE THE REAL ROOTS OF A QUADRATIC EQUATION
 ENTER A,B,C AS IN A*X**2 + B*X + C = 0
?1,-2,3
 THE ROOTS ARE IMAGINARY
 ENTER 1 OR 2 TO CONTINUE OR TERMINATE
?1
```

```
COMPUTE THE REAL ROOTS OF A QUADRATIC EQUATION
ENTER A,B,C AS IN A*X**2 + B*X + C = 0
?1,-2,1
X1=              1
X2=              1
ENTER 1 OR 2 TO CONTINUE OR TERMINATE
?1




COMPUTE THE REAL ROOTS OF A QUADRATIC EQUATION
ENTER A,B,C AS IN A*X**2 + B*X + C = 0
?1,-3,-4
X1=              4
X2=             -1
ENTER 1 OR 2 TO CONTINUE OR TERMINATE
?1




COMPUTE THE REAL ROOTS OF A QUADRATIC EQUATION
ENTER A,B,C AS IN A*X**2 + B*X + C = 0
?1,-9,3
X1=              8.653312
X2=              0.3466881
ENTER 1 OR 2 TO CONTINUE OR TERMINATE
?1




COMPUTE THE REAL ROOTS OF A QUADRATIC EQUATION
ENTER A,B,C AS IN A*X**2 + B*X + C = 0
?-3,-2,1
X1=             -1
X2=              0.3333333
ENTER 1 OR 2 TO CONTINUE OR TERMINATE
?2
```

EX. [5]: THE BREAK-EVEN ANALYSIS

The break-even point for a product is a function of the sales price (**S**), the variable cost (**V**), and the total fixed cost (**F**) of that product. If the sales price is smaller than the total variable cost, one should cease operating, to avoid losing money.

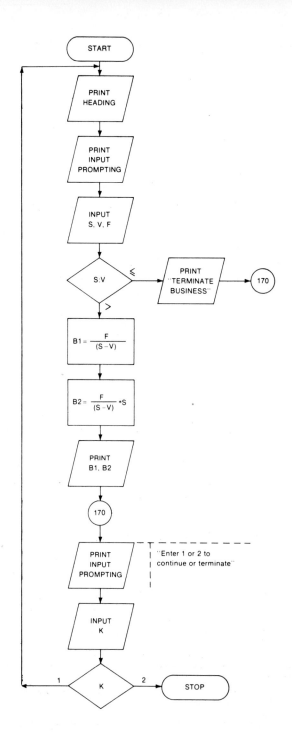

The break-even point can be calculated in sales volume (**B1**) or dollar value (**B2**).

In sales volume, the break-even point is:

$$\mathbf{B1} = \frac{\mathbf{F}}{\mathbf{S - V}}$$

In dollar value, the break-even point is:

$$\mathbf{B2} = \left(\frac{\mathbf{F}}{\mathbf{S - V}}\right) \mathbf{S}$$

The following procedure is used to calculate the break-even point and to decide whether the operation is profitable.

1. Obtain information of the product in terms of: sales price (**S**), variable cost (**V**), and total fixed cost (**F**).
2. If **S** is less than or equal to **V**, do not operate.
3. If **S** is larger than **V**, operate.

$$\mathbf{B1} = \frac{\mathbf{F}}{\mathbf{(S - V)}}$$

$$\mathbf{B2} = \frac{\mathbf{F}}{\mathbf{(S - V)}} \cdot \mathbf{S}$$

4. Write out all appropriate information.

Above procedure, as represented by the flowchart, is coded in **BASIC** as follows:

```
10 PRINT "1BREAKEVEN ANALYSIS"
20 PRINT " ENTER SALE PRICE PER UNIT"
30 INPUT S
40 PRINT " ENTER VARIABLE COST PER UNIT"
50 INPUT V
60 PRINT " ENTER TOTAL FIXED COSTS"
70 INPUT F
80 IF S>V THEN 120
90 PRINT " SALE PRICE DOES NOT COVER VARIABLE COST.   TERMINATE"
100 PRINT " BUSINESS OPERATION TO AVOID A LOSS!"
110 GOTO 170
120 B1=F/(S-V)
130 B2=(F/(S-V))*S
140 PRINT " SALE PRICE, V. COST, F. COST",S,V,F
150 PRINT " B.E. IN UNITS",B1
160 PRINT " B.E. IN $ SALES",B2
170 PRINT " ENTER 1 TO CONTINUE, 2 TO TERMINATE"
180 INPUT K
190 GOTO (10,200),K
200 PRINT " IT HAS BEEN A PLEASURE TO SERVE YOU!"
210 STOP
```

The following output is generated:

```
 BREAKEVEN ANALYSIS
 ENTER SALE PRICE PER UNIT
?10
 ENTER VARIABLE CØST PER UNIT
?9
 ENTER TØTAL FIXED CØSTS
?100
 SALE PRICE, V. CØST, F. CØST  10              9            100
 B.E. IN UNITS  100
 B.E. IN $ SALES              1000
 ENTER 1 TØ CØNTINUE, 2 TØ TERMINATE
?1




 BREAKEVEN ANALYSIS
 ENTER SALE PRICE PER UNIT
?9
 ENTER VARIABLE CØST PER UNIT
?10
 ENTER TØTAL FIXED CØSTS
?1000
 SALE PRICE DØES NØT CØVER VARIABLE CØST.  TERMINATE
 BUSINESS ØPERATIØN TØ AVØID A LØSS!
 ENTER 1 TØ CØNTINUE, 2 TØ TERMINATE
?1




 BREAKEVEN ANALYSIS
 ENTER SALE PRICE PER UNIT
?17.95
 ENTER VARIABLE CØST PER UNIT
?14.50
 ENTER TØTAL FIXED CØSTS
?25000
 SALE PRICE, V. CØST, F. CØST  17.95          14.5         25000
 B.E. IN UNITS  7246.377
 B.E. IN $ SALES              130072.5
 ENTER 1 TØ CØNTINUE, 2 TØ TERMINATE
?2
 IT HAS BEEN A PLEASURE TØ SERVE YØU!
```

TYPE 2

The general form of the **Type 2 IF-THEN** statement is:

IF exp1, reln exp2 THEN (n_1, n_2, n_3, . . ., n_m), exp3

where: **(n_1, n_2, n_3, . . ., n_m)** is an ordered list of line numbers, just as in a computed GOTO

exp1, exp2 and exp3 are arithmetic expressions
reln is a relational operator
exp1 reln exp2 is a logical expression

Again one of the before-mentioned relational operators can be used, in the logical expression of this second type of IF-THEN statement (=, >, <, <>, <=, >=). In the logical expression, arithmetic expression number 1 and arithmetic expression number 2 are evaluated and the results are compared to see whether they satisfy the relational operator. If the relation does not hold (or is **FALSE**), then control passes to the next executable statement. If the relation holds (or is **TRUE**), then control is transferred to one of the line numbers in the list of **(n_1, n_2, n_3, . . ., n_m)** according to the value of exp3, as follows:

if the truncated value of exp3 equals **1**, then transfer is made to n_2

if the truncated value of exp3 equals **2**, then transfer is made to n_2

-
-
-

if the truncated value of exp3 equals **m,** then transfer is made to n_m.

Again, the truncated value of exp3 must be between one and the number of line numbers, to avoid termination of execution. Example [6] illustrates the use of this IF-THEN statement.

EX. [6] THE SALARY INCREASE PROBLEM

The following flowchart illustrates the updating of employee's data records for a salary increase.

If an employee has worked 1 year, his salary increase is $100
If an employee has worked 2 years, his salary increase is $100 more, or $200
If an employee has worked 3 years, his salary increase is $200 more, or $400
If an employee has worked 4 years, his salary increase is $200 more, or $600
If an employee has worked 5 years, his salary increase is $400 more, or $1,000
If an employee has worked 6 years, his salary increase is $500 more, or $1,500

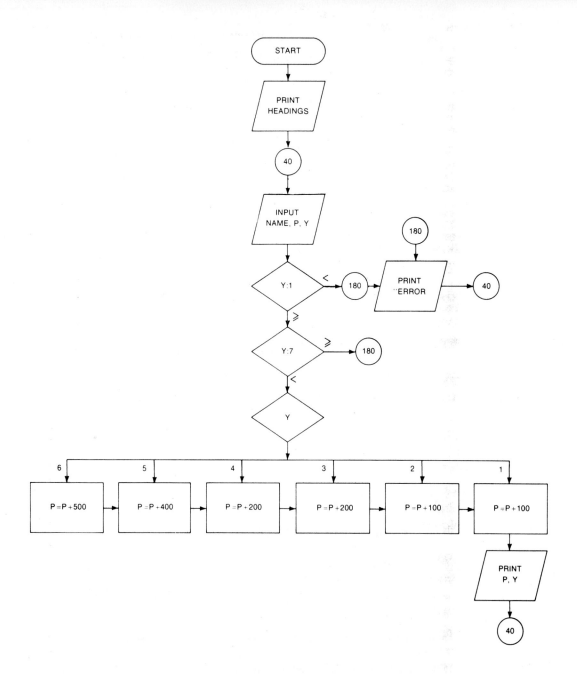

It is known that all employees have been with the company for at least one year, but none for more than 6 years. If someone's record shows less than one year, then an error message should be given.

The information that is read in for each employee contains his name, his yearly income (**P**), and the number of years he has served the company.

The flowchart and the program contain several transfers. The first transfer (line 50 in the program) checks whether the number of years (**Y**) is less than one. If it is, then transfer is made to a statement that prints **ERROR**.

If the years (**Y**) is larger than 1, transfer is made to the next line (line 60) in which the number of years are checked for being larger than 6. If **Y** is larger than 6, transfer is made to a statement that prints **ERROR**. Otherwise, the computed **GOTO**, which is part of the **IF-THEN** statement on line 60 is executed and the appropriate salary increase is calculated, using an accumulative procedure.

The flowchart is coded in BASIC as follows:

```
10 PRINT "1 FØR EACH EMPLØYEE, ENTER HIS LAST NAME, HIS PAY AND"
15 PRINT " YEARS SERVICE (0<YEARS SERVICE<7)"
20 PRINT "1EMPLØYEE RECØRD"
30 PRINT "                          PAY        YEARS"
40 INPUT SKP(1),P,Y
50 IF Y<1 THEN 70
60 IF Y<7 THEN (130,120,110,100,90,80),Y
70 GØTØ 180
80 P=P+500
90 P=P+400
100 P=P+200
110 P=P+200
120 P=P+100
130 P=P+100
140 PRINT "                      ",P,Y
150 GØTØ 40
180 PRINT "+","ERRØR"
190 GØTØ 40
```

This program generated the following output:

```
    FØR EACH EMPLØYEE, ENTER HIS LAST NAME, HIS PAY AND
    YEARS SERVICE (0<YEARS SERVICE<7)




    EMPLØYEE RECØRD
                                    PAY           YEARS
    ?DUMB,1500,0
                    ERRØR
    ?MILLER,1500,1
                                    1600            1
    ?JØNES,1500,2
                                    1700            2
    ?KLIEN,1500,3
                                    1900            3
    ?LAGRANGE,1500,4
                                    2100            4
    ?SMITH,1500,5
                                    2500            5
    ?SMITHE,1500,6
                                    3000            6
    ?DUMBER,1500,7
                    ERRØR
    ?%ENDFILE
```

TYPE 3

The last type of **IF-THEN** statement has the following general form:

IF exp1 reln exp2 THEN: S

where: **S** is a BASIC executable statement

exp1 and exp2 are two arithmetic expressions

exp1 reln exp2 is a logical expression

reln is a relational operator

Again one of the six relational operators can be used in the logical expression.

In the logical expression, arithmetic expression number 1 and arithmetic expression number 2 are evaluated and the results are compared to see whether they satisfy the relational operator. If the relation does not hold (or is **FALSE**), then control passes to the next executable statement. If the relation holds (or is **TRUE**), then control is transferred to statement **S**.

Statement S must be an executable statement, such as:

an INPUT statement

a PRINT statement

a STOP statement

a LET statement

a READ statement

a GOTO statement

or even another IF-THEN statement

EX. [7] THE SIMPLIFIED FEDERAL TAX EXAMPLE

Consider the federal tax example as illustrated in the flowchart on page 104 and as summarized in the following steps:

1. Read in the number of hours (**H**), the rate per hour (**R**), and the number of dependents (**D**).
2. Calculate the gross pay (**G**).
3. Calculate the federal tax (**F**) through a standard formula.
4. Check whether the calculated federal tax is negative. If it is negative, put it equal to zero.
5. Print **H, P, G,** and **F.**
6. Calculate and print the net pay, which equals the difference between the gross pay (**G**) and the federal tax (**F**).

```
10 PRINT "1COMPUTE GROSS AND NET PAY.  ALSO FEDERAL TAX."
20 PRINT " ENTER HOURS WORKED, PAY RATE AND # OF DEPENDENTS"
30 INPUT H,P,D
40 G=H*P
50 F=.18*(G-13*D)
60 IF F<0 THEN: F=0
70 PRINT " HOURS WORKED",H
80 PRINT " PAY RATE",P
90 PRINT " GROSS PAY",G
100 PRINT " FEDERAL TAX",F
110 PRINT " NET PAY",G-F
120 PRINT " ENTER 1 OR 2 TO TERMINATE OR CONTINUE"
130 INPUT K
140 GOTO (150,10),K
150 STOP
```

This program features the use of the **IF-THEN** statement in line number 60:

60   IF F<0 THEN: F=0

It checks whether **F** (which is the variable name used for federal tax) is less than zero. If it is, then the executable statement following **THEN:** is executed

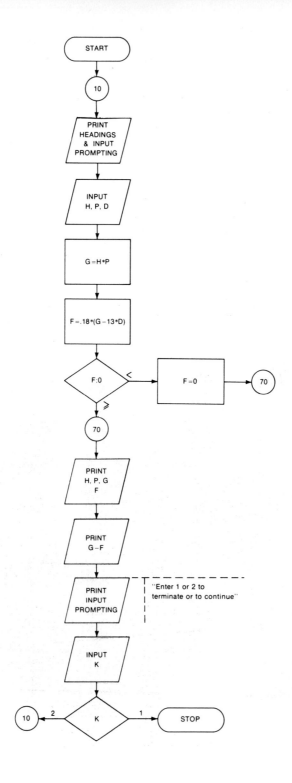

which puts **F** equal to zero. If **F** is not less than zero, then the remainder of that statement is not executed and control passes to the executable statement in line 70.

Again lines 120 and 130 provide for the input of a constant **K**, which is checked in the computed **GOTO** statement in line 140. The execution of this program stops if **K** equals **1**, since control then is passed to line 150 which contains the **STOP** statement. If **K** equals **2**, a new set of data will be read in, since control then is passed to line 10.

The following output is generated for three different sets of data.

```
COMPUTE GROSS AND NET PAY.  ALSO FEDERAL TAX.
ENTER HOURS WORKED, PAY RATE AND # OF DEPENDENTS
?40,3.5,1
HOURS WORKED    40
PAY RATE        3.5
GROSS PAY       140
FEDERAL TAX     22.86
NET PAY         117.14
ENTER 1 OR 2 TO TERMINATE OR CONTINUE
?2




COMPUTE GROSS AND NET PAY.  ALSO FEDERAL TAX.
ENTER HOURS WORKED, PAY RATE AND # OF DEPENDENTS
?36,2.75,0
HOURS WORKED    36
PAY RATE        2.75
GROSS PAY       99
FEDERAL TAX     17.82
NET PAY         81.18
ENTER 1 OR 2 TO TERMINATE OR CONTINUE
?2




COMPUTE GROSS AND NET PAY.  ALSO FEDERAL TAX.
ENTER HOURS WORKED, PAY RATE AND # OF DEPENDENTS
?28,1,3
HOURS WORKED    28
PAY RATE        1
GROSS PAY       28
FEDERAL TAX     0
NET PAY         28
ENTER 1 OR 2 TO TERMINATE OR CONTINUE
?1
```

Construction of Loops with Transfer Statements

In conclusion, let us consider the construction of loops to execute a set of statements several times.

In examples [3], [4], [5], and [7] of this chapter a computed **GOTO** statement is used for this purpose, whereas in examples [1], [2], and [6] an unconditional **GOTO** statement transferred control back to the input prompting statement which results in a loop. These two methods certainly work well when one works in conversational mode on the teletype, since the user can respond with an appropriate constant (**K**) or a **%ENDFILE** (or **CONTROL C**) to terminate execution of the BASIC program.

However, BASIC programs can be batch processed. In order to BATCH process a BASIC program, the programmer must submit the BASIC program and all pertinent data with the appropriate BASIC job commands to the system's operator. The same loop methods (the computed **GOTO** and the unconditional **GOTO** statement with **%ENDFILE**) may not be appropriate or convenient to use. Here follows a third method which is explained through Example [8]. It utilizes a counter (**J**), an **IF-THEN** statement and an unconditional **GOTO** transfer.

EX. [8]

Employees at several divisions of Ford Motor Company took a test. The following data has been prepared:

Data Statements	Content of Data Statement
First	1. Control value giving the number of employees who took the exam (N).
	2. One of the division numbers (D).
Remaining	1. Employee's number (S)
	2. Division number ($D1$)
	3. Score (P)

This data has to be processed in order to compute and output the average score obtained by the employees whose division number appears in the first data statement.

The corresponding BASIC program is:

```
10   READ N, D
20   LET T = 0
30   LET K = 0
40   LET J = 0
50   LET J = J+1
60   READ S, D1, P
70   IF D< > D1 THEN 100
80   LET T = T+P
```

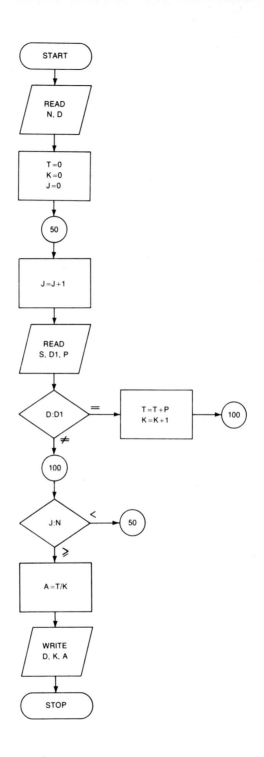

90	LET K = K+1
100	IF J<N THEN 50
110	LET A = T/K
120	PRINT TAB(5); "DIVISION NUMBER:"; D
130	PRINT TAB(5); "PEOPLE TAKING EXAM:"; K
140	PRINT TAB(5); "AVERAGE SCORE:"; A
150	DATA 10, 13
160	DATA 17, 1, 77, 12, 13, 89, 4, 13, 60, 99, 4, 56
170	DATA 26, 13, 91, 11, 1, 81, 14, 13, 79, 51, 4, 90
180	DATA 29, 4, 100, 30, 13, 54
190	STOP

Statements 40, 50, and 100 control the loop. According to **DATA** statement 150, 10 employees did the exam. Their scores are read in through statement number 60. This READ statement is executed 10 times, as controlled by the explicit built-in loop; statement 40 (**LET J = 0**) sets up a counter **J** and initializes it to ZERO; statement 50 (**LET J = J+1**) augments that counter by one just before the first score is read in; and finally statement 100 (**IF J<N THEN 50**) checks whether the counter J is smaller than N (the number of employees who took the exam). If **J** is smaller than **N**, then more information has to be read in and control is passed to line 50. The counter **J** will equal the value of **N** when all information is read in and then control passes to statement 110. At that point the average can be calculated and the results printed out.

Summary of Transfers

If one wishes to alter the logical sequential flow of execution three sets of transfers can be used:

1. The **unconditional GOTO** statement
2. The **conditional GOTO** statement
3. The **IF-THEN** statements

1.   **GOTO n**

This is the unconditional transfer statement, that offers the opportunity to transfer control to the statement that is numbered or labeled **n**

2.   **GOTO (n_1, n_2, n_3, . . ., n_m), exp**

          or

                    ON exp GOTO n_1, n_2, n_3, . . ., n_m

This is the **conditional GOTO** statement that provides us with a m-way check and a single transfer, based upon the truncated value of the expression (**exp**):

if truncated value of the expression equals 1, transfer is made to n_1;
if truncated value of the expression equals 2, transfer is made to n_2;

•

•

•

if truncated value of the expression equals m, transfer is made to n_m.

3.   **IF-THEN** statements
   Type 1:   **IF exp1 reln exp2 THEN n**

The **IF** in this type of statement is followed by a relationship to be tested that consists of two expressions or operands (**exp1 and exp2**) separated by a relational symbol ($<$, $<=$, $>$, $>=$, $=$, $<>$).
If the relationship is true, then control is made to statement number **n**. If the relationship is not true, then control goes to the next line in sequence.

   Type 2:   **IF exp1 reln exp2 THEN (n_1, n_2, n_3, . . ., n_m), exp3**

If the relationship (**exp1 reln exp2**) is true then control is transferred to one of the line numbers (n_1, n_2, n_3, . . ., n_m) according to the value of **exp3**. Otherwise, control passes to the next executable statement.

   Type 3:   **IF exp1 reln exp2 THEN: S**

If the relationship (**exp1 reln exp2**) is true then statement **S** is executed. If the relationship is not true, then control passes immediately to the next executable statement.

Exercises

PROBLEM #1

Write BASIC statements to accomplish the following:

a. If A is less than B, greater than 0, and not equal to C, or if A equals 100, transfer control to statement 120, otherwise transfer to statement 50.
b. If a variable name called E has a value greater than 10^{12}, transfer control to statement 58; otherwise, continue with the next statement.
c. If the square root of X is less than or equal to 400, proceed to the next statement; otherwise, terminate the program.

PROBLEM #2

Consider the following program, which reads 20 constants and computes the sum of all positive constants.

```
10   LET S=0
20   LET I=0
30   INPUT X
40   IF X > =0, THEN: S=S+X
50   I=I+1
60   IF I<20, THEN 30
70   PRINT S
80   STOP
```

Draw a correct flowchart for this program.

PROBLEM #3

Write BASIC statements for the following:

a. Determine whether the constant G, which is an integer, is odd or even. Proceed to step 100 if it is odd, proceed to step 200 if it is even.

b. If the number of dependents is greater than 3 and not greater than 6, and if the number of years of service is bracketed between 35 and 50, reduce the retirement contribution by 6%; otherwise go on.

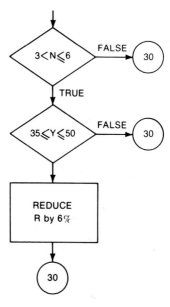

c. If S=0, assign the larger of A or B to C, otherwise, set S=0.

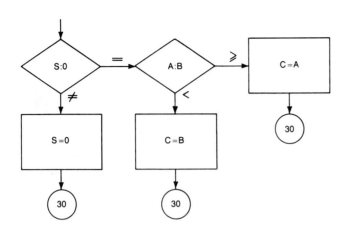

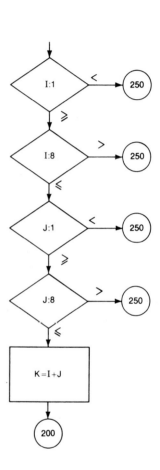

d. If I lies between 1 and 8 inclusive, and if at the same time J also lies between 1 and 8 inclusive, set the contents of K equal to I+J; otherwise, proceed to statement 250.

PROBLEM #4

What will be the value of L at the conclusion of this program? Draw a correct flowchart.

```
10    LET L=3
20    LET L=INT(L/4)*4+L
30    IF L>=5, THEN 70
40    LET L=L-1
50    IF L>=(3*INT(L/4)), THEN 70
60    LET L=L-1
70    STOP
```

PROBLEM #5

Indicate and correct all errors in the following statements.

```
10    GOTO (17, 14, 4, 3, 1, 77) C1
20    IF TAX = 0.18*(G-13*D) GOTO 12
      IF A<B OR >C, THEN D=E+F
30    IF I=B, THEN GOTO 7
```

PROBLEM #6

Write a BASIC program for the flowchart as exhibited in Example [1] of Chapter 2. (Note: choose workable variable names). Run the program with data from the terminal or on batch.

PROBLEM #7

Write a BASIC program, to be run from the terminal, for the flowchart as exhibited in Example [2] of Chapter 2. Do not use a DATA statement for data input.

PROBLEM #8

Write a BASIC program, to be run from the terminal, for the flowchart as exhibited in Example [3] of Chapter 2. Prompt yourself for input.

PROBLEM #9

Write a BASIC program, to be run from the terminal, for the flowchart as exhibited in Example [4] of Chapter 2. Prompt yourself for all input.

PROBLEM #10

Write two complete BASIC programs (one for terminal use, the other for batch use) that will compute the difference in minutes between two times, both expressed in hours and minutes since midnight, such as 01:45, 11:30, or 23:50, for 10 sets of times. You are guaranteed that the first time is earlier than the second time and that they are less than 24 hours apart. You are *not* guaranteed that they are in the same day: for instance, 23:50 before midnight is earlier than 02:00 after midnight of the same night.

Note, your data consists of the hours portion of the first time (H1), the minutes portion of the first time (M1), the hours portion of the second time (H2), and the minutes portion of the second time (M2). Your output should reflect the two times and the difference between them in minutes. Make your program, that will be run from the terminal, a conversational one!

PROBLEM #11

In the "Good Samaritan Hospital," a record of all blood donors of the village is kept on DATA cards. Each card contains the name of donor, age of donor, and blood code according to the following table (all information separated by commas):

Blood Code	Type
1	A
2	B
3	AB
4	O

An emergency occurs wherein AB blood is needed by an injured person.

You are supposed to draw a flowchart and write a BASIC program to be run from batch to print out a listing of the names of all AB donors.

PROBLEM #12

You are required to read values of x, perform certain checkings on x, and compute a value of y according to the following step function:

$$y = \begin{cases} 8.72 \text{ if } 0 < x \le 10.9 \\ 16.19 \text{ if } 10.9 < x \le 21.6 \\ 24.07 \text{ if } 21.6 < x \le 50 \end{cases}$$

The values of x and y are then to be printed. If x<0 or x>50 we are to stop the processing. The last x value that you process has a value of x greater than 50, which will terminate the processing. Draw the flowchart and write a BASIC program to be run either from batch or from a terminal.

PROBLEM #13

You are requested to read in *ten* sets of two numbers. Each set of two numbers represent a different bank. The first number reflects the bank's total deposits (in millions) as of January 1, 1978, and the second number represents the bank's total deposits (in millions) as of January 1, 1979. Prepare a flowchart and a conversational BASIC program to output the following:

1. the average deposits as of January 1, 1978.
2. the average deposits as of January 1, 1979.
3. the range between the above two averages.
4. the average January 1, 1979, deposits of all banks that suffered a *decline* in total deposits during 1978.
5. the average January 1, 1979, deposits of all banks that incurred an *incline* in total deposits during 1978.
6. the number of banks that started off 1978 *and* 1979 with total deposits which exceeded $100 million.

PROBLEM #14

You must read in ten sets of three numbers from the terminal. Each set of three numbers includes:

a section number (1, 2, or 3) (N)

grade on test #1 (T1)

grade on test #2 (T2)

Process this information to obtain:

1. for each section the average grade the student obtained on test #1.

2. the average grade on test #1 of all students who obtained a grade less than 65 on test #2.
3. the number of students in Section 1 who averaged more than 75 points. Label all output.

PROBLEM #15

Consider the following ten numbers (5, −6, −8, 2, 1, −1, 1, −3, 4, 5). Write a BASIC program to be run on batch to process these numbers in order to count the number of times a negative number is followed by a positive number. Flowchart your solution procedure first and process the above data through the flowchart in the form of a procedure to check the logic.

8
Looping

The FOR-NEXT Loop

The last example in Chapter 7 illustrates one way of constructing a loop. Since quite often statements have to be executed over and over again, BASIC provides us with a concise loop structure: the **FOR-NEXT** loop structure. The **FOR-NEXT** statements are control statements that allows one to set up a simple iterative loop in two statements. The general form of the **FOR-NEXT** statements is as follows:

$$\textbf{FOR} \quad i = e_1 \ \textbf{TO} \ e_2 \ \textbf{STEP} \ e_3$$
$$\textbf{NEXT i}$$

where **i** is a numeric nonsubscripted loop variable

e_1, e_2, e_3 are arithmetic expressions

e_1 is an arithmetic expression, whose value is used as initial value for i.

e_2 is an arithmetic expression, whose value is used as the largest or smallest value of i, which is not necessarily always reached.

e_3 is an arithmetic expression, whose value is used as increment value for i.

The **FOR-NEXT** statements cause the repeated execution of all statements which are sandwiched in between the **FOR** and the **NEXT** statements. The first time the statements are executed, the first expression e_1 is evaluated and its numeric value is assigned to **i.** Each succeeding time the statements are executed, e_2 and e_3 are reevaluated and **i** is incremented by the numeric value of e_3. Repeated execution continues as long as $e_1 \leqslant i \leqslant e_2$ **for** $e_3 > 0$ or as long as $e_2 \leqslant i \leqslant e_1$ **for** $e_3 < 0$. This rather complex rule will be illustrated in several examples. If the increment, e_3, is not specified, it is assumed to be equal to one. In this case, the general form of the **FOR-NEXT** statements are:

$$\textbf{FOR} \quad i = e_1 \ \textbf{TO} \ e_2$$
$$\textbf{NEXT i}$$

The **"NEXT i"** marks the end of the range of the loop and must come after its corresponding **FOR** statement.

The four statements which are necessary to iterate a sequence of statements are built in the **FOR-NEXT** statements. These four statements are:

1. Initialize a counter: $i = e_1$
2. Increment the counter: $i = i + e_3$ or $i = i + 1$
3. Test the counter: if $i > e_2$ (if e_3 is positive) or if $i < e_2$ (if e_3 is negative) transfer control to the executable statement following the "NEXT i" statement.
4. Define the ending statement in the loop: the statement preceding the "NEXT i" statement.

There are two ways of representing a loop in a flowchart: by using either the processing symbol or the preparation symbol. The preparation symbol will be used in this text.

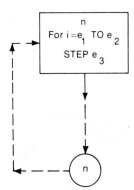
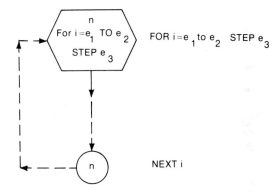

EX. [1]

Here follow two ways for evaluating the sum of the first five squared integers

$$\left(\sum_{I=1}^{5} I^2 \right)$$

```
10    LET I = 0
20    FOR J = 1 TO 5 STEP 1
30    LET I = I + J**2
40    NEXT J
50    PRINT I
60    STOP
```

The above **FOR-NEXT** loop is executed five times, at which time transfer is made to the PRINT statement, which is the first executable statement following the **FOR-NEXT** loop. In this example the loop counter **J** is used in the arithmetic expression in line 30 of the loop. Execution in the above example proceeds as follows: Upon entering the **FOR-NEXT** loop, **1** is assigned to the loop index **J**. The limiting value **5** is then compared with **J**. If **J** is greater than **5**, the loop terminates and control is passed to the PRINT statement, since it follows the **NEXT J** statement. If **J** is smaller than or equal to **5**, the loop is entered. The following table illustrates the complete procedure.

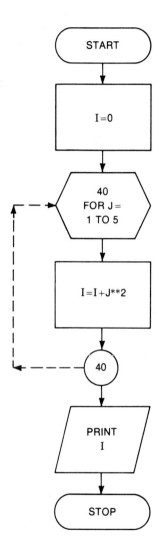

TABLE 8.1.

Line Number	Procedure	Result
10	Assign 0 to I	I = 0
20	Initialize J to 1	J = 1
	Compare J to 5	J = 1 ≤ 5, OK †
30	Augment I with J**2	I = 1
40	Augment J with STEP 1	J = 2
20	Compare J to 5	J = 2 ≤ 5, OK †
30	Augment I with J**2	I = 1 + 2**2 = 5
40	Augment J with STEP 1	J = 3
20	Compare J with 5	J = 3 ≤ 5, OK †
30	Augment I with J**2	I = 5 + 3**2 = 14
40	Augment J with STEP 1	J = 4
20	Compare J with 5	J = 4 ≤ 5, OK †
30	Augment I with J**4	I = 14 + 4**2 = 30
40	Augment J with STEP 1	J = 5
20	Compare J with 5	J = 5 ≤ 5, OK †
30	Augment I with J**2	I = 30 + 5**2 = 55
40	Augment J with STEP 1	J = 6
20	Compare J with 5	J = 6 > 5, transfer to 50 †
50	PRINT I	55
60	STOP	

†Note that on some machines (i.e., GE) statements in the **FOR-NEXT** loop are executed at least once, since on these machines the **FOR** statement only assigns e_1 to the loop index and at the **NEXT** statement the index is augmented by e_3 and compared to e_2. If the index is larger than e_2, it is reduced by e_3 and transfer is made to the first executable statement following the loop.

Note that at the end of this procedure the index of the **FOR-NEXT** loop equals **6**, which is larger than the maximum value **5**. At any time, inside the loop or after the loop is executed, this variable **J** can be used. If one were not able to use the **FOR-NEXT** index **J**, then the solution procedure would be slightly different, as illustrated by the following flowchart and BASIC program.

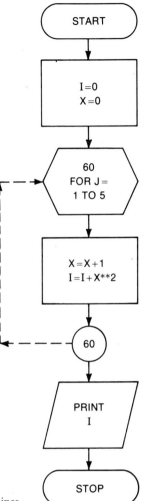

```
10   LET I = 0
20   LET X = 0
30   FOR J = 1 TO 5 STEP 1
40   LET X = X + 1
50   LET I = I +X**2
60   NEXT J
70   PRINT I
80   STOP
```

Following values are finally generated:

$$I = 55$$
$$X = 5$$
$$J = 6‡$$

‡On most IBM machines J would be 6, however on other machines, like GE machines, this value of J would be 5.

FOR-NEXT Loop Rules

RULE 1

All loop statements are sandwiched in between the **FOR** and the **NEXT** statements. The **NEXT** statement always follows its **FOR** statement and corresponding **FOR-NEXT** statements carry the same loop variable.

RULE 2

If the step variable, e_3, equals 1, then it may be omitted in the **FOR** statement. Therefore, Example [1] can be rewritten to eliminate Step 1 as follows.

EX. [2]

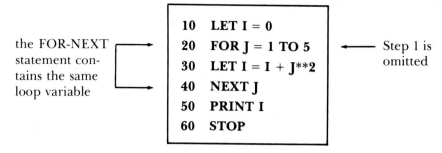

the FOR-NEXT statement contains the same loop variable

10	LET I = 0
20	FOR J = 1 TO 5
30	LET I = I + J**2
40	NEXT J
50	PRINT I
60	STOP

◄—— Step 1 is omitted

RULE 3

A **FOR-NEXT** loop can be put within the range of another **FOR-NEXT** loop, but all statements of the inner **FOR-NEXT** loop must be within the range of the outer **FOR-NEXT** loop.

EX. [3]

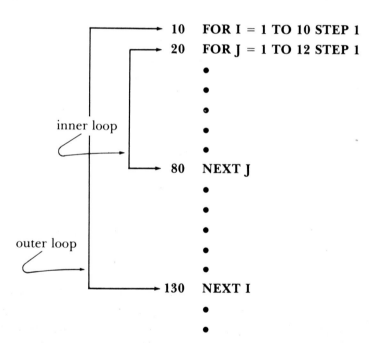

inner loop

outer loop

10	FOR I = 1 TO 10 STEP 1
20	FOR J = 1 TO 12 STEP 1
	•
	•
	•
	•
	•
80	NEXT J
	•
	•
	•
	•
	•
130	NEXT I
	•
	•

Here the inner loop is in the range of the outer loop and the loop variable "**I**" and "**J**" are different.

EX. [4]

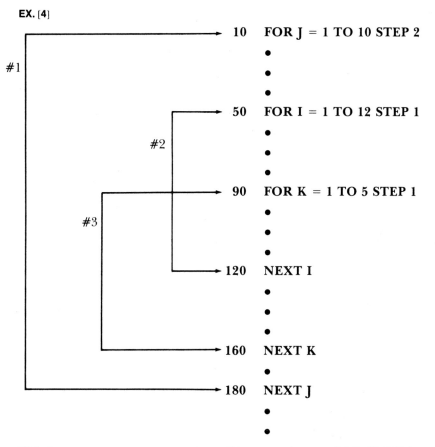

#1	10	FOR J = 1 TO 10 STEP 2
		•
		•
		•
#2	50	FOR I = 1 TO 12 STEP 1
		•
		•
		•
#3	90	FOR K = 1 TO 5 STEP 1
		•
		•
		•
	120	NEXT I
		•
		•
		•
	160	NEXT K
		•
	180	NEXT J

This is not a proper construction of inner and outer **FOR-NEXT** loops since Rule 3 is violated by the two inner loops #2 and #3.

RULE 4

The general form of the **FOR** statement indicates the presence of three possible expressions:

$$\text{FOR i} = e_1 \text{ TO } e_2 \text{ STEP } e_3$$

By expressions are meant arithmetic expressions: variables and/or constants with operators. If any or all of these expressions are fixed values, which do not change during the execution of the loop, then it is more efficient to define these values in a LET statement prior to entering the **FOR** statement. Thus, the resulting values can then be assigned to variables which take the place of e_1, e_2, and e_3 respectively.

RULE 5

Since the loop parameters, e_2 and e_3, are always reevaluated before the repetition of the loop, they can be changed inside or outside its loop. However, they should not be changed to cause an indefinite loop, which would prove to be disastrous.

RULE 6

A transfer out of the range of any **FOR-NEXT** loop is permissible at any time, as long as the limit of the loop has not been reached. This transfer may be followed by a transfer back into the loop.

Any departure from within the loop allows the loop variable to be used outside the loop, with the value it had at the time of departure.

EX. [5]

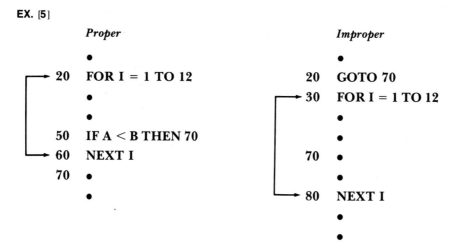

Proper

```
        •
→ 20    FOR I = 1 TO 12
        •
        •
  50    IF A < B THEN 70
→ 60    NEXT I
  70    •
        •
```

Improper

```
        •
  20    GOTO 70
→ 30    FOR I = 1 TO 12
        •
        •
  70    •
        •
→ 80    NEXT I
        •
        •
```

If "**A < B**," then control is transferred out of the range of the FOR-NEXT loop to line number 70. The "GOTO 70" statement makes transfer into the loop. This is not allowed, unless transfer was made previously out of that loop.

RULE 7

Control must not be transferred into the range of an inner loop from its outer loop. However, it is quite permissible to transfer control from a statement within an inner loop to a statement within its outer loop.

EX. [6]

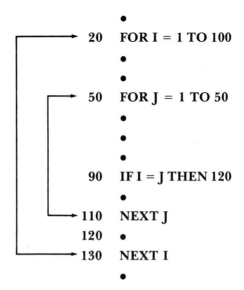

●

20   FOR I = 1 TO 100

●

●

50   FOR J = 1 TO 50

●

●

●

90   IF I = J THEN 120

●

110 NEXT J

120 ●

130 NEXT I

●

The above transfer from the inner **FOR-NEXT** loop to the outer **FOR-NEXT** loop is correct.

EX. [7]

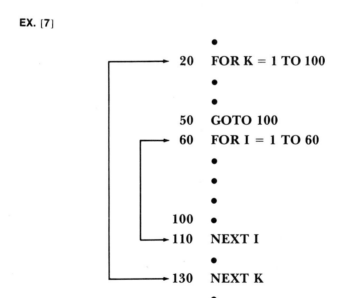

●

20   FOR K = 1 TO 100

●

●

50   GOTO 100

60   FOR I = 1 TO 60

●

●

●

100 ●

110 NEXT I

●

130 NEXT K

●

The above transfer "GOTO 100" is not quite correct since the inner **FOR-NEXT** loop index **I** has not been initialized properly.

RULE 8

In summary of Rules 6 and 7 one may say that a transfer into the range of any **FOR-NEXT** loop is not permitted if the loop index in the FOR statement has not been initialized properly.

RULE 9

A negative **STEP** value e_3 is allowed in any **FOR** statement of a loop.

$$\textbf{FOR I = A TO B STEP } -1$$

This is executed by reducing **I** by the **STEP** value **−1**; the resulting **I** is then compared to **A** and **B** as follows:

$$\textbf{B} \leqslant \textbf{I} \leqslant \textbf{A}$$

So the statements within the **FOR-NEXT** loop are carried out as long as **B** $\leqslant$ **I** $\leqslant$ **A**. If **A** is smaller than **B** (**A<B**) then the loop will be ignored.

Many of the above rules are illustrated through a set of examples in the next section.

EXAMPLES OF FOR-NEXT LOOPING

EX. [8] SUM-OF-THE-YEARS-DIGITS DEPRECIATION (SINGLE LOOP)

As opposed to the straight-line and the declining-balance method, the sum-of-the-years-digits method applies a declining rate to a constant base, the cost of the asset minus the salvage value.

For the three assets which are considered in this example it is assumed that the salvage value equals zero. The declining rate depends on the life of the asset and the depreciation year. For example: if an asset has to be depreciated over four years, then the sum-of-the-years-digits equals $4 + 3 + 2 + 1$ = 10. This depreciation method will therefore depreciate $\frac{4}{10}$ of the asset the first year, $\frac{3}{10}$ of the asset the second year, $\frac{2}{10}$ of the asset the third year, and $\frac{1}{10}$ or the remainder of the asset the fourth or last year. If N is the life of the asset then calculus teaches us that the sum of the years can be calculated with the following formula:

$$S = \frac{N*(N + 1)}{2}$$

Therefore, the depreciation at the end of each year I equals:

$$\frac{N + 1 - I}{S} * P$$

where: **P:** is the asset value.

S: is the sum-of-the-years-digits.

N: is the live of the asset.

I: is the depreciation year, $1 \leq I \leq N$.

The following flowchart gives the detailed solution procedure:

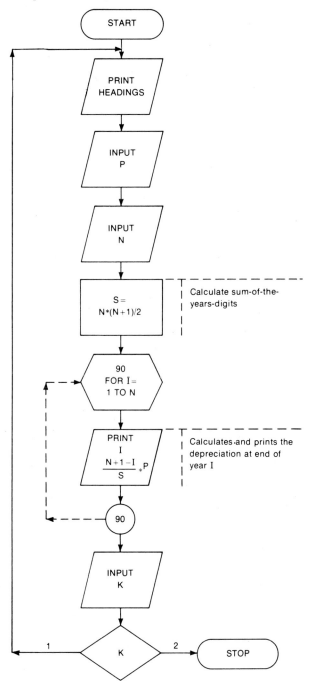

The BASIC program for the flowchart above is as follows:

```
10 PRINT "1SUM OF YEARS DIGITS DEPRECIATION SCHEDULE"
20 PRINT " ENTER ASSET VALUE"
30 INPUT P
40 PRINT " ENTER ASSET LIFE TO THE NEAREST WHOLE YEAR"
50 INPUT N
60 S=N*(N+1)/2
70 FOR I=1 TO N
80 PRINT " DEPRECIATION IN YEAR",I,((N+1-I)/S)*P
90 NEXT I
100 PRINT " ENTER 1 TO CONTINUE, 2 TO TERMINATE"
110 INPUT K
120 GOTO (10,130),K
130 PRINT " IT HAS BEEN A PLEASURE TO SERVE YOU!"
140 STOP
```

This program features:

1. Input promptings: lines 20, 40, and 100.
2. An Arithmetic Assignment: line 60, to calculate sum-of-the-years-digits.
3. One **FOR-NEXT** loop: lines 70 through 90.

> **70 FOR I = 1 TO N**
> **80 PRINT "DEPRECIATION IN YEAR," I, ((N + 1 − I)/S) *P**
> **90 NEXT I**

Note that the loop is executed **N** times (**N** is equal to the life of the asset) since the initial index value of **I** equals 1 and the default **STEP** equals 1. Line 80 simultaneously prints and calculates the depreciation value for each of the **I** years.

4. A computed GOTO statement (line 120) controls the termination of this program.

The BASIC program generates the following output:

```
SUM ØF YEARS DIGITS DEPRECIATIØN SCHEDULE
ENTER ASSET VALUE
?600
ENTER ASSET LIFE TØ THE NEAREST WHØLE YEAR
?3
DEPRECIATIØN IN YEAR          1          300
DEPRECIATIØN IN YEAR          2          200
DEPRECIATIØN IN YEAR          3          100
ENTER 1 TØ CØNTINUE, 2 TØ TERMINATE
?1




SUM ØF YEARS DIGITS DEPRECIATIØN SCHEDULE
ENTER ASSET VALUE
?1000
ENTER ASSET LIFE TØ THE NEAREST WHØLE YEAR
?4
DEPRECIATIØN IN YEAR          1          400
DEPRECIATIØN IN YEAR          2          300
DEPRECIATIØN IN YEAR          3          200
DEPRECIATIØN IN YEAR          4          100
ENTER 1 TØ CØNTINUE, 2 TØ TERMINATE
?1




SUM ØF YEARS DIGITS DEPRECIATIØN SCHEDULE
ENTER ASSET VALUE
?125000
ENTER ASSET LIFE TØ THE NEAREST WHØLE YEAR
?17
DEPRECIATIØN IN YEAR          1          13888.89
DEPRECIATIØN IN YEAR          2          13071.9
DEPRECIATIØN IN YEAR          3          12254.9
DEPRECIATIØN IN YEAR          4          11437.91
DEPRECIATIØN IN YEAR          5          10620.92
DEPRECIATIØN IN YEAR          6          9803.922
DEPRECIATIØN IN YEAR          7          8986.928
DEPRECIATIØN IN YEAR          8          8169.935
DEPRECIATIØN IN YEAR          9          7352.941
DEPRECIATIØN IN YEAR          10         6535.948
DEPRECIATIØN IN YEAR          11         5718.954
DEPRECIATIØN IN YEAR          12         4901.961
DEPRECIATIØN IN YEAR          13         4084.967
DEPRECIATIØN IN YEAR          14         3267.974
DEPRECIATIØN IN YEAR          15         2450.98
DEPRECIATIØN IN YEAR          16         1633.987
DEPRECIATIØN IN YEAR          17         816.9935
ENTER 1 TØ CØNTINUE, 2 TØ TERMINATE
?2
IT HAS BEEN A PLEASURE TØ SERVE YØU!
```

EX. [9] SUM-OF-THE-YEARS-DIGITS DEPRECIATION (NESTED LOOP)

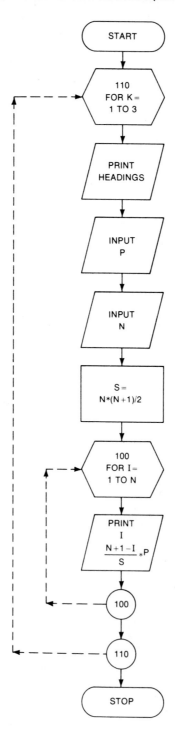

In the previous example the sum-of-the-digits depreciation program is executed for three sets of data. The repetition is governed by the computed GOTO statement in line 120. This statement transfers control to line 10 (if continuation is desired or if K equals 1) or to line 130 (if no continuation is desired or if K equals 2). Here, the flowchart and the BASIC program is reconstructed with a loop to execute the sum-of-the-years-digits depreciation program three times. The resulting output is basically the same.

BASIC PROGRAM

```
 10   FOR K = 1 TO 3
 20   PRINT "1SUM OF YEARS DIGITS DEPRECIATION SCHEDULE"
 30   PRINT "ENTER ASSET VALUE"
 40   INPUT P
 50   PRINT "ENTER ASSET LIFE TO THE NEAREST WHOLE YEAR"
 60   INPUT N
 70   S = N*(N + 1)/2
 80   FOR I = 1 TO N
 90   PRINT "DEPRECIATION IN YEAR," I, ((N + 1 - I)/S)*P
100   NEXT I
110   NEXT K
120   STOP
```

Note the structure of the two loops.

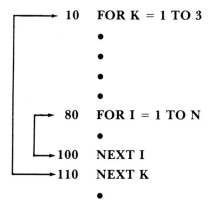

The inner loop (80-100) is completely contained within its outer loop (10-110).

EX. [10] LARGEST COMMON INTEGER DIVISOR

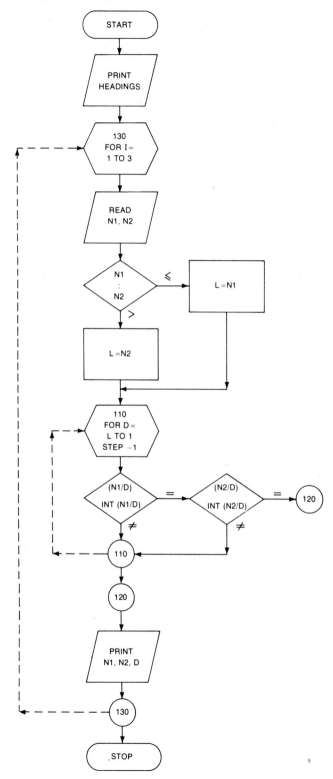

Given two integer numbers, **N1** and **N2**, then the largest common integer divisor, **D**, of these numbers cannot be larger than the min(**N1, N2**), or:

$$1 \leq D \leq \min(N1, N2).$$

The largest common integer divisor, **D**, equals 1 if both **N1** and **N2** are prime numbers. The largest common integer divisor, **D**, equals min(**N1, N2**) if one of the two numbers is a multiple of the other. Clearly, to find the largest common divisor of **N1** and **N2**, one must start with the min(**N1, N2**) and work backwards until one divisor is found, as illustrated in this flowchart and the BASIC program that follows.

The preceding flowchart is translated in BASIC as follows:

```
10 PRINT "1FIRST NUMBER","SECOND NUMBER","COMMON DIVISOR"
20 FOR I=1 TO 3
30 READ N1,N2
40 IF N1<=N2 THEN 70
50 LET L=N2
60 GOTO 80
70 LET L=N1
80 FOR D=L TO 1 STEP -1
90 IF (N1/D)<>INT(N1/D)THEN 110
100 IF (N2/D)=INT(N2/D) THEN 120
110 NEXT D
120 PRINT N1,N2,D
130 NEXT I
140 DATA 187,221,132,44,45,105
150 STOP
```

FOR-NEXT loop Rules 2, 3, 7, and 9 are illustrated in this example.

Rule 2: If the STEP variable, e_3, equals 1, then it may be omitted in its **FOR** statement. This is the case in line 20.

20   FOR I = 1 TO 3

Rule 3: A **FOR-NEXT** loop can be put within the range of another **FOR-NEXT** loop. Note that the second FOR-NEXT loop (lines 80 through 110) is completely contained within its outer loop (lines 20 through 130).

Rule 7: It is quite permissible to transfer control from a statement within an inner loop to a statement within its outer loop. The BASIC statement in line 100 of the inner loop may result in transferring control into the range of its outer loop:

100   IF (N2/D) = INT(N2/D) THEN 120

If the logical expression:

(N2/D) = INT(N2/D)

is true, then control is passed to statement 120, which is a statement in the outer **FOR-NEXT** loop. However, if that logical expression does not hold then transfer is made to the next statement, which is the **NEXT** statement of the inner loop.

Rule 9: A negative **STEP** value e_3 is allowed in the **FOR** statement of a loop:

80   FOR D = L TO 1 STEP −1

This allows us to work backwards, until the largest common divisor **D** is found.

Initially **D** takes on the largest possible common divisor **L**, min(**N1**, **N2**), and is decremented by 1 (STEP −1).

Note that: **L** ⩾ **1** at all times;
and: **1** ⩽ **D** ⩽ **L** at all times.

The following output is generated by this program:

```
FIRST NUMBER   SECOND NUMBER   COMMON DIVISOR
187            221             17
132            44              44
45             105             15
```

EX. [11] RANGE OF SALES VOLUME

The range of sales volume is a measure of sales dispersion and is obtained by subtracting from the largest sales volume the smallest one. Under the assumption that the number of sales (**N**) which are made is read in, the flowchart exhibits the logic of computing the range of the sales volume.

The **FOR-NEXT** loop provides for reading in the **N** sales volumes, one at a time, and for changing the **S** value (variable that ultimately stores the smallest volume) and the **B** value (variable that ultimately stores the big value).

Note that before the loop is entered **B** and **S** are initialized, by giving **B** a very small value (**B = 0**) and by assigning a very large value to **S** (**S = 10000000**). The first time the loop is executed the first sales volume, **S1**, is assigned to **B** and to **S**, since:

B = 0<S1<10000000 = S

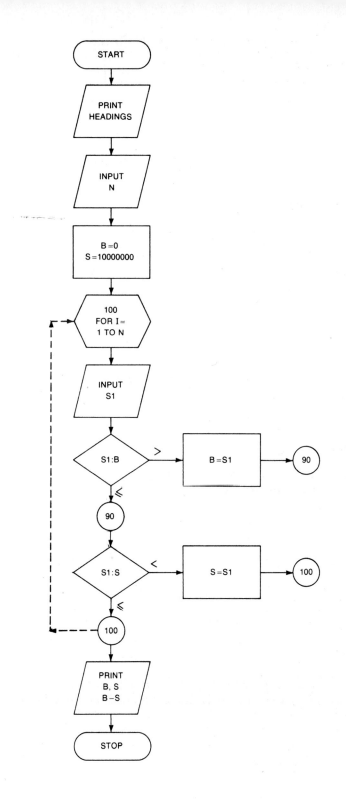

When the loop is executed **N** times, the variable **B** contains the largest sales volume, whereas the variable name **S** contains the smallest sales volume. Therefore, the difference between **B** and **S** represents the range of the **N** sales volumes.

The BASIC program, corresponding to the preceding flowchart is as follows:

```
10 PRINT "1CØMPUTE THE RANGE ØF SALES VØLUMES"
20 PRINT " ENTER THE NUMBER ØF SALES VØLUMES TØ CØNSIDER"
30 INPUT N
40 LET B=0
50 LET S=10000000
55 PRINT " ENTER THE SALES VØLUMES, ØNE PER LINE"
60 FØR I=1 TØ N
70 INPUT S1
80 IF S1>B THEN: B=S1
90 IF S1<S THEN: S=S1
100 NEXT I
110 PRINT " SMALLEST SALES VØLUME", S
120 PRINT " LARGEST SALES VØLUME", B
130 PRINT " RANGE", B-S
140 PRINT "1"
150 STØP
```

The program generates the following output:

```
 CØMPUTE THE RANGE ØF SALES VØLUMES
 ENTER THE NUMBER ØF SALES VØLUMES TØ CØNSIDER
?10
 ENTER THE SALES VØLUMES, ØNE PER LINE
?25
?49
?44
?109
?39
?555
?555557
?90
?16
?2
 SMALLEST SALES VØLUME          2
 LARGEST SALES VØLUME           555557
 RANGE            555555
```

Summary of Looping

The **FOR-NEXT** statements are control statements that allows one to set up a single iterative loop in two statements:

$$\textbf{FOR} \quad \textbf{i} = \textbf{e}_1 \textbf{ TO } \textbf{e}_2 \textbf{ STEP } \textbf{e}_3$$
$$\textbf{NEXT i}$$

The **FOR-NEXT** statements cause the repeated execution of all statements which are sandwiched in between the **FOR** and the **NEXT** statements. The first time the statements are executed, the first expression e_1 is evaluated and its numeric value is assigned to **i**. Each succeeding time the statements are executed, e_2 and e_3 are reevaluated and **i** is incremented by the numeric value of e_3. Repeated execution continues as long as $e_1 \leq i \leq e_2$ for $e_3 > 0$ or as long as $e_2 \leq i \leq e_1$ for $e_3 < 0$.

FOR-NEXT LOOP RULES:

Rule 1: All loop statements are sandwiched in between the **FOR** and the **NEXT** statements. The **NEXT** statement always follows its **FOR** statement and corresponding **FOR-NEXT** statements carry the same loop variable.

Rule 2: If the step variable, e_3, equals 1, then it may be omitted in the **FOR** statement.

Rule 3: A **FOR-NEXT** loop can be put within the range of another **FOR-NEXT** loop, but all statements of the inner **FOR-NEXT** loop must be within the range of the outer **FOR-NEXT** loop.

Rule 4: The general form of the **FOR** statement indicates the presence of three possible expressions: e_1, e_2 and e_3.

Rule 5: Since the loop parameters, e_2 and e_3, are always reevaluated before the repetition of the loop, they can be changed inside or outside its loop. However, they should not be changed to cause an infinite loop.

Rule 6: A transfer out of the range of any **FOR-NEXT** loop is permissible at any time, as long as the limit of the loop has not been reached. This transfer may be followed by a transfer back into the loop.

Rule 7: Control must not be transferred into the range of an inner loop from its outer loop. However, it is quite permissible to transfer control from a statement within an inner loop to a statement within its outer loop.

Rule 8: In summary of rules 6 and 7 one may say that a transfer into the range of any **FOR-NEXT** loop is not permitted if the loop index in the **FOR** statement has not been initialized properly.

Rule 9: A negative **STEP** value e_3 is allowed in any **FOR** statement of a loop.

Exercises

PROBLEM #1

Rewrite the following program without the use of a FOR-NEXT loop.

```
10   FOR I=1 TO 10
20   FOR J=1 TO 10
30   FOR K=1 TO 10
40   K1=K1+I*J*K
50   NEXT K
60   NEXT J
70   NEXT I
80   PRINT K1
90   STOP
```

PROBLEM #2

Rewrite the following program by using as many FOR-NEXT loops as possible.

```
10   INPUT X
20   IF X<=0, THEN 40
30   S=S+X
40   I=I+1
45   IF I<20, THEN 10
50   PRINT S
60   STOP
```

Draw a flowchart for your rewritten program.

PROBLEM #3

(The following problem was provided by Professor J. Daniel Couger, University of Colorado.) Peter Minuit, governor of the Dutch West India Company, is reputed to have purchased Manhattan Island from the Indians for $24 in 1626. Assume that the Indians invested their receipts at 6 percent compounded annually. Write a BASIC program which would determine and print out the value of their investment at the end of each of the following years: 1676, 1726, 1776, 1826, 1876, 1926, and 1976. In your print-out, identify the year associated with each investment value.

PROBLEM #4

A sample of 200 people was taken to obtain income statistics. Find the percentage of people sampled whose annual income is greater than $10,000, and calculate the overall average and the average income of the people whose income is above $10,000. Draw a flow diagram and write a complete BASIC program to accomplish this.

PROBLEM #5

Use a FOR-NEXT loop to process the ten sets of two numbers as indicated in Problem #13 of Chapter 7.

PROBLEM #6

Use a FOR-NEXT loop to process the ten sets of three numbers as indicated in Problem #14 of Chapter 7.

PROBLEM #7

Use a FOR-NEXT loop to process the ten numbers as indicated in Problem #15 of Chapter 7.

PROBLEM #8

Consider the following ten integer constants:

25311	27346
12345	20405
22446	12121
34008	52035
55555	99999

Process this data through a BASIC program to define the constant M. M denotes the number of constants that must be read to find three numbers that are either evenly divisible by 5 or that have a 4 as their third digit. If three such numbers do not occur among this data set, output a message to that effect.

PROBLEM #9

The input for processing the payroll of the ABC company consists of the following data items:

1. N: indicating the number of employees in the ABC company.
2. N sets of data for each employee consisting of:
   - the employee's ID number (I)
   - his hourly pay rate (R), and
   - five numbers, representing the number of hours that the employee worked each day of the previous week. (H1, H2, H3, H4, H5).

Give the flowchart and a BASIC program that will:

1. calculate the paycheck amount for each employee and output the ID, total hours (H), pay rate and paycheck amount (P).

2. calculate and output the total of the paychecks and the average hourly rate (A) paid to the employees (divide total pay by total hours).

Check your flowchart and program with the following data items:

$$3$$
$$2045, 2.25, 6, 8, 5, 3, 11$$
$$4653, 2.75, 8, 8, 4, 9, 5$$
$$2655, 3.80, 9, 9, 4, 9, 5$$

PROBLEM #10

Process twenty sets of information. Each set contains three closing stock prices for companies A, B, and C. In this manner you are given the closing prices (per share) of the stock of three companies on twenty successive days. Give the flowchart and a BASIC program that will determine and output the following:

1. The number of times that Company A stock closed higher than that of either Company B or Company C.
2. The number of times that a buyer could have purchased one share of stock from each company for a total of less than $100.
3. The average price of Company B stock on the days that stock was selling for less than Company A stock.

PROBLEM #11

Calculating the checking service charge.

Give a flowchart and a BASIC program that calculates and prints the checking service charge and the final balance. Checking charges are calculated on the basis of the following specifics:

1. A charge of $.04 is made for each deposit.
2. A charge of $.05 is made for each withdrawal.
3. If the amount becomes negative, a $3.00 charge occurs. This charge is accessed only once, regardless of the number of times the account becomes negative.
4. No charges are made if a minimum balance of $150 is maintained.
5. All checks are honored even if the balance is negative.

The input consists of: 1. a DATA card containing two numbers (N and B). N represents the number of transactions (deposits and checks) and B reflects the starting balance; 2. N DATA cards representing a number: if the number is positive it then represents a deposit; if the number is negative, however, it represents a withdrawal.

PROBLEM #12

Consider the flowchart and the following data: 6, 3, −4, 1, 4, 2, −6. Process this data through the flowchart in the form of a procedure.

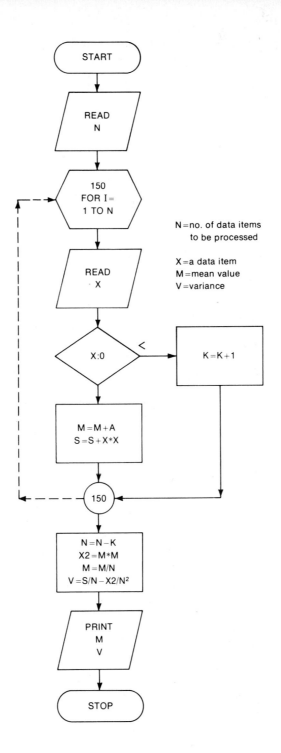

N = no. of data items
    to be processed

X = a data item
M = mean value
V = variance

Write a BASIC program and run it with the given data.
Describe what the flowchart or program does for you.

PROBLEM #13

You are requested to draw a flowchart and to write a BASIC program to generate a summary report for NO WORRY FINANCE COMPANY. Your summary report should contain the following information:

1. Average balance of all accounts.
2. Average balance of all accounts which are past due for more than a month (at least 30 days).
3. Average number of days past due of all accounts.
4. Average number of days past due of all accounts with a current balance greater than $1,000.
5. Average number of days past due of all accounts with a current balance of less than or equal to $1,000.
6. Number of past due accounts having a current balance greater than $1,000.
7. Number of past due accounts having a current balance less than $1,000.

Your data consists of N followed by N cards, where N denotes the number of account holders. Each of the N cards contains an account number, its current balance and the number of days that account is past due.

Run your BASIC program with self-constructed data.

PROBLEM #14

A major Northwestern university accepts students into its MBA program based on their undergraduate grade-point average (G) and their quantitative (Q) and verbal (V) ATGSB scores.

To be accepted the student must satisfy *one* of the following conditions:

1. The sum of his two ATGSB scores must be greater than 100 *and* his grade point average (G) must be greater than 3.5.
2. Each ATGSB score must be at least 600.
3. His grade point average must be at least 3.9.

For the following data draw a flowchart and a BASIC program to generate a listing of all accepted students.

DATA

Name	ID	G	Q	V
Johnson, J.	1345	3.95	400	390
Adams, A.	1993	2.90	615	370
Brown, C.	4566	2.50	650	700
Dickson, I.	2234	3.40	480	560
Nelson, A.	3190	3.80	500	500

9

Use of Subscripts

Subscripts are used to form arrays. An array is an ordered set of quantities, called elements of the array. The elements of an array are all referred to by the same name and are distinguished by their subscripts.

Type of Arrays

BASIC allows for the use of one-dimensional and two-dimensional arrays. The dimension size refers to a special arrangement of elements. A general discussion of one-dimensional and two-dimensional arrays follows.

EX. [1] A ONE-DIMENSIONAL ARRAY

In statistics, a discrete random variable is a variable that can take on several values, known as the elements of that random variable. The random variable is given a general name, **X**. The elements of the random variable **X** are referred to by subscripts.

x_1 is the first element

x_2 is the second element

x_3 is the third element

•

•

x_n is the nth element

So, if **X** represents the random variable describing the outcome of tossing a dice, then its elements are 1, 2, 3, 4, 5, and 6. In statistics this is represented by the use of a one-dimensional array:

$$\mathbf{X} = \{\mathbf{1,2,3,4,5,6}\} \text{ with}$$

$$x_1 = 1$$
$$x_2 = 2$$
$$x_3 = 3$$
$$x_4 = 4$$
$$x_5 = 5$$
$$x_6 = 6$$

EX. [2] A TWO-DIMENSIONAL ARRAY

Consider the three linear equations:

$$3x_1 + 4x_2 + 6x_3 = 14$$
$$2x_1 + 9x_2 + 4x_3 = 22$$
$$7x_1 + 2x_2 + 4x_3 = 13$$

This can be rewritten in matrix algebra as follows:

$$\begin{pmatrix} 3 & 4 & 6 \\ 2 & 9 & 4 \\ 7 & 2 & 4 \end{pmatrix} \begin{pmatrix} x_1 \\ x_2 \\ x_3 \end{pmatrix} = \begin{pmatrix} 14 \\ 22 \\ 13 \end{pmatrix}$$

where:

$$\begin{pmatrix} 3 & 4 & 6 \\ 2 & 9 & 4 \\ 7 & 2 & 4 \end{pmatrix} = \begin{pmatrix} A_{1,1} & A_{1,2} & A_{1,3} \\ A_{2,1} & A_{2,2} & A_{2,3} \\ A_{3,1} & A_{3,2} & A_{3,3} \end{pmatrix}$$

is the set of coefficients of the above linear equations, and form a 3×3 two-dimensional array, with $A_{1,1} = 3$, $A_{1,2} = 4$, $A_{1,3} = 6$, $A_{2,1} = 2$, $A_{2,2} = 9$, $A_{2,3} = 4$, $A_{3,1} = 7$, $A_{3,2} = 2$, and $A_{3,3} = 4$;

$$\begin{pmatrix} x_1 \\ x_2 \\ x_3 \end{pmatrix}$$

is a one-dimensional array, with x_1 being the first x-value, x_2 the second x-value, and x_3 the third x-value.

$$\begin{pmatrix} 14 \\ 22 \\ 13 \end{pmatrix} = \begin{pmatrix} B_1 \\ B_2 \\ B_3 \end{pmatrix}$$

is a one-dimensional array, with $B_1 = 14$, $B_2 = 22$, and $B_3 = 13$.

A two-dimensional array has a column and row arrangement. In the above example of a two-dimensional array the columns and rows are as follows:

	Column 1	*Column 2*	*Column 3*
Row 1	3	4	6
Row 2	2	9	4
Row 3	7	2	4

The columns run vertically, and the rows run horizontally. The first subscript of a two-dimensional array refers to the row, and the second subscript refers to the column:

$A_{2,3}$ is the element of the second row and the third column, and therefore equals 4.

In this chapter frequent reference will be made to one-dimensional arrays or vectors and to two-dimensional arrays or matrixes.

BASIC Representation of Subscripts of Vectors and Matrixes

In BASIC we refer to the elements of a vector or a matrix by putting the subscripts in parentheses.

EX. [3]

Algebra	BASIC	
X_i	$X(I)$	is the element i in vector X
$A_{i,j}$	$A(I,J)$	is the element in the row i and column j of the matrix A.
$A_{5,4}$	$A(5,4)$	is the element in the fifth row and the fourth column of the two-dimensional array, or matrix, A.

Most BASIC systems allow for the use of single letters only to name a one-dimensional (vector) or a two-dimensional array (matrix). Therefore, a BASIC program cannot contain more than twenty-six subscripted variables. In a program, the same single letter name can be used to reference a simple nonsubscripted variable and to reference a vector or a matrix. Therefore, it is perfectly all right to use **A** and **A(10)** in the same program. The statement context in which the name is used will convey to the system whether either elements of the array are referenced or the nonsubscripted variable is considered. The subscripts of arrays can be constants, variables, and even complicated expressions. It is the truncated value of these constants, variables, or expressions which serve as the actual subscript, referencing an element of the array.

Dimension Statement

Certain information must be supplied to the BASIC interpreter when using vectors or matrixes, such as:

—How many subscripts (one or two) are there for each subscripted variable?
—What is the maximum size of each subscript?

This information is given in a dimension statement, which has the following general form:

DIMENSION v, v, v, . . .

where: the **v's** stand for variable names followed by parentheses, enclosing 1 or 2 integer constants, giving the maximum size of each subscript.

10   DIMENSION X(10), A(2), B(3,4)

When BASIC processes a **DIMENSION** statement, it will set aside enough storage locations to contain the vectors or matrixes. In the above **DIMENSION** statement, the BASIC translator assigns **ten** storage locations for the one-dimensional array **X**, **two** storage locations for the vector **A** and 3×4 = **12** storage locations for the matrix **B**. Storage assignments are made in a special order. With respect to the matrix B in Example [4]; the assignments are made in the following order.

B(1,1), B(1,2), B(1,3), B(1,4), B(2,1), B(2,2),
B(2,3), B(2,4), B(3,1), B(3,2), B(3,3), B(3,4)

A **DIMENSION** statement is a nonexecutable statement. It only provides information for the BASIC translator. It must occur prior to any other BASIC statement in which the subscripted variable name is used.

DIMENSION, in the dimension statement may be abbreviated as follows:

10   DIM X(10), A(2), B(3,4)

Example [4] dimensions two arrays, **X** and **A**, and one matrix. As indicated before, **ten** cells are allocated to **X**, **two** cells are allocated to **A**, and **twelve** cells are allocated to **B**. This is the case on most systems. However, some systems allow for a zero subscript. If this is the case, the above dimension statement provides **eleven** cells for **X** (X(0), X(1), X(2), X(3), X(4), X(5), X(6), X(7), X(8), X(9), X(10)); **three** cells for **A** (A(0), A(1), A(2)), and finally 4×5 = **20** cells for **B** (B(0,0), B(0,1), B(0,2), B(0,3), B(1,4), B(1,0), B(1,1), B(1,2), B(1,3), B(1,4), B(2,0), B(2,1), B(2,2), B(2,3), B(2,4), B(3,0), B(3,1), B(3,2), B(3,3), and B(3,4)). Zero subscripts will not be considered in this text.

BASIC dimensions by default. However, if there are no dimensions given only ten cells are provided for each vector or 10×10 spaces are provided for each undimensioned matrix. If this allocation does not suffice, explicit dimensions must be given.

Example [5] shows an incorrect way of dimensioning the vector **A**:

EX. [5]

10   LET K = 25
20   DIMENSION A(K)

Recall that the statement on line 10 is executed during the execution of the BASIC program, or after the entire program is compiled. Since the **DIMENSION** statement is a nonexecutable statement, it is considered during the compilation of the entire program. For the above example, during the translation of the BASIC program, the system will not know the value of K and, therefore, no cells can be allocated to the vector A. Most systems will flag an error when the above type of **DIMENSION** statement occurs in a BASIC program.

Input/Output Statements for Subscripted Variables

There are many ways to input and output the elements of vectors or matrixes. Several of these methods are discussed in this section. All input/output forms, which are discussed here, are equally efficient. It is up to the user to elect the form that suits his particular problem best.

INPUT/OUTPUT OF ONE ELEMENT OF AN ARRAY

The following general forms indicate how one element of an array can be read into core memory or can be printed out:

$$\text{READ} \quad \langle \text{list } (e_i) \rangle$$
$$\text{INPUT} \quad \langle \text{list } (e_i) \rangle$$
$$\text{PRINT} \quad \langle \text{list } (e_i) \rangle$$

where: **list** is a list of names of BASIC arrays which can be either single or double subscripted variable names.

e_i are arithmetic expressions for each of the subscripts of the array. The truncated value of these expressions references a particular element of the array.

Clearly, if the array is a one-dimensional array or a vector, then only one expression is needed to identify the element under consideration. Since two subscripts are needed to identify an element of a matrix (the row and the column subscript), two expressions are necessary to identify the element.

The following example illustrates the above.

EX. [6]

```
10   DIMENSION A(15), B(10, 20), C(2,3)
     •
     •
     •
20   INPUT A(14)
     •
     •
     •
30   LET D = 2*3.25
40   LET E = 2
     •
     •
50   INPUT A(E), A(D*E), B(D,E)
     •
     •
     •
```

60   PRINT B(5, D + 3), C(1,2)

70   STOP

Statement 10 gives arrays **A**, **B**, and **C** dimensions. During compilation, **fifteen** cells are allocated to **A**, $10 \times 20 = 200$ cells are set aside for **B**, and $2 \times 3 = 6$ storage locations are reserved for the matrix **C**. Line 20 inputs one single constant and places it in the 14th cell of the one-dimensional array **A**, since this cell is indicated in the INPUT statement. The value of **D** is calculated in statement 30 and equals 6.50, whereas line 40 assigns the constant 2 to the basic variable **E**. Both of these constants are used in the INPUT statement in line 50: **A(E)** refers to the second element of **A**, **A(D*E)** refer to the (6.5*2) 13th element of A, and, finally, **B(D,E)** refers to the element in the sixth row (truncated value of **D**) and the second (**E**) column of the matrix **B**. The PRINT statement in line 60 results in the printing of two constants: an element of the matrix **B** which represents the fifth row and the ninth column (truncated value of **D + 3**), and the element in the first row and the second column of matrix **C**.

The **MAT READ** and the **MAT INPUT** statements can also be used to read arrays of strings. This is handy for reading messages in memory as follows:

10   DIM R$ (70)

20   MAT READ R$

The above pair of statements are sufficient for reading 70 strings in an array called **R$**.

INPUT/OUTPUT OF AN ARRAY, USING THE FOR-NEXT LOOP

The above input/output procedure is used to output one element of a vector or an array. The FOR-NEXT loop can be used to input or output part or an entire array. If this is the case, then the index of the loop is also used as the index of the subscript of the array. Changing the index from 1 (one) up to the maximum dimension size enables us to read, to input, or to print the entire one-dimensional array. Likewise, a matrix can be read, inputted, or printed through the use of two loops, where the inner loop reflects the column or row index and the outer loop reflects the row or column index. These procedures are illustrated in the following examples.

EX. [7]

10   DIMENSION A(8)

20   FOR J = 1 TO 8

30   INPUT A(J)

40   NEXT J

•

•

Example [7] illustrates how eight elements can be read from terminal input. During compilation **eight** cells are allocated to the vector **A** and during execution **eight** constants are assigned to these cells through the INPUT statement in line 30. Notice the use of the FOR-NEXT loop index **J** in the input statement! As indicated in the section of the **DIMENSION** statement, it is not necessary to dimension a vector that consists of no more than ten elements. Therefore, one could omit the **DIMENSION** statement in Example [7]. Consequently, the vector **A** would have an implied size of ten. However, the user should realize that storage space can be saved when using the **DIMENSION** statement for vectors which are smaller than ten, and for matrixes which are smaller than 10×10.

EX. [8]

Consider the following table which represents three test grades which eight students obtained in a course on BASIC programming.

	Student	Test 1	Test 2	Test 3
Row 1	1	40	33	45
Row 2	2	81	90	88
Row 3	3	90	91	68
Row 4	4	81	75	75
Row 5	5	55	76	74
Row 6	6	85	95	83
Row 7	7	83	62	47
Row 8	8	85	89	77
		Column 1	Column 2	Column 3

The above information can be stored in an 8×3 matrix and is read into a matrix by either of the following sets of BASIC statements.

```
10   DIMENSION A(8,3)
20   FOR I = 1 TO 8
30   FOR J = 1 TO 3
40   READ A(I, J)
50   NEXT J
60   NEXT I
70   DATA 40, 33, 45, 81, 90, 88, 90, 91, 68, 81, 75, 75
80   DATA 55, 76, 74, 85, 95, 83, 83, 62, 47, 85, 89, 77
     •
     •
```

In the above set of BASIC statements the data is read into core row by row. If one wishes to read the data column by column, then the following statement organization is necessary:

```
10    DIMENSION A(8,3)
20    FOR J = 1 TO 3
30    FOR I = 1 TO 8
40    READ A(I, J)
50    NEXT I
60    NEXT J
70    DATA 40, 81, 90, 81, 55, 85, 83, 85, 33, 90, 91, 75
80    DATA 76, 95, 62, 89, 45, 88, 68, 75, 74, 83, 47, 77
      •
      •
```

Notice how the list of the data in the **DATA** statements is reorganized to insure proper input: column by column or test by test. Again, the **DIMENSION** statement in the above example is optional, since **A** is not larger than 10 × 10. A total number of 8 × 3 = 24 cells are allocated to the matrix **A**. This is a significant reduction from 100 cells, which would be assigned if no **DIMENSION** were given.

MAT INPUT/OUTPUT STATEMENTS

MAT statements make the input and output of matrixes very convenient. Through one **MAT** statement an entire array can be read into core or printed out. The general form of the **MAT** input statements is:

> MAT   READ ⟨list⟩
> MAT   INPUT ⟨list⟩ **for terminal input**

⟨**list**⟩ represents a list of BASIC array names, separated by commas. A dimension statement indicates the size of the array that will be read in. Matrixes are read in row-by-row.

EX. [9]

```
10    DIMENSION A(8,3)
20    MAT READ A
30    DATA 40, 33, 45, 81, 90, 88, 90, 91, 68, 81, 75, 75
40    DATA 55, 76, 74, 85, 95, 83, 83, 62, 47, 85, 89, 77
      •
      •
```

Example [9] reads into core the same matrix as in Example [8]. When the **MAT INPUT** statement is used, continuous question mark promptings occur, until the entire array is supplied to the system.

The general form of the **MAT PRINT** statement is:

MAT PRINT ⟨**list**⟩

⟨**list**⟩ represents a list of BASIC array names, separated by commas or semi-colons. Matrixes are printed row-by-row, with each row starting a new line. Recall that only five constants can be printed on a terminal output line. How-ever, if the matrix name is followed by a semicolon, then the printing is packed and consequently more than five elements of one matrix row can be printed on one output line.

For reasons of efficiency, one-dimensional arrays or vectors are printed out as row-vectors; in other words the elements are printed out just like the elements of rows of matrix.

The array names in a **MAT READ** or a **MAT INPUT** statement can be followed by one- or two-dimensional subscripts. In this case the subscripts must be defined and can not have a dimension larger than the original number of cells which were set aside for the array through the **DIMENSION** statement. If the name of an array is followed by above mentioned subscripts, then the array is redimensioned before the elements are read in.

EX. [10]

Again, consider the data of Example [8] which represents three test grades obtained by eight students. Assume that we wish to read in and write out the first two test grades obtained by the eight students. Under the assump-tion that the original dimension of 8 × 3 is given, the following BASIC program accomplishes the above.

```
10 DIMENSIØN A(8,3)
20 MAT READ A(8,2)
30 MAT PRINT A
40 DATA 40,33,81,90,90,91,81,75
50 DATA 55,76,85,95,83,62,85,89
60 STØP
```

This program generates the following output:

```
40          33
81          90
90          91
81          75
55          76
85          95
83          62
85          89
```

The **DIMENSION** statement reserves 8×3 or 24 cells for matrix **A**. Only $8 \times 2 = 16$ elements are read into core, since **MAT READ A(8,2)** redimensions the matrix **A** and reads in $8 \times 2 = 16$ constants. By observing the output it is clear that the matrix **A** consists of eight rows and only two columns, rather than eight rows and three columns as indicated in the **DIMENSION** statement of line 10.

Vector and Matrix Operations

The BASIC language lends itself very well for certain matrix operations. The nine operations which are to be discussed in this section are: the addition of two matrixes; the subtraction of two matrixes; the unary negation of matrix elements; the scalar multiplication; the multiplication of two matrixes; solution to simultaneous linear equations; the matrix assignment; the inverse of a matrix; the transpose of a matrix. Note however, that not all BASICs recognize the full set of matrix operations.

ADDITION OF TWO MATRIXES

Two matrixes **A** and **B** can be added to form the matrix **C**, if and only if matrix **A** and matrix **B** are of the same size. Therefore, matrix **A** must have the same number of rows and the same number of columns as matrix **B** has. The resulting matrix **C** will be of the same size as matrix **A** or **B**, since corresponding elements of the **A** and **B** matrixes are added to form matrix **C** (i.e.: $c_{ij} = a_{ij} + b_{ij}$). This is illustrated in the following example:

$$A = \begin{bmatrix} 1 & 2 & 3 \\ 4 & 5 & 6 \\ 7 & 8 & 9 \end{bmatrix} \quad B = \begin{bmatrix} 9 & 8 & 7 \\ 6 & 5 & 4 \\ 3 & 2 & 1 \end{bmatrix} \quad A+B = \begin{bmatrix} 1+9 & 2+8 & 3+7 \\ 4+6 & 5+5 & 6+4 \\ 7+3 & 8+2 & 9+1 \end{bmatrix} = C = \begin{bmatrix} 10 & 10 & 10 \\ 10 & 10 & 10 \\ 10 & 10 & 10 \end{bmatrix}$$

The general BASIC form for adding two matrixes **A** and **B** is:

$$\text{MAT LET C} = \text{A} + \text{B}$$

where: **A, B, and C** are different matrix names.
+ is the matrix addition operator.
LET is the optional assignment key word.

The above matrix addition is illustrated in the following BASIC program.

```
10 DIMENSIØN A(3,3),B(3,3),C(3,3)
20 MAT READ A,B
30 MAT LET C=A+B
40 PRINT "MATRIX A EQUALS:"
50 MAT PRINT A;
60 PRINT "MATRIX B EQUALS:"
70 MAT PRINT B;
80 PRINT "MATRIX C EQUALS:"
90 MAT PRINT C;
100 DATA 1,2,3,4,5,6,7,8,9
110 DATA 9,8,7,6,5,4,3,2,1
120 STØP
```

```
MATRIX A EQUALS:
1 2 3
4 5 6
7 8 9
MATRIX B EQUALS:
9 8 7
6 5 4
3 2 1
MATRIX C EQUALS:
10 10 10
10 10 10
10 10 10
```

Several observations can be made from the above example: Note that matrixes are read in row-by-row and printed out in that same manner. The packed matrix output stems from the use of a semicolon behind the matrix names in the various print statements.

SUBTRACTION OF TWO MATRIXES

Just as is the case in adding two matrixes, matrix **A** and **B** can be subtracted from each other to form the matrix **C**, if and only if the matrix **A** is of the same order (same number of rows and columns) as matrix **B**. Corresponding elements of **A** and **B** matrixes are subtracted to form matrix **C** (i.e.: $c_{ij} = a_{ij} - b_{ij}$). Under the assumption that the minuend matrix is the **A** matrix and that the subtrahend matrix is the **B** matrix, the subtraction is illustrated in the following example:

$$A = \begin{bmatrix} 1 & 2 & 3 & 4 \\ 5 & 6 & 7 & 8 \\ 9 & 10 & 11 & 12 \end{bmatrix} \quad B = \begin{bmatrix} 12 & 11 & 10 & 9 \\ 8 & 7 & 6 & 5 \\ 4 & 3 & 2 & 1 \end{bmatrix} \quad A - B = \begin{bmatrix} 1-12 & 2-11 & 3-10 & 4 \\ 5-8 & 6-7 & 7-6 & 8 \\ 9-4 & 10-3 & 11-2 & 12 \end{bmatrix}$$

$$A - B = C = \begin{bmatrix} -11 & -9 & -7 & -5 \\ -3 & -1 & 1 & 3 \\ 5 & 7 & 9 & 11 \end{bmatrix}$$

The general BASIC form for subtracting two matrixes **A** and **B** is:

$$\textbf{MAT LET C} = \textbf{A} - \textbf{B}$$

where: **A, B, and C** are different matrix names.
           − is the matrix subtraction operator.
           LET is the optional assignment key word.

The above matrix subtraction is illustrated in the following BASIC program.

EX. [12] MATRIX SUBTRACTION

```
10  DIMENSIØN A(3,4),B(3,4),C(3,4)
20  MAT READ A,B
30  MAT LET C=A-B
40  PRINT "MATRIX A EQUALS:"
50  MAT PRINT A
60  PRINT "MATRIX B EQUALS:"
70  MAT PRINT B
80  PRINT "MATRIX C EQUALS:"
90  MAT PRINT C
100 DATA 1,2,3,4,5,6,7,8,9,10,11,12
110 DATA 12,11,10,9,8,7,6,5,4,3,2,1
120 STØP


MATRIX A EQUALS:
1                 2                 3                 4
5                 6                 7                 8
9                 10                11                12
MATRIX B EQUALS:
12                11                10                9
8                 7                 6                 5
4                 3                 2                 1
MATRIX C EQUALS:
-11               -9                -7                -5
-3                -1                1                 3
5                 7                 9                 11
```

The matrix printing in this example is not packed. A packed output would not look quite well in this example, since the elements of the resulting matrix **C** do not occupy an equal amount of space.

UNARY NEGATION OF MATRIX ELEMENTS

The sign of all elements in a matrix or a vector can be changed through the unary negation operator (−). The following illustrates this algebraically:

$$A = \begin{bmatrix} 1 & 2 & 3 \\ 4 & 5 & 6 \\ 7 & 8 & 9 \end{bmatrix} \quad -A = - \begin{bmatrix} 1 & 2 & 3 \\ 4 & 5 & 6 \\ 7 & 8 & 9 \end{bmatrix} \quad -A = B = \begin{bmatrix} -1 & -2 & -3 \\ -4 & -5 & -6 \\ -7 & -8 & -9 \end{bmatrix}$$

The general BASIC form for the unary negation of a matrix **A** is:

$$\textbf{MAT LET B} = -\textbf{A}$$

where: **A and B** are different matrix names.

    − is the unary minus operator.

    LET is the optional assignment key word.

The above matrix negation is illustrated in the following BASIC program.

```
10 DIMENSIØN A(3,3),B(3,3)
20 MAT READ A
30 MAT LET B=-A
40 PRINT "MATRIX A EQUALS:"
50 MAT PRINT A;
60 PRINT "MATRIX B EQUALS:"
70 MAT PRINT B;
80 DATA 1,2,3,4,5,6,7,8,9
90 STØP


MATRIX A EQUALS:
1  2  3
4  5  6
7  8  9
MATRIX B EQUALS:
-1 -2 -3
-4 -5 -6
-7 -8 -9
```

The program and output are self-explanatory. Again, notice the packed printing!

SCALAR MULTIPLICATION

All elements in a matrix can be multiplied by a constant through scalar multiplication.

The following illustrates scalar multiplication algebraically.

$$A = \begin{bmatrix} 1 & 2 & 3 & 4 \\ 5 & 6 & 7 & 8 \\ 9 & 10 & 11 & 12 \end{bmatrix} \quad (2) \times A = \begin{bmatrix} 2\times1 & 2\times 2 & 2\times 3 & 2\times 4 \\ 2\times5 & 2\times 6 & 2\times 7 & 2\times 8 \\ 2\times9 & 2\times10 & 2\times11 & 2\times12 \end{bmatrix}$$

$$(2) \times A = B = \begin{bmatrix} 2 & 4 & 6 & 8 \\ 10 & 12 & 14 & 16 \\ 18 & 20 & 22 & 24 \end{bmatrix}$$

The general BASIC form for scalar multiplication of a matrix **A** is:

MAT LET B = (exp)*A.

where: **A and B** are different matrix names.

exp is the expression, which becomes the multiplier.

* is the multiplication operator.

LET is the optional assignment key word.

Note that the expression must be enclosed within parentheses. The above scalar multiplication is illustrated in the following program.

```
10 DIMENSIØN A(3,4),B(3,4)
20 MAT READ A
30 MAT LET B=(2)*A
40 PRINT "MATRIX A EQUALS:"
50 MAT PRINT A
60 PRINT "MATRIX B EQUALS:"
70 MAT PRINT B
80 DATA 1,2,3,4,5,6,7,8,9,10,11,12
90 STØP


MATRIX A EQUALS:
1               2               3               4
5               6               7               8
9               10              11              12
MATRIX B EQUALS:
2               4               6               8
10              12              14              16
18              20              22              24
```

MULTIPLICATION OF TWO MATRIXES

Two matrixes **A** and **B** can be multiplied (**A** × **B**) if and only if matrix **A** has as many columns as matrix **B** has rows. An element **c**$_{ij}$ in the resulting **C** matrix is obtained by making the scalar product of the **ith** row of matrix **A** with the **jth** column of matrix **B**. Algebraically, given an **m X n** matrix **A** and an **n X p** matrix **B**, then the product of **A** × **B** results in an **m X p** matrix **C**, with elements defined by:

$$c_{ij} = \sum_{k=1}^{n} a_{ik} b_{kj} \qquad \begin{array}{l} \text{for all i and j} \\ i = 1, 2, 3, \ldots, m \\ j = 1, 2, 3, \ldots, p \end{array}$$

The above rather complicated definition is illustrated in the following example:

$$A = \begin{bmatrix} 1 & 2 & 3 & 4 \\ 5 & 6 & 7 & 8 \\ 9 & 10 & 11 & 12 \end{bmatrix} \quad B = \begin{bmatrix} 12 & 11 & 10 \\ 9 & 8 & 7 \\ 6 & 5 & 4 \\ 3 & 2 & 1 \end{bmatrix} \quad C = A \times B$$

$$C = \begin{bmatrix} (1\times12)+(2\times9)+(3\times6)+(4\times3) & (1\times11)+(2\times8)+(3\times5)+(4\times2) & (1\times10)+(2\times7)+(3\times4)+(4\times1) \\ (5\times12)+(6\times9)+(7\times6)+(8\times3) & (5\times11)+(6\times8)+(7\times5)+(8\times2) & (5\times10)+(6\times7)+(7\times4)+(8\times1) \\ (9\times12)+(10\times9)+(11\times6)+(12\times3) & (9\times11)+(10\times8)+(11\times5)+(12\times2) & (9\times10)+(10\times7)+(11\times4)+(12\times1) \end{bmatrix}$$

$$A \times B = \begin{bmatrix} 1 & 2 & 3 & 4 \\ 5 & 6 & 7 & 8 \\ 9 & 10 & 11 & 12 \end{bmatrix} \times \begin{bmatrix} 12 & 11 & 10 \\ 9 & 8 & 7 \\ 6 & 5 & 4 \\ 3 & 2 & 1 \end{bmatrix} = \begin{bmatrix} 60 & 50 & 40 \\ 180 & 154 & 128 \\ 300 & 258 & 216 \end{bmatrix} = C$$

Note that $c_{3,2} = 258 = \sum_{k=1}^{4} a_{3,k} b_{k,2} = (9 \times 11) + (10 \times 8) + (11 \times 6) + (12 \times 2)$

So the element in the third row and the second column of matrix **C** is obtained by making the sum of the paired products of elements in the third row of matrix **A** with the elements in the second column of matrix **B**.

The general BASIC form of matrix multiplication of **A** and **B** is as follows:

$$\text{MAT LET C} = \text{A*B}$$

where: **A, B, and C** are different matrix names.

* is the multiplication operator.

LET is the optional assignment key word.

The above tedious multiplication process is illustrated in the following BASIC program. Note its simplicity, since BASIC has taken the "thinking process" out of it!

EX. [15] MATRIX MULTIPLICATION

```
10 DIMENSIØN A(3,4),B(4,3),C(3,3)
20 MAT READ A
30 MAT READ B
40 MAT LET C=A*B
50 PRINT "MATRIX A EQUALS:"
60 MAT PRINT A
70 PRINT "MATRIX B EQUALS:"
80 MAT PRINT B
90 PRINT "MATRIX C EQUALS:"
100 MAT PRINT C
110 DATA 1,2,3,4,5,6,7,8,9,10,11,12
120 DATA 12,11,10,9,8,7,6,5,4,3,2,1
130 STØP


MATRIX A EQUALS:
1               2               3               4
5               6               7               8
9               10              11              12
MATRIX B EQUALS:
12              11              10
9               8               7
6               5               4
3               2               1
MATRIX C EQUALS:
60              50              40
180             154             128
300             258             216
```

SOLUTION TO SIMULTANEOUS LINEAR EQUATIONS

Consider the following simultaneous linear equations,

$$2x_1 + x_2 + 4x_3 = 16$$
$$3x_1 + 2x_2 + x_3 = 10$$
$$x_1 + 3x_2 + 3x_3 = 16$$

which can be written in matrix algebra as follows:

$$\begin{bmatrix} 2 & 1 & 4 \\ 3 & 2 & 1 \\ 1 & 3 & 3 \end{bmatrix} = \begin{bmatrix} x_1 \\ x_2 \\ x_3 \end{bmatrix} = \begin{bmatrix} 16 \\ 10 \\ 16 \end{bmatrix} \Rightarrow B \times X = A$$

If one wishes to solve the above simultaneous linear equations for $X = [x_1, x_2, x_3]$, then one must go through the following steps:

Step #1: Divide both sides by the square matrix B.

$$\frac{\begin{bmatrix} 2 & 1 & 4 \\ 3 & 2 & 1 \\ 1 & 3 & 3 \end{bmatrix} \times \begin{bmatrix} x_1 \\ x_2 \\ x_3 \end{bmatrix}}{\begin{bmatrix} 2 & 1 & 4 \\ 3 & 2 & 1 \\ 1 & 3 & 3 \end{bmatrix}} = \frac{\begin{bmatrix} 16 \\ 10 \\ 16 \end{bmatrix}}{\begin{bmatrix} 2 & 1 & 4 \\ 3 & 2 & 1 \\ 1 & 3 & 3 \end{bmatrix}}$$

Step #2: Reduce both sides by dividing numerator and denominator by same matrix.

$$\begin{bmatrix} x_1 \\ x_2 \\ x_3 \end{bmatrix} = \frac{\begin{bmatrix} 16 \\ 10 \\ 16 \end{bmatrix}}{\begin{bmatrix} 2 & 1 & 4 \\ 3 & 2 & 1 \\ 1 & 3 & 3 \end{bmatrix}} = X = A/B$$

Note that $B \times X = A$ is equivalent to $X = A/B$, which gives the solution to the above simultaneous equations. In matrix algebra $\dfrac{1}{[B]} = [B]^{-1}$ is called the inverse of the matrix B. Many BASIC systems provide us with the following general form to find the solution to simultaneous equations:

MAT LET X = A/B

where: **X** is an n X 1 matrix.
       A is an n X 1 matrix.
       B is an X n nonsingular square matrix.
       / is the division operator.
   LET is the optional assignment key word.

Note that it is absolutely necessary to define **X** and **A** as **n X 1** matrixes, rather than vectors with n elements. The above simultaneous equations are solved in the following BASIC program.

EX. [16] SIMULTANEOUS LINEAR EQUATIONS

```
10 DIMENSIØN A(3,1),B(3,3),X(3,1)
20 MAT READ A
30 MAT READ B
40 MAT LET X=A/B
50 PRINT "VECTØR A EQUALS:"
60 MAT PRINT A;
70 PRINT "MATRIX B EQUALS:"
80 MAT PRINT B;
90 PRINT "RESULTING VECTØR X EQUALS:"
100 MAT PRINT X;
110 DATA 16,10,16
120 DATA 2,1,4,3,2,1,1,3,3
130 STØP


VECTØR A EQUALS:
16
10
16
MATRIX B EQUALS:
2  1  4
3  2  1
1  3  3
RESULTING VECTØR X EQUALS:
1
2
3
```

MATRIX ASSIGNMENT

A matrix **A** can be assigned to the matrix **B** by use of the matrix assignment statement. The general form of the BASIC matrix assignment statement is:

MAT LET B = A

where: **A and B** are different matrix names.

LET is the optional assignment key word.

Example [17] illustrates the matrix assignment.

```
10 DIMENSIØN A(3,3),B(3,3)
20 MAT READ A
30 MAT LET B=A
40 PRINT "MATRIX A EQUALS:"
50 MAT PRINT A;
60 PRINT "MATRIX B EQUALS:"
70 MAT PRINT B;
80 DATA 1,2,3,4,5,6,7,8,9
90 STØP


MATRIX A EQUALS:
1  2  3
4  5  6
7  8  9
MATRIX B EQUALS:
1  2  3
4  5  6
7  8  9
```

A matrix **A** can be assigned to another matrix **B** if and only if the two matrixes are of the same order (have the same number of rows and same number of columns).

Some BASIC systems do not recognize the matrix assignment statement. If this is the case, then the user must enable himself of the following scalar multiplication.

30   MAT LET B = (1)*A

MATRIX INVERSE

The inverse of a matrix **A** can be calculated if and only if matrix **A** is a nonsingular square matrix. The resulting matrix **B** is then also a nonsingular square matrix of the same order as the matrix **A**.

Matrix inversion is obtained by the following general statement:

MAT LET B = INV(A)

where: **A and B** are different matrix names.

INV is the matrix function that defines the inverse of A.

LET is the optional assignment key word.

$$\text{Let } A = \begin{bmatrix} 2 & 1 & 4 \\ 3 & 2 & 1 \\ 1 & 3 & 3 \end{bmatrix}, \text{ then } B = \frac{\begin{bmatrix} 1 & 0 & 0 \\ 0 & 1 & 0 \\ 0 & 0 & 1 \end{bmatrix}}{\begin{bmatrix} 2 & 1 & 4 \\ 3 & 2 & 1 \\ 1 & 3 & 3 \end{bmatrix}} = \begin{bmatrix} 2 & 1 & 4 \\ 3 & 2 & 1 \\ 1 & 3 & 3 \end{bmatrix}^{-1}$$

Example [18] calculates the inverse of the above matrix.

EX. [18] MATRIX INVERSE

```
10 DIMENSION A(3,3),B(3,3)
20 MAT READ A
30 MAT LET B=INV(A)
40 PRINT "MATRIX A EQUALS:"
50 MAT PRINT A
60 PRINT "THE INVERSE OF A EQUALS:"
70 MAT PRINT B
80 DATA 2,1,4,3,2,1,1,3,3
90 STOP


MATRIX A EQUALS:
2                 1                 4
3                 2                 1
1                 3                 3
THE INVERSE OF A EQUALS:
0.1153846         0.3461538         -0.2692308
-0.3076923        7.692308E-2       0.3846154
0.2692308         -0.1923077        3.846154E-2
```

Since some BASIC systems do not allow for calculating the solution to simultaneous equations as illustrated by Example [16], it is necessary to obtain this solution through the inverse method.

Reconsider Example [16]: Find the vector $X = [x_1, x_2, x_3]$ s.t.

$$2x_1 + x_2 + 4x_3 = 16$$
$$3x_1 + 2x_2 + x_3 = 10$$
$$x_1 + 3x_2 + 3x_3 = 16$$

or, in matrix algebra notation:

$$\begin{bmatrix} 2 & 1 & 4 \\ 3 & 2 & 1 \\ 1 & 3 & 3 \end{bmatrix} \times \begin{bmatrix} x_1 \\ x_2 \\ x_3 \end{bmatrix} = \begin{bmatrix} 16 \\ 10 \\ 16 \end{bmatrix} => B \times X = A$$

The above can be solved by premultiplying both sides of the equality by the inverse of B.

$$\begin{bmatrix} 2 & 1 & 4 \\ 3 & 2 & 1 \\ 1 & 3 & 3 \end{bmatrix}^{-1} \times \begin{bmatrix} 2 & 1 & 4 \\ 3 & 2 & 1 \\ 1 & 3 & 3 \end{bmatrix} \times \begin{bmatrix} x_1 \\ x_2 \\ x_3 \end{bmatrix} = \begin{bmatrix} 2 & 1 & 4 \\ 3 & 2 & 1 \\ 1 & 3 & 3 \end{bmatrix}^{-1} \times \begin{bmatrix} 16 \\ 10 \\ 16 \end{bmatrix}$$

$$\begin{bmatrix} x_1 \\ x_2 \\ x_3 \end{bmatrix} = \begin{bmatrix} 2 & 1 & 4 \\ 3 & 2 & 1 \\ 1 & 3 & 3 \end{bmatrix}^{-1} \times \begin{bmatrix} 16 \\ 10 \\ 16 \end{bmatrix} => X = B^{-1} \times A$$

So, after reading in matrixes **A** and **B** one must calculate the inverse of **B**, or B^{-1}, store it under matrix **C** and then calculate **X** by multiplying **C** and **A**, as illustrated in the next example.

EX. [19] SIMULTANEOUS LINEAR EQUATIONS THROUGH MATRIX INVERSE

```
10 DIMENSIØN A(3,1),B(3,3),C(3,3),X(3,1)
20 MAT READ A
30 MAT READ B
40 MAT LET C=INV(B)
50 MAT LET X=C*A
60 PRINT "VECTØR A EQUALS:"
70 MAT PRINT A
80 PRINT "MATRIX B EQUALS:"
90 MAT PRINT B;
100 PRINT "RESULTING VECTØR X EQUALS:"
110 MAT PRINT X;
120 DATA 16,10,16
130 DATA 2,1,4,3,2,1,1,3,3
140 STØP


VECTØR A EQUALS:
16
10
16
MATRIX B EQUALS:
2 1 4
3 2 1
1 3 3
RESULTING VECTØR X EQUALS:
1
2
3
```

Note that it is necessary to calculate the inverse separate (Line 40). Line 50 is a straightforward multiplication of two matrixes. It is not legal to combine lines 40 and 50 as follows:

45   MAT LET X = INV(B)*A

TRANSPOSE OF A MATRIX

The transpose of an **m X n** matrix **A** results in an **n X m** matrix **B**, since rows and columns are interchanged through this operation. So, the transpose of a matrix **A** is a matrix **B** which is formed by interchanging rows and columns, such that **row j** of matrix **A** becomes **column j** in the transposed matrix **B**. The following example illustrates this concept:

$$A = \begin{bmatrix} 1 & 2 & 3 & 4 \\ 5 & 6 & 7 & 8 \\ 9 & 10 & 11 & 12 \end{bmatrix} \quad B = \begin{bmatrix} 1 & 5 & 9 \\ 2 & 6 & 10 \\ 3 & 7 & 11 \\ 4 & 8 & 12 \end{bmatrix}$$

Matrix transposition is obtained by the following general statement:

MAT LET B = TRN(A)

where: **A and B** are different matrix names.

TRN is the matrix function that defines the transpose of A.

LET is the optional assignment key word.

Example [20] illustrates the above matrix transposition.

EX. [20] MATRIX TRANSPOSE

```
10 DIMENSIØN A(3,4),B(4,3)
20 MAT READ A
30 MAT LET B=TRN(A)
40 PRINT "MATRIX A EQUALS:"
50 MAT PRINT A
60 PRINT "THE TRANSPØSE ØF A EQUALS:"
70 MAT PRINT B
80 DATA 1,2,3,4,5,6,7,8,9,10,11,12
90 STØP


MATRIX A EQUALS:
1               2               3               4
5               6               7               8
9               10              11              12
THE TRANSPØSE ØF A EQUALS:
1               5               9
2               6               10
3               7               11
4               8               12
```

As already pointed out in this section, but not explicitly stated, the programmer who uses matrix operations must be very careful in assigning correct dimensions in **DIMENSION** statements, since matrix operations do not dimension any resulting matrixes.

Redimensioning and Special Matrix Assignments

RDM, CON, IDN, and **ZER** are four BASIC functions to make special matrix assignments. **RDM** redimensions a previously dimensioned matrix,

CON assigns ones to all elements of a matrix, **IDN** defines a square matrix as an identity matrix, and **ZER** assigns zeroes to all elements of a matrix.

The general form of the BASIC redimension statement is:

$$\textbf{MAT LET A = RDM (exp1, exp2)}$$

where: **A** is any matrix name.

RDM is the redimensioning function.

exp1 and exp2 are basic expressions.

LET is the optional assignment key word.

When the above redimensioning statement is executed, the system evaluates, truncates and tests the expressions **exp1** and **exp2**. The truncated value of the first expression, **exp1**, represents the new row dimension, whereas the truncated value of the second expression, **exp2**, represents the new column dimension. These new dimensions may not exceed the original dimensions.

The following are the general forms for the CON, IDN, and ZER assignments.

$$\textbf{MAT LET A = CON}$$
$$\textbf{MAT LET A = CON(exp1, exp2)}$$
$$\textbf{MAT LET A = IDN}$$
$$\textbf{MAT LET A = IDN(exp1, exp2)}$$
$$\textbf{MAT LET A = ZER}$$
$$\textbf{MAT LET A = ZER(exp1, exp2)}$$

where: **A** is a matrix name.

CON, IDN, and ZER are special matrix assignments as previously indicated.

exp1 and exp2 are optional expressions for row and column redimensioning.

LET is the optional assignment key word.

When redimensioning takes place, the new dimensions should not exceed the original dimensions of the matrix. If **exp1** and **exp2** are omitted, then the current dimensions are used. Redimensioning and special matrix assignments are illustrated in the following example:

```
10 DIMENSIØN A(8,8)
20 MAT READ A
30 PRINT "MATRIX A EQUALS:"
40 MAT PRINT A;
50 MAT LET A=RDM(5,5)
60 PRINT "MATRIX A NØW IS EQUAL TØ:"
70 MAT PRINT A;
80 MAT LET A=CØN
90 PRINT "MATRIX A EQUALS:"
100 MAT PRINT A;
110 MAT LET A=IDN(2*2,4)
120 PRINT "MATRIX A IS THE IDENTITY MATRIX:"
130 MAT PRINT A;
140 MAT LET A=ZER
150 PRINT "MATRIX A IS FILLED UP WITH ZERØS:"
160 MAT PRINT A;
170 DATA 1,2,3,4,5,6,7,8,9,1,2,3,4,5,6,7,8,9
180 DATA 1,2,3,4,5,6,7,8,9,1,2,3,4,5,6,7,8,9
190 DATA 1,2,3,4,5,6,7,8,9,1,2,3,4,5,6,7,8,9
200 DATA 1,2,3,4,5,6,7,8,9,1
210 STØP
```

The original dimensions of matrix **A** is 8×8, as defined in line 10. When the matrix is redimensioned, 5×5, in line 50, it is obvious from the output that it does not refer to the first five rows and five columns of the original 8×8 matrix. During the execution of line 80 the "current" size of the matrix **A** is 5×5, therefore "ones" will be assigned to the 5×5 square matrix **A**, as is shown by the printout statement in line 100. The identity matrix is assigned to the redimensioned 4×4 matrix **A** in line 110 and, finally, zeros are assigned to that same 4×4 matrix **A** in statement 140.

```
MATRIX A EQUALS:
1  2  3  4  5  6  7  8
9  1  2  3  4  5  6  7
8  9  1  2  3  4  5  6
7  8  9  1  2  3  4  5
6  7  8  9  1  2  3  4
5  6  7  8  9  1  2  3
4  5  6  7  8  9  1  2
3  4  5  6  7  8  9  1
MATRIX A NØW IS EQUAL TØ:
0  0  0  1  2
4  5  6  7  8
9  1  2  3  4
6  7  0  8  9
2  3  4  5  6
MATRIX A EQUALS:
1  1  1  1  1
1  1  1  1  1
1  1  1  1  1
1  1  1  1  1
1  1  1  1  1
MATRIX A IS THE IDENTITY MATRIX:
1  0  0  0
0  1  0  0
0  0  1  0
0  0  0  1
MATRIX A IS FILLED UP WITH ZERØS:
0  0  0  0
0  0  0  0
0  0  0  0
0  0  0  0
```

Examples with Subscripted Variables

In conclusion, here are two business examples where subscripted variables are used.

EX. [22] COMPUTATION OF MARKET STATISTICS

Consider the following estimated distribution of stainless plates in net tons by states.

ALA	173	MAINE	55	OHIO	1868
ARIZ	33	MD	255	OKLA	150
ARK	32	MASS	852	OREG	152
CALIF	1418	MICH	1170	PA	1817
COLO	86	MINN	233	RI	103
CONN	714	MISS	106	SC	76
DEL	55	MO	373	SDAK	11
FLA	146	MONT	12	TENN	265
GA	150	NEBR	49	TEX	522
IDAHO	14	NEV	8	UTAH	59
ILL	1844	NH	67	VT	15
IND	660	NJ	926	VA	196
IOWA	191	NMEX	16	WASH	217
KANS	118	NY	1687	WVA	71
KY	227	NC	152	WIS	816
LA	133	NDAK	7	WYO	8
				DC	8

A program is written here to analyze above data in order to generate the following statistics:

$$\text{TOTAL (S2)}$$
$$\text{AVERAGE (M)}$$
$$\text{VARIANCE (V)}$$
$$\text{RANGE (R)}$$

The TOTAL (**S2**) reflects the total estimated production in net tons of stainless plates in the United States.

The AVERAGE (**M**) is the average estimated production in net tons of stainless plates for the above 49 states.

The VARIANCE (**V**) gives the discrepancy of the estimated production over the 49 states and is equal to the sum of the squared differences between the observed production and mean production, divided by the number of observations (49).

The RANGE (**R**) is the difference between the largest (**B**) and the smallest observation (**S1**).

The procedure for calculating these statistics is outlined in the following flowchart, where **P** is the observed production for the different states. **P** is dimensioned as a vector with a maximum of 50 elements; 49 of these are used in the program, since there are only 49 states to consider.

The flowchart is self-explanatory. Notice that it is necessary to remember all production data, as this data is reused in the second loop to calculate the VARIANCE (**V**), after the AVERAGE (**M**) value is calculated in the first loop.

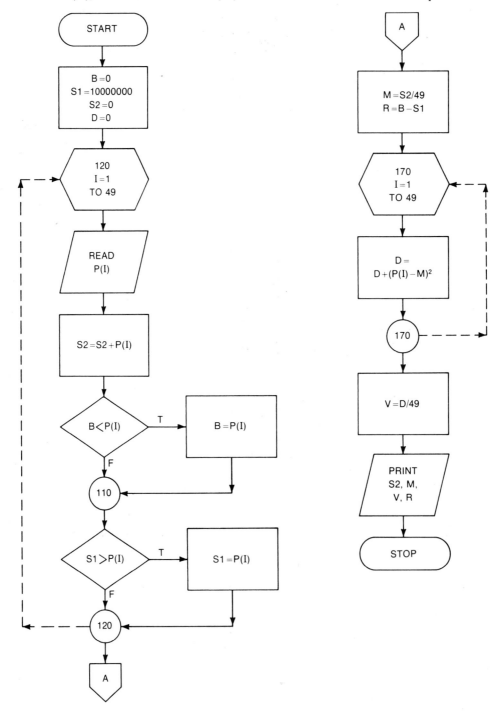

```
10 PRINT "1COMPUTE MARKET STATISTICS"
20 DIMENSION P(50)
30 LET B=0 /* BIGGEST ELEMENT
40 LET S1=10000000 /* SMALLEST ELEMENT
50 LET S2=0 /* SUM OF ELEMENTS
60 LET D=0 /* SQUARE OF DIFFERENCES (SUM)
70 FOR I=1 TO 49
80 READ P(I)
90 S2=S2+P(I)
100 IF B<P(I) THEN: B=P(I)
110 IF S1>P(I) THEN: S1=P(I)
120 NEXT I
130 M=S2/49 /* MEAN OF P(I)'S
140 R=B-S1 /* RANGE OF P(I)'S
150 FOR I=1 TO 49
160 D=D+(P(I)-M)**2
170 NEXT I
180 V=D/49 /* VARIANCE OF P(I)'S
190 PRINT " TOTAL=",S2
200 PRINT " AVERAGE=",M
210 PRINT " VARIANCE=",V
220 PRINT "RANGE=",R
230 PRINT "1"
240 DATA 173,33,32,1418,86,714,55,146,150,14,1844,660,191,119,227,133,5
*5
250 DATA 255,852,1170,233,106,373,12,49,8,67,926,16,1687,152,7,1868,150
 260 DATA 152,1817,103,76,11,265,522,59,15,106,217,71,916,8,8
270 STOP




COMPUTE MARKET STATISTICS
TOTAL=         18316
AVERAGE=       373.7959
VARIANCE=      281092.6
RANGE=          1861
```

EX. [23] INTEREST FOR FRACTIONAL YEAR

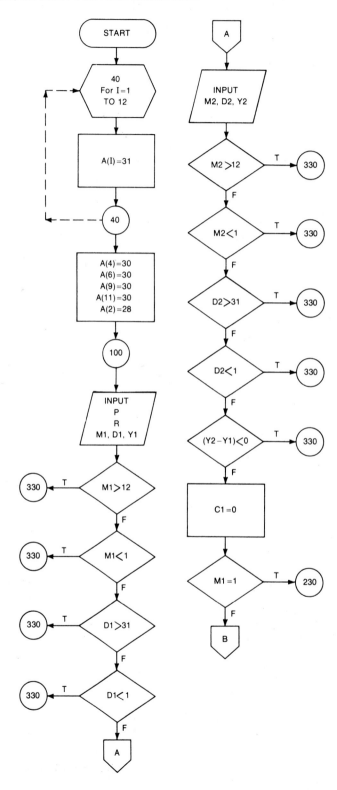

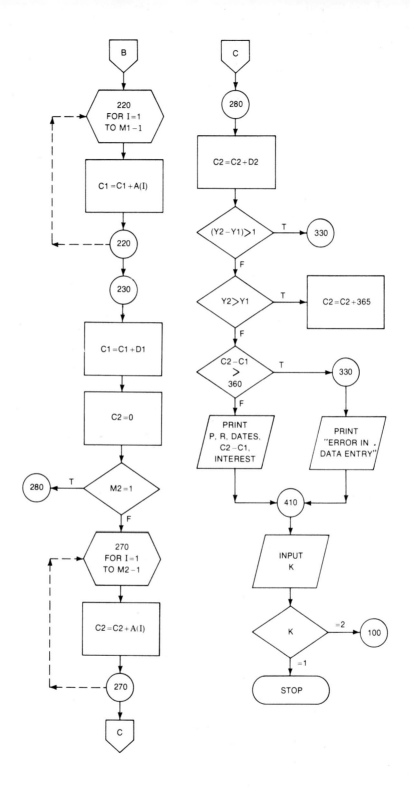

The preceding is the flowchart for the following program. A vector or a one-dimensional matrix **A** is set up, representing the number of days in each of the twelve months. The correct number of days are assigned to the twelve cells of **A** in lines 20 through 90. Data is inputted in lines 120, 140, 160, and 180:

P stands for the principal value.

R stands for the annual interest rate.

M1 stands for the month in which the loan was opened.

D1 stands for the day of the month in which the loan was opened.

Y1 stands for the year in which the loan was opened.

M2 stands for the month in which the loan was closed.

D2 stands for the day of the month in which the loan was closed.

Y2 stands for the year in which the loan was closed.

The opening and closing dates of the loan are checked for correctness in lines 161 through 164, lines 181 through 185, and line 290. The calendar day number that the loan was opened is calculated in lines 190 through 230, whereas the calendar day number that the loan was closed is calculated in lines 240 through 280. If the loan is closed in the calendar year following the opening year, then 365 days are added to the calendar day number that the loan was closed. If the difference between the two calendar days is larger than 360, then an error message is produced via lines 310 and 330.

Finally, all pertinent information is printed in lines 350 through 390, including the principal, the interest rate, the dates, the difference in days, and the interest.

```
10 DIMENSIØN A(12)
20 FØR I=1 TØ 12
30 A(I)=31
40 NEXT I
50 A(4)=30
60 A(6)=30
70 A(9)=30
80 A(11)=30
90 A(2)=28
100 PRINT "1CØMPUTE INTEREST FØR FRACTIØNAL YEAR"
110 PRINT "ENTER PRINCIPLE"
120 INPUT P
130 PRINT " ENTER ANNUAL INTEREST RATE"
140 INPUT R
150 PRINT " ENTER DATE LØAN WAS ØPENED, IE. 09,24,73"
160 INPUT M1,D1,Y1
161 IF M1>12 THEN 330
162 IF M1<0 THEN 330
163 IF D1>31 THEN 330
164 IF D1<0 THEN 330
170 PRINT " ENTER DATE LØAN WAS CLØSED, IE. 10,23,73"
180 INPUT M2,D2,Y2
181 IF M2>12 THEN 330
182 IF M2<0 THEN 330
183 IF D2>31 THEN 330
184 IF D2<0 THEN 330
185 IF Y2-Y1<0 THEN 330
190 C1=0
200 FØR I=1 TØ M1
210 C1=C1+A(I)
220 NEXT I
230 C1=C1+D1
240 C2=0
250 FØR I=1 TØ M2
260 C2=C2+A(I)
270 NEXT I
280 C2=C2+D2
290 IF (Y2-Y1)>1 THEN 330
300 IF Y2>Y1 THEN: C2=C2+365
310 IF (C2-C1)>360 THEN 330
320 GØTØ 350
330 PRINT " ERRØR IN DATE ENTRY"
340 GØTØ 400
350 PRINT " PRINCIPLE",P
360 PRINT " INTEREST RATE",R
370 PRINT " DATES",Y1+100*D1+10000*M1,Y2+100*D2+10000*M2
380 PRINT " DAYS DIFFERENCE",C2-C1
390 PRINT " INTEREST",P*R*(C2-C1)/360
400 PRINT " ENTER A 1 TØ TERMINATE, 2 TØ CØNTINUE"
410 INPUT K
420 GØTØ (430,100),K
430 STØP
```

```
 CØMPUTE INTEREST FØR FRACTIØNAL YEAR
 ENTER PRINCIPLE
?2500
 ENTER ANNUAL INTEREST RATE
?.05
 ENTER DATE LØAN WAS ØPENED, IE. 09,24,73
?2,21,72
 ENTER DATE LØAN WAS CLØSED, IE. 10,23,73
?7,10,72
 PRINCIPLE       2500
 INTEREST RATE   0.05
 DATES           22172          71072
 DAYS DIFFERENCE                142
 INTEREST        49.30556
 ENTER A 1 TØ TERMINATE, 2 TØ CØNTINUE
?2




 CØMPUTE INTEREST FØR FRACTIØNAL YEAR
 ENTER PRINCIPLE
?1700
 ENTER ANNUAL INTEREST RATE
?.06
 ENTER DATE LØAN WAS ØPENED, IE. 09,24,73
?9,15,72
 ENTER DATE LØAN WAS CLØSED, IE. 10,23,73
?7,13,73
 PRINCIPLE       1700
 INTEREST RATE   0.06
 DATES           91572          71373
 DAYS DIFFERENCE                302
 INTEREST        85.56667
 ENTER A 1 TØ TERMINATE, 2 TØ CØNTINUE
?1
```

Summary of Subscripts

The Dimension statement is used to tell the translator how many subscripts there are for each subscripted variable and what the maximum size of each subscript is:

$$\text{DIMENSION } v_1, v_2, v_3, \ldots$$

INPUT/OUTPUT STATEMENTS FOR SUBSCRIPTED VARIABLES

Input/Output of one element of an Array:

$$\text{READ} \quad \langle \text{list}(e_i) \rangle$$
$$\text{INPUT} \quad \langle \text{list}(e_i) \rangle$$
$$\text{PRINT} \quad \langle \text{list}(e_i) \rangle$$

Input/Output using the **FOR-NEXT** loop
MAT Input/Output statements

$$\text{MAT READ} \quad \langle \text{list} \rangle$$
$$\text{MAT INPUT} \quad \langle \text{list} \rangle$$
$$\text{MAT PRINT} \quad \langle \text{list} \rangle$$

VECTOR AND MATRIX OPERATIONS

Addition:

$$\text{MAT LET C} = A + B$$

Subtraction:

$$\text{MAT LET C} = A - B$$

Unary Negation:

$$\text{MAT LET B} = -A$$

Scalar Multiplication:

$$\text{MAT LET B} = (\text{exp})*A$$

Multiplication of two Matrixes:

$$\text{MAT LET C} = A*B$$

Matrix Assignment:

$$\text{MAT LET B} = A$$

Matrix Inverse:

$$\text{MAT LET B} = \text{INV}(A)$$

Transpose of Matrix:

$$\text{MAT LET B} = \text{TRN}(A)$$

Redimensioning:

$$\text{MAT LET A} = \text{RDM(exp1, exp2)}$$

Assigning Ones:

$$\text{MAT LET A} = \text{CON}$$
$$\text{MAT LET A} = \text{CON(exp1, exp2)}$$

Define Identity Matrix:

$$\text{MAT LET A} = \text{IDN}$$
$$\text{MAT LET A} = \text{IDN(exp1, exp2)}$$

Assigning Zeroes:

$$\text{MAT LET A} = \text{ZER}$$
$$\text{MAT LET A} = \text{ZER (exp1, exp2)}$$

Exercises

PROBLEM #1

Are the following subscripts correct (C) or illegal (I), and why?

a. X(N1*3)

b. Y(M1, M2)

c. Z(LI+1)

d. AA(K1, K2) or A$(K1, K2)

e. B(K1, K2, K3)

f. Q(AA)

PROBLEM #2

Are the following pair of statements in the same program consistent? If not, why?

a. 10   DIMENSION X(5, 6), L(20, 3), A(10, 20)

•

•

•

•

40   LET Y = X+7.*A(I, J)

•

•

b. 10   LET B = A(K, I)*12.**8

      •

      •

      •

    20   LET C = B+X−A(10)

      •

      •

c. 10   LET C = D(1, I)*12.+3

    20   MAT LET D = RDM(12)

      •

      •

      •

      •

    60   LET K = D(1, 4)+2

      •

      •

PROBLEM #3

Rewrite the following program without the use of any FOR-NEXT loop.

```
 10    DIM A(10, 20), B(20, 5), C(10, 5)
 20    MAT INPUT A
 30    MAT INPUT B
 40    FOR I = 1 TO 10
 50    FOR J = 1 TO 5
 60    FOR K = 1 TO 20
 70    LET C(I, J) = C(I, J) + A(I, K)*B(K, J)
 80    NEXT K
 90    NEXT J
100    NEXT I
110    MAT PRINT C
120    STOP
```

Before you rewrite this program be careful—first find out what it does; it might be helpful!

PROBLEM #4

Construct a flowchart that would aid you in writing a BASIC program for the following problem and then write and run the BASIC program. INPUT an array of N constants and calculate the sum of the differences between adjacent numbers.

PROBLEM #5

Write all the BASIC statements to accomplish the following:

Set up a two-dimensional array with five rows and five columns. (A(5, 5)). The numbers to be stored in the elements of the array are the products of the row and column designations of the elements. For example, the element A(3, 4) would have the value 12(4 × 3). Write out this two-dimensional array, taking care that you write row by row, so that the first printed line is row 1 and the fifth printed line is row 5.

PROBLEM #6

Write a BASIC segment which will set the value of the variable K, equal to the number of elements in an array, H, which are greater than 2,345. Assume that the array has been defined by DIMENSION H(50, 30).

PROBLEM #7

Write a program which will set the variable I equal to the number of even numbers in the array named N. All the values in the array N are positive integer constants. Assume that the array N is defined by

DIMENSION N (50, 100).

PROBLEM #8

Give the flowchart for a BASIC program that inputs an M × N matrix A and that loads the content of matrix, A, in a vector, V, such that the last column of the matrix A, is at the beginning of the vector, V, followed by the next to last column, etc., up to the first column. Then output the vector, V.

Run your BASIC program for the following data:

$$\text{Matrix A:} \quad \begin{matrix} 6 & 2 & 5 & 6 \\ 9 & 1 & 8 & 2 \\ 5 & 2 & 9 & 7 \end{matrix}$$

PROBLEM #9

Give the flowchart for a BASIC program that will input an N-position vector A, and create two new vectors: B and C. Vector B should contain all odd elements of A and vector C should contain all even elements of A. The one-dimensional array A contains positive integer constants.

PROBLEM #10

Input twenty values in a one-dimensional array A and interchange these elements pairwise, that is:

A(1) is to contain A(2) and A(2) is to contain A(1)

A(3) is to contain A(4) and A(4) is to contain A(3)

. . . . . .

. . . .

A(19) is to contain A(20) and A(20) is to contain A(19)

Print out the rearranged array.

PROBLEM #11

Read in a 4 × 4 matrix and find the 4th power efficiently. Print the original and the resulting matrix.

PROBLEM #12

Input twenty values in a one-dimensional array B and do the following:

1. Make the sum of all elements of B which have an even subscript, and call this sum S1.
2. Make the sum of all elements of B which have an odd subscript, and call this sum S2.
3. Make the difference between S1 and S2 (S1−S2), and call this difference D.
4. Print the array B, S1, S2, and D.

PROBLEM #13

An instructor gives a 30-question multiple-choice exam. There are five possible answers given for each question (1, 2, 3, 4 or 5). You are supposed to write a BASIC program to grade the exam. The data consists of:

1. one DATA card containing 30 integers separated by commas, reflecting the 30 correct answers to the 30 questions (A).
2. one DATA card indicating the number of students in the class who took the exam (N).
3. N DATA cards each containing the student's Social Security number (S) and 30 answers ("0" indicates that the student did not answer the question).

Your BASIC program should generate the following information:

1. A listing of the student's Social Security number, the number of wrong (W) and correct (C) answers and his final grade based on the following formula: $2(C-W/5)$. If the grade has a fraction larger than or equal to .5, then round the grade up to the next integer, otherwise drop the fraction.

2. The class average.
3. A listing indicating for each question the percentage of the students who answered it correctly (C1), incorrectly (W1), or left it blank (B1).

PROBLEM #14

Consider the following sales transactions:

Identification (I)	Sales Quantity S	Price/Unit
510	12	3.50
29	17	4.45
79	2	3.30
510	52	3.50
65	6	10.59
79	17	3.30
83	19	10.99
83	20	10.99
30	26	1.77

You are supposed to write a BASIC program that outputs:

1. a total income from these transactions.
2. how many items were involved in more than one sale.
3. a listing of all items involved in the sale and identify the total sales quantity of each item.

10
Subprograms in BASIC

Economies in programming can only be obtained by using programs which have been written by others and are already prepared. These "canned" programs are called subprograms. For calculations that are needed frequently by many users, it is possible to determine an efficient method. Once that efficient method has been determined, its equivalent BASIC program can be written and placed in a library, where other users can call for it through their own programs. The user is now in a position to concentrate his programming knowledge and skills on those portions of his program which are uniquely suited to his particular problem.

These subprograms are especially advantageous if they are required and can be used over and over again in the same program. The calculation of square roots, logarithms, absolute values, factorials, minima, maxima, and the like fall in this category. In the case of large programs, the savings in memory space or in complexity of programming are most significant. A subprogram is inserted into the computer core memory only once, even though it may be used over and over again. This chapter will explore and explain the manner in which subprograms are written in the BASIC language. Basically, these subprograms can be classified under four major groups:

1. Built-in functions.
2. User defined internal functions.
3. User defined internal subroutines.
4. User defined external subroutines.

A detailed discussion of the first three types of subprograms follows.

Note: As there are several versions of BASIC in use, they differ in subprogram capability. The discussion here assumes a fairly complete BASIC such as might be used on intermediate and large machines. The predefined processing symbol is used in flowcharting to refer to a user-defined internal subroutine. A separate flowchart is then developed to specify all steps and operations for the user-defined internal subroutine.

```
Function
or
Subroutine
```

Built-In, or Library Functions

Most BASICS have a family of built-in functions which are part of the BASIC language. They are used to generate, in an efficient way, commonly used mathematical functions. Special BASIC names are used to call these library functions, such as:

SQR can be used to calculate the square root of a numeric expression

$$[SQR(13) \rightarrow \sqrt{13}], \ [SQR(A*B+14) \rightarrow \sqrt{A \cdot B + 14}]$$

LOG can be used to calculate the natural log of a numeric expression that results in a positive constant

$$[LOG(14.3) \rightarrow \log_e 14.3], \ [LOG(A*B) \rightarrow \log_e (A \cdot B)]$$

SIN can be used to calculate the trigonometric sine of a numeric expression that reflects the angle in radians

$$[SIN(3.14) \rightarrow \sin 180°]$$

COS can be used to calculate the trigonometric cosine of a numeric expression that reflects the angle in radians

$$[COS(3.14) \rightarrow \cos 180°]$$

INT can be used to truncate the result of a numeric expression

$$[INT(13.7) \rightarrow 13]$$

In tables 10.1 and 10.2 is a listing of library functions used in trigonometry and other fields.

TABLE 10.1
Trigonometric BASIC Functions

Name	Content	Argument	Result	Example
ACS	angle in radians whose trigonometric cosine is the argument (arccosine)	numeric expression	angle in radians	ACS(.54)
ASN	angle in radians whose trigonometric sine is the argument (arcsine)	numeric expression	angle in radians	ASN(.33)
ATN	angle in radians whose trigonometric tangent is the argument (arctangent)	numeric expression	angle in radians	ATN(2.33)
COS	cosine of argument in radians	numeric expression	numeric constant	COS(3.14)
HTN	hyperbolic tangent of argument in radians	numeric expression	numeric constant	HTN(1.20)
SIN	sine of argument in radians	numeric expression	numeric constant	SIN(3.14)
TAN	tangent of argument in radians	numeric expression	numeric constant	TAN(1.5)

TABLE 10.2
Other BASIC Nonstring Functions

Name	Content	Argument	Result	Example
ABS	absolute value of an argument	numeric expression	positive numeric constant	ABS(A*B)
EXP	e (2.7183) raised to a power, which is the argument	numeric expression	numeric constant	EXP(10.2)
INT	truncates the result of the argument (drops the decimal part)	numeric expression	integer constant	INT(A*7.1)
LGT or **CLG**	common log of a positive argument (logarithm in base 10)	numeric expression	numeric constant	LGT(A)
LOG	natural log of a positive argument (logarithm in base e)	numeric expression	numeric constant	LOG(10)
RND	generates a random number (see simulation for its use)	simple numeric variable	numeric constant $0 < C < 1$	RND(K)
SGN	sign of the argument argument <0, sign is −1 argument =0, sign is 0 argument >0, sign is +1	numeric expression	−1, 0, or +1	SGN(X)
SQR	square root value of positive argument	numeric expression	numeric constant	SQR(A+4)

The square root function (**SQR**) could have been used in example [3] and [4] of Chapter 4, as follows:

4-[3]   **40   LET E1=SQR(2*F*C1/C2)**

for the economic borrowing amount

4-[4]   **20   LET X1=(−B+SQR(D))/(2*A)**
          30   LET X2=(−B−SQR(D))/(2*A)

for the roots of a quadratic equation

Once again, note that the arguments are placed within parentheses behind the name of the function. As indicated in the tables, most arguments of a built-in function may be a constant, a variable name, or an arithmetic expression with or without built-in functions; however, a built-in function may not be an argument of itself. Examples of correct built-in functions are:

10   LET E1=LOG(ABS(A*7.1))

20   LET E2=INT(SQR(B1))

If one wishes to calculate the 4th root out of the constant **A**, then:

$$\sqrt[4]{A}=\sqrt{\sqrt{A}}$$

The following is incorrect.

10   LET B=SQR(SQR(A))

Two BASIC statements are necessary to achieve the above,

10   LET C=SQR(A)

20   LET B=SQR(C)

since the built-in function SQR cannot be an argument of itself.

The **INT** function is illustrated in Chapter 4, examples [12] and [13], and in Chapter 6, example [4] (the remainder of a division). Another typical use of the **INT** function is illustrated in the following example.

EX. [1] THE LOTTERY EXAMPLE

The Q-T Candy Store sponsors a lottery. Each customer can buy a lottery ticket with a hidden number between 1 and 5,000. There are two types of winners, the BIG winners and the SMALL winners. Winners are determined as follows:

BIG winner: if the lottery number ends in 1 and is divisible by 13.
SMALL winner: if the lottery number is even and is either less than 50 or greater than or equal to 4,500.

The following principles are used in the development of the solution procedure as illustrated in the next flowchart:

1. A lottery number (**L**) is divisible by **13** if:

$$INT(L/13)*13=L,$$

2. A lottery number (**L**) ends in 1 if (**L−1**) is divisible by **10**, or if:

$$INT((L-1)/10)*10=L-1$$

3. A lottery number (**L**) is even if (**L**) is divisible by **2**, or if:

$$INT(L/2)*2=L$$

4. A BIG winner cannot at the same time be a SMALL winner.

The flowchart reads in the customer's identification number and the lottery number and processes all submitted numbers.

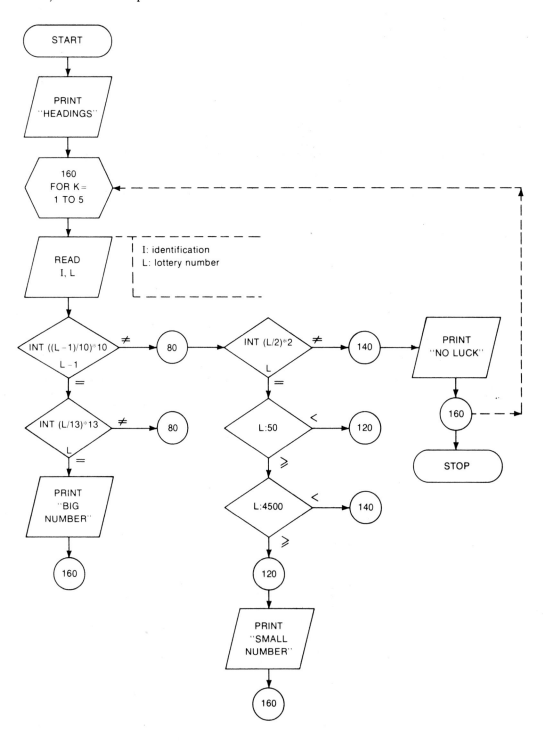

```
10 PRINT "1IDENT.","LØT NUMBER","TYPE"
20 FØR K=1 TØ 5
30 READ I,L
40 REM CHECK FØR BIG WINNER
50 IF INT((L-1)/10)*10<>L-1, THEN 100
60 IF INT(L/13)*13<>L, THEN 100
70 PRINT I,L,"BIG WINNER"
80 GØTØ 160
90 REM CHECK FØR SMALL WINNER
100 IF INT(L/2)*2<>L,THEN 150
110 IF L<50, THEN 130
120 IF L<4500, THEN 150
130 PRINT I,L,"SMALL WINNER"
140 GØTØ 160
150 PRINT I,L,"NØ LUCK"
160 NEXT K
170 DATA 1234,3380,2134,91,1324,4759,1243,101,2143,14
180 STØP
```

IDENT.	LØT NUMBER	TYPE
1234	3380	NØ LUCK
2134	91	BIG WINNER
1324	4759	NØ LUCK
1243	101	NØ LUCK
2143	14	SMALL WINNER

User-Defined Internal Functions

The programmer can define functions which are different from the library functions. These functions are called user-defined internal functions and are one-statement subprograms. As these functions appear in the BASIC program, they are translated along with the program and therefore can only be used during the execution of the program in which they are located.

Like the built-in functions, the user-defined internal functions save considerable storage space and simplify writing statements. They are of great help when they are complex statements, have many arguments and parameters, and are used many times in the same program. Note, however, that not all BASICs allow user-defined functions and some allow only one per program.

The **DEF** or definition statement is used to define the internal function. The syntax of the **DEF** statement is as follows:

$$\textbf{DEF FN}\alpha\textbf{(d)=exp}$$

where: $\boldsymbol{\alpha}$ is a letter of the alphabet; therefore, there are a maximum of 26 functions.

d dummy variable or argument.

exp arithmetic expression to be evaluated; it may or may not contain the argument.

The one-line function definition statement may appear anywhere in the BASIC program, since they are nonexecutable statements. It is, however, good practice to place them in the very beginning of the BASIC program. Any user-defined function within the BASIC program starts with **FN** and is followed by a single letter of the alphabet.

EX. [2]

```
10    DEF FNA(X)=3*X+2

.

.

.

50    LET Y=FNA(4)

.

.

.
```

Note that in line 10 **FNA** is defined and has one dummy argument **X**. In line 50 the function **FNA** is referenced and the dummy argument **X** is defined to be equal to 4; therefore, the constant **14(3*4+2)** is assigned to **Y** at the execution of line 50.

EX. [3]

$$10 \quad DEF \ FNQ(X)=A*X+B$$

•

•

$$40 \quad LET \ B=3$$
$$60 \quad LET \ A=INT \ (B/2+.5)$$
$$70 \quad LET \ Y=FNQ(2*A)$$

•

•

In line 10 **FNQ** is defined. The variable **A** and **B** are program variables or parameters. It is perfectly all right to have parameters, such as **A** and **B**, in a function definition statement. The variable **X** is the dummy argument. When line 70 is executed, the parameters **A** and **B** must be defined, which is the case in the example:

$$B=3$$
$$A=INT(B/2+.5)=INT(3/2+.5)=2$$

After line 70 is executed the value of **Y** equals:

$$Y=FNQ(2*A)=FNQ(2*2)=FNQ(4)=A*4+B$$
$$=2*4+3=8+3=11$$

EX. [4] THE DERIVATIVE EXAMPLE

Consider the following function:

$$F(X)=4X^3+3X^2-X+1$$

The first derivative of the above function can be calculated at any point of **X** (**X=a**) for any small ΔX or **H** as follows:

$$\left.\frac{dF(X)}{dX}\right|_{X=a}=F'(a)=\frac{F(a+H)-F(a)}{H}$$

Here follows a flowchart and a BASIC program that calculates this first derivative of **F(X)** for **X=5** and for three values of $\Delta X=H(H=.001, H=.01, H=.1)$. A function **FNX(X)** is defined as follows:

$$20 \quad DEF \ FNX(X)=4*X**3+3*X**2-X+1$$

This function is then used twice to calculate for different values of **H** at **X=5** the first derivative as follows:

$$60 \quad LET \ D(I)=(FNX(5+H)-FNX(5))/H$$

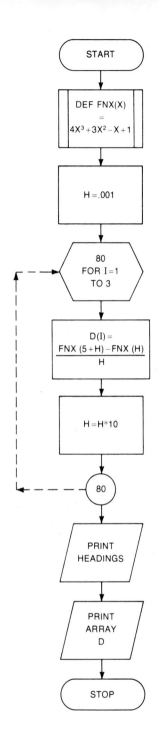

```
10 DIM D(3)
20 DEF FNX(X)=4*X**3+3*X**2-X+1
30 LET H=.001
40 FØR I=1 TØ 3
50 REM CALCULATE THE FIRST DERIVATIVE
60 LET D(I)=(FNX(5+H)-FNX(5))/H
70 H=H*10
80 NEXT I
90 PRINT "DERIVATIVES AT X=5"
100 PRINT "X=5,H=.001","X=5,H=.01","X=5,H=.1"
110 MAT PRINT D
120 STØP
DERIVATIVES AT X=5
X=5,H=.001      X=5,H=.01       X=5,H=.1
329.063         329.6304        335.34
```

A one-dimensional matrix or array is dimensioned in line 10. This establishes three storage locations which will be used to store the first derivative of **f(X)** at **X=5** for **H=.001**, **.01**, and **.1**. Line 20 contains the user-defined internal **f(X)** function. This function is called for in line 60 for the calculation of the first derivatives. Lines 30 and 70

> **30   LET H=.001**
>
> •
>
> •
>
> **70   LET H=H*10**

define and redefine the different values of **ΔX**,

$$\Delta X = H = .001$$
$$\Delta X = H = .01$$
$$\Delta X = H = .1$$

which are used in the calculation of the first derivative in line 60.

Some systems permit more than one argument in user-defined internal functions. These arguments must then be distinct and separated by commas.

EX. [5] CUMULATIVE SAVINGS

> **10**   **DEF FNS(A,N)=A*(1.+B)**N**
>
> •
>
> •
>
> •
>
> •
>
> **60**   **LET S1=FNS(C1,Y1)**
>
> •
>
> •
>
> •
>
> **100**   **LET S2=FNS(C1+C2,Y2)**
>
> •
>
> •
>
> •
>
> •
>
> **150**   **LET S3=FNS(C,17)**
>
> •
>
> •
>
> •

Note that in the above function **B** is not listed as an argument of the user-defined internal function in line 10. As indicated before the variable **B** is a parameter. The current values of the actual arguments (**C1** and **Y1** in line 60, **C1+C2** and **Y2** in line 100, and **C** and 17 in line 150) and the current value of the parameter **B** are used when the internal function is called in lines 60, 100, and 150. Therefore, one can change the values of the parameters or the arguments between calls for the internal function **FNS**.

A user-defined internal function may not contain itself; however, a user-defined function may contain a BASIC built-in function.

EX. [6] CALCULATING A BASE 10 LOG VALUE

Some systems have the base 10 log function as a built-in BASIC function, others do not.

If the base **10 log function ($\log_{10}$)** is missing, then the user can define an internal function for it, based on the following relation:

$$LOG_{10}(X) = LOG_{10}(e) \cdot LOG_e(X)$$

since

$$LOG_{10}(e) = 0.43429448190325183,$$

the above relation can be reduced to:

$$LOG_{10}(X) = .4343*LOG_e(X)$$

The following user-defined internal function can now be defined:

10   DEF FNL(X)=.4343*LOG(X),

where **LOG(X)** is a built-in BASIC function. Note that the argument of the built-in BASIC function is the same argument that is used for the user-defined internal function!

User-Defined Internal Subroutines

The structure of a user-defined internal subroutine is quite different from the user-defined internal function or built-in function. The user-defined internal subroutine is used when the subprogram cannot be expressed by one single BASIC statement. Here the user defines the set of statements within its main BASIC program, so the internal subroutine is compiled with the BASIC program in which it is embedded. Transfer to the subroutine is obtained via the **GOSUB** statement, which has the following general form:

GOSUB n

where: **n** is the line number of the first executable statement of the subroutine to which control is to be given.

After the subroutine is executed, control is returned to the main BASIC program through the **RETURN** statement in the subroutine. When the **RETURN** statement is issued, then control is returned to the statement following the **GOSUB** statement that called that subroutine. In this respect, the **GOSUB** is different from the **GOTO** statement.

A subroutine has access to all data items in the running program, because it is internal to that running program.

A separate flowchart is used to represent the logical flow of a subroutine. The start symbol can contain the name of the subroutine or **SUBROUTINE**. The last block in the flowchart is the terminal block that indicates the **RETURN** to the main program.

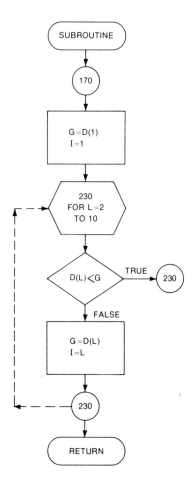

EX. [7] THE DIFFERENCE BETWEEN THE LARGEST ELEMENTS OF TWO ARRAYS

Consider two one-dimensional arrays **A** and **B**. Assume that the largest element in array **A** equals **A(L1)** and the largest element in array **B** equals **B(L2)**. The difference between these two elements, **A(L1) − B(L2)**, is the goal of this example. A user-defined internal subroutine defines these two largest elements, **A(L1)** and **A(L2)**.

```
10 DIM A(10),B(10),D(10)
20 MAT READ A,B
30 REM DEFINE LARGEST VALUE IN A:A(L1)
40 MAT LET D=A
50 GØSUB 170
60 LET L1=I
70 REM DEFINE LARGEST VALUE ØF B:B(L2)
80 MAT LET D=B
90 GØSUB 170
100 LET L2=I
110 LET D1=A(L1)-B(L2)
120 PRINT "1 THE LARGEST VALUE IN A EQUALS: ";A(L1)
130 PRINT " THE LARGEST VALUE IN B EQUALS: ";B(L2)
140 PRINT " THE DIFFERENCE BETWEEN A(L1) AND B(L2) EQUALS: ";D1
150 STØP
160 REM DEFINING THE SUBSCRIPT ØF THE LARGEST VALUE IN ARRAY D
170 G=D(1)
180 I=1
190 FØR L=2 TØ 10
200 IF D(L)<G ,THEN 230
210 G=D(L)
220 I=L
230 NEXT L
240 RETURN
250 DATA 17,15,99,2,4,47,19,100,22,51
260 DATA 71,51,99,2,4,74,91,1,22,15
270 END




 THE LARGEST VALUE IN A EQUALS:   100
THE LARGEST VALUE IN B EQUALS:   99
THE DIFFERENCE BETWEEN A(L1) AND B(L2) EQUALS:   1
```

In this BASIC program, the internal subroutine is located in lines 170 through 240. This subroutine defines the index of **I** of an array **D**, where the largest value of **D** is stored.

This subroutine is called for (**GOSUB 170**) from two locations in the main BASIC program: from line 50 and from line 90.

Before calling the subroutine from line 50, a matrix assignment statement is used to assign the input array **A** to the subroutine array **D**. To remember the index where the largest value of **A** is stored, the subroutine index **I** is assigned to **L1** in line 60. A similar procedure is used for the **B**-array (lines 80 through 100).

The **STOP** statement in line 150 prevents entry into the subroutine from a statement other than the **GOSUB** statement.

EX. [8] THE SQUARE ROOT SUBROUTINE

Suppose that the square root function is missing from the built-in functions and it is our task to calculate the fourth root out of ten numbers. An internal subroutine can be constructed that employs Newton's algorithm for defining the square root value of a positive constant.

Under the assumption that one wishes to calculate the square root of N, the following formulas summarize Newton's method:

let $\quad A_{(i+1)} = \frac{1}{2} (A_i + N/A_i)$

where $A_1 = N$

$\quad A_{(i+1)} \approx \sqrt{N}$ **when** $A_{(i+1)} - A_i < 0.0001$

The following BASIC statements reflect a BASIC subroutine that follows Newton's algorithm for calculating square roots.

```
100    REM NEWTON'S ALGORITHM FOR SQUARE ROOT CALCULATION
110    A1=N
120    A2=1/2*(A1+N/A1)
130    IF ABS(A2-A1) < 0.0001, THEN 160
140    A1=A2
150    GOTO 120
160    RETURN
```

This routine is used in the following BASIC program to calculate the fourth root of ten constants.

```
10 PRINT "1CØNSTANT","FØURTH RØØT"
20 FØR K=10 TØ 100 STEP 10
30 LET N=K
40 GØSUB 110
50 LET N=A2
60 GØSUB 110
70 PRINT K,A2
80 NEXT K
90 STØP
100 REM NEWTØN'S ALGØRITHM FØR SQUARE RØØT CALCULATIØN
110 A1=N
120 A2=1/2*(A1+N/A1)
130 IF ABS(A2-A1)<.0001 ,THEN 160
140 A1=A2
150 GØTØ 120
160 RETURN
170 END
```

```
CØNSTANT        FØURTH RØØT
10              1.778279
20              2.114743
30              2.340347
40              2.514867
50              2.659148
60              2.783158
70              2.892508
80              2.990698
90              3.08007
100             3.162278
```

EXAMPLES OF FREQUENTLY USED SUBROUTINES

EX. [9] COMPUTATION OF N! (N FACTORIAL)

If N represents an integer constant, then N! is also an integer constant, which is obtained by multiplying all integer constants that do not exceed N. Clearly:

$$N! = 1 \times 2 \times 3 \times 4 \times \ldots \times (N-1) \times N$$

Typically:

$$0! = 1$$
$$1! = 1$$
$$2! = 1 \times 2 = 2$$
$$3! = 1 \times 2 \times 3 = 6$$
$$4! = 1 \times 2 \times 3 \times 4 = 24$$

and so on

Under the above assumptions, the following subroutine calculates N!

```
100   REM CALCULATION OF N! (N=FACTORIAL=F)
110   F=1
120   IF N<=1, THEN 160
130   FOR I=2 TO N
140   F=F*I
150   NEXT I
160   RETURN
```

Notice, that the variable **N** is the input value and must have been defined in the main BASIC program when this subroutine is called for.

This subroutine can be used in statistical exercises for calculating hypergeometric probabilities, binomial probabilities, poison probabilities, and others.

EX. [10] CONVERSION OF DEGREES (D), MINUTES (M), SECONDS (S) TO RADIANS (R)

As there are 60 minutes in one degree and 3600 seconds in one degree, and as there are 3.14 radians in 180 degrees, the following subroutine represents the conversion of degrees, minutes, seconds to radians.

```
100   REM CONVERSION TO RADIANS
110   D=D+M/60+S/3600
120   R=D*3.14/180
130   RETURN
```

The input values for this subroutine are **D** (degrees), **M** (minutes), and **S** (seconds).

The following user-defined internal function accomplishes the same as the above subroutine.

```
10    DEF FNR(D,M,S)=(D+M/60+S/3600)*3.14/180
      where D,M,S are the arguments
```

The subroutine and function are handy for calculating trigonometric values, such as **COSINE**, **SINE**, or **TANGENT**, because the argument of the corresponding trigonometric BASIC functions (**COS**, **SIN**, or **TAN**) must be in radians.

EX. [11] CONVERSION OF RADIANS (R) TO DEGREES (D), MINUTES (M), AND SECONDS (S)

Under the assumption that there are 180 degrees in 3.14 radians, 60 minutes in 1 degree and 60 seconds in 1 minute, the following subroutine makes the conversion possible. It breaks the radians (**R**) down into degrees (**D**), minutes (**M**), and seconds (**S**).

```
100   REM CONVERSION OF RADIANS IN DEGREES, MINUTES, SECONDS
110   D1=(180/3.14)*R
120   D=INT(D1)
130   M1=60*(D1-D)
140   M=INT(M1)
150   S1=60*(M1-M)
160   S=INT(S1+.5)
170   RETURN
```

There is only one input value for this subroutine: **R** (the radians). The output values are **D** (the degrees), **M** (the minutes), and **S** (the seconds).

Since the arccosine (**ACS**), the arcsine (**ASN**), and the arctangent (**ATN**) generate results in radians, the above subroutine may be used to convert that result in terms of degrees (**D**), minutes (**M**), and seconds (**S**) rounded to the nearest second.

EX. [12] COMPUTATION OF THE VARIANCE

The statistical measure, variance, is the average of the squared differences of all elements from the mean and can be expressed as follows:

$$V = \frac{\sum_{i=1}^{N} (M - A_i)^2}{N}, \text{ where } \mathbf{M}: \text{ is the mean}$$

$$\mathbf{A_i} \text{ is the ith element}$$

$$M = \frac{\sum_{i=1}^{N} A_i}{N}$$

```
      10 DIM A(100)
      20 READ N
      30 FØR K=1 TØ N
      40 READ A(K)
      50 NEXT K
      60 GØSUB 110
      70 PRINT "1AVERAGE= ";M
      80 PRINT "VARIANCE= ";V
      90 STØP
     100 REM SUB FØR CALCULATING THE VARIANCE (V)
     110 T=0
     120 GØSUB 210
     130 FØR I=1 TØ N
     140 T=T+(M-A(I))**2
     150 NEXT I
     160 V=T/N
     170 RETURN
     200 REM SUB FØR CALCULATING THE MEAN (M)
     210 S=0
     220 FØR J=1 TØ N
     230 S=S+A(J)
     240 NEXT J
     250 M=S/N
     260 RETURN
     270 DATA 10,1,11,22,33,44,55,66,77,88,99
     280 END




     AVERAGE=   49.6
     VARIANCE=  988.44
```

The BASIC **MEANVAR** program contains two subroutines. The first subroutine runs from line 110 to line 170 and calculates the variance, **V**. This subroutine is called for from line 60 in the main BASIC program. The second subroutine runs from line 210 to line 260 and calculates the mean, **M**. This subroutine is called for from line 120, which is in the first subroutine.

Note, therefore, that it is quite all right to call a subroutine from a subroutine. When the **RETURN** statement is executed, the system remembers to which statement to transfer. It will transfer to the executable statement following the last **GOSUB**. So when the **RETURN** at line 260 is reached, the system will return to the executable statement following the last executed **GOSUB**, or to statement 130. The execution procedure is indicated on the left of the BASIC program with the use of lines and arrows.

Summary of Subprograms

Subprograms in BASIC are classified under four major groups:

1. Built-in functions.
2. User-defined internal functions.
3. User-defined internal subroutines.
4. User-defined external subroutines.

BUILT-IN, OR LIBRARY FUNCTIONS

Built-in or library functions are used to generate, in an efficient way, commonly used mathematical functions (**SQR** for the square root function, **LOG** for the natural log function, **SIN** for the trigonometric sine, **INT** for the integer function to truncate the result, and others . . .).

USER-DEFINED INTERNAL FUNCTIONS

The programmer can define functions which are different from the library functions. These functions are called user-defined internal functions and are one-statement subprograms. As these functions appear in the BASIC program, they are translated along with the program and therefore can only be used during the execution of the program in which they are located.

The **DEF** or definition statement is used to define the internal function:

$$\textbf{DEF FN } \alpha\textbf{(d)=exp}$$

where: α is a letter of the alphabet (max 26 functions)
d is for dummy variables or arguments
exp is an arithmetic expression

USER-DEFINED INTERNAL SUBROUTINES

The user-defined internal subroutine is used when the subprogram cannot be expressed by one single BASIC statement. Here the user defines a set of statements within the main program. Transfer to the subroutine is obtained via the **GOSUB** statement:

$$\textbf{GOSUB n}$$

where: **n** is a statement number

After the subroutine is executed, control is returned to the main BASIC program through the **RETURN** statement:

$$\textbf{RETURN}$$

Exercises

PROBLEM #1

Write a single BASIC statement for each of the following:

1. $y = \sqrt{\dfrac{(a+b)^2 - 1}{|i|(c+d)^2}}$

2. $y = \sqrt{|\tan \phi - \frac{1}{2}|}$ where $\phi = 45°$

3. $y = 4 \cos^2 x + 2 \sin x$ where x is expressed in degrees

4. calculate the square root of the absolute value of A and assign it to Y.

5. calculate the third root of x and assign it to y:

$$y = \sqrt[3]{x} = x^{1/3} = x^{.333}$$

Note, however, that the following BASIC expression results in an error if $x < 0$:

$$\text{LET } Y = X^{**}.333$$

PROBLEM #2

Define a user-defined function to calculate the following:

$$\log_4(17), \ \log_{16}(999), \ \log_{19}(333)$$

From calculus we know the following:

$$\log_A (B) = \frac{\log_e (B)}{\log_e (A)} = \frac{\log_{10} (B)}{\log_{10} (A)}$$

PROBLEM #3

The function

$$Z = \frac{N \tan^2 \phi}{\sqrt{N+X^2}} \left| e^{X/N} + e^{-X/N} \right| \text{ where } \phi = 60°$$

is to be evaluated for all combinations of

N: 1.0(0.1)5.0   i.e., N = 1.0, 1.1, 1.2, . . ., 4.9, 5.0
X: −1.0(0.05)1.0   i.e., X = −1.0, −T0.95, −0.90, . . ., 0.95, 1.0

For each combination of N and X, write a line giving the values of N, X, and Z. Write a complete BASIC program to accomplish this.

PROBLEM #4

The function

$$F = \frac{\sin X + \cos Y}{\log_e (X+Y)}$$

is to be evaluated for all combinations of

$$X: -1.0(0.05)0.0$$
$$Y: 10.0(0.5)25.0$$

For each combination of X and Y, write a line giving the values of X, Y, and F. Write a complete BASIC program to accomplish this.

PROBLEM #5

Write a BASIC program with two user-defined internal subroutines to calculate the range of the sales volume, which is equal to the difference between the largest and the smallest sales volume. The first subroutine must define the largest sales volume, and the second subroutine must define the smallest sales volume.

PROBLEM #6

Write a BASIC program with one user-defined internal subroutine. The main program should read the size of a matrix: M and N (M = number of rows, N = number of columns) and the matrix itself: A.

The subroutine should calculate the elements of a vector B, consisting of M elements. Each element represents the sum of the elements in each of the M rows of the matrix A. Matrix A and vector B are originally over-dimensioned:

$$A(50, 50), B(50)$$

As soon as their size is known, redimensioning is necessary.
Note: If your system does not allow redimensioning, ignore this last requirement.

11
Sorting Data

In the literature of Computer Programming Languages and Numerical Methods the activity of sorting, the process of ordering data, is an essential subject. One can sort from the smallest element to the largest one, or from the largest number to the smallest one. Numerous techniques have been developed in an attempt to sort efficiently. Here, two sorting programs are discussed. The first is considerably less efficient than the second, as will be obvious after the development. Both programs sort unordered numerical constants in an increasing order, and print out the ordered array, in which the ordered numbers are stored.

The First Program

The sorting problem, as considered here, can be formulated as follows:

Given a one-dimensional array **A(I)**;
This array needs to be ordered, beginning with the smallest element
and ending with the largest;
The ordered set has to be placed in another one-dimensional array
B(I);

The ordering procedure in this program selects the smallest element of the array **A** and places it at the beginning of the **B**-array. Choosing the same (smallest) element over and over again can be avoided by reassigning an arbitrary large value to that element of the **A**-array after its value is placed in order in the **B**-array. The reassigned value has to be larger than any value in the random list of the **A**-array.

The flowchart and the program accomplish the above procedure. The **REM** statements fully explain the programming procedure. It is assumed that the **A**-array does not contain more than 50 elements.

The average number of passes through the most inner loop (lines 110 through 170) equals N^2. In Table 11.1, through the use of an example, the program is illustrated for a one-dimensional array **A(5)**, containing the following constants: **A(1) = 7, A(2) = 1, A(3) = 10, A(4) = 12, and A(5) = 9.**

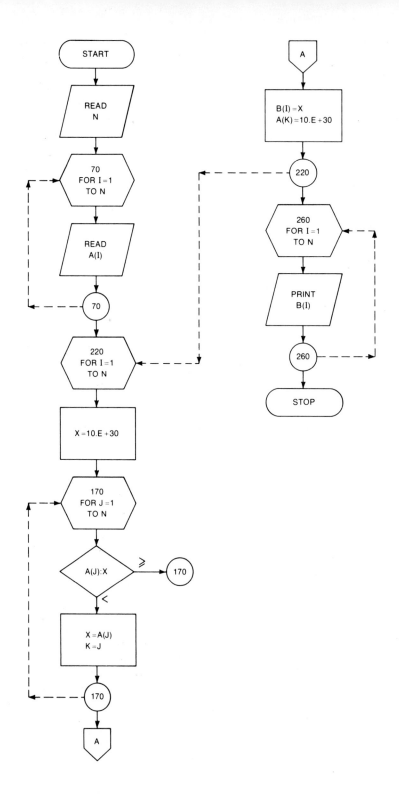

```
10 DIM A(50),B(50)
20 REM READ IN THE NUMBER OF CONSTANTS TO BE ORDERED
30 READ N
40 REM READ IN ALL N CONSTANTS TO BE ORDERED
50 FOR I=1 TO N
60 READ A(I)
70 NEXT I
80 FOR I =1 TO N
90 REM ASSIGN A VERY LARGE CONSTANT TO THE DUMMY X
100 X=10.E+30
110 FOR J=1 TO N
120 IF A(J)>=X ,THEN 170
130 REM REMEMBER THE SMALLEST VALUE
140 X=A(J)
150 REM DETERMINE THE LOCATION IN ARRAY FOR LATER REFERENCE
160 K=J
170 NEXT J
180 REM ASSIGN THE SMALLEST ELEMENT IN THE B-ARRAY
190 B(I)=X
200 REM ASSIGN A LARGE CONSTANT TO SMALLEST ELEMENT IN A-ARRAY
210 A(K)=10.E+30
220 NEXT I
230 PRINT "THE ORDERED ARRAY IS AS FOLLOWS:"
240 FOR I=1 TO N
250 PRINT B(I)
260 NEXT I
270 DATA 20
280 DATA 19.9,52.9,28.6,62.0,87.5,29.4,91.5,46.3,84.8,86.0
290 DATA 25.2,97.7,23.9,11.1,86.8,24.3,42.1,96.9,19.6,29.1
310 STOP
THE ORDERED ARRAY IS AS FOLLOWS:
11.1
19.6
19.9
23.9
24.3
25.2
28.6
29.1
29.4
42.1
46.3
52.9
62
84.8
86
86.8
87.5
91.5
96.9
97.7
```

TABLE 11.1
Illustration of the First Sorting Program

Program Reference	I	J	X	K	B(I)	Changes in A(I)
80 FOR I = 1 TO N	1				[B(1)]	
100 X = 10.E+30			10.E+30			
110 FOR J = 1 TO N		1	7	1		A(1) = 7
L		2	1	2		A(2) = 10.E30
O		3	1	2		A(3) = 10
O		4	1	2		A(4) = 12
P		5	1	2		A(5) = 9
170 NEXT J						
190 B(I) = X					1	
80 FOR I = 1 TO N	2				[B(2)]	
100 X = 10.E+30			10.E+30			
110 FOR J = 1 TO N		1	7	1		A(1) = 10.E30
L		2	7	1		A(2) = 10.E30
O		3	7	1		A(3) = 10
O		4	7	1		A(4) = 12
P		5	7	1		A(5) = 9
170 NEXT J						
190 B(I) = X					7	
80 FOR I = 1 TO N	3				[B(3)]	
100 X = 10.E+30			10.E+30			
110 FOR J = 1 TO N		1	10.E+30			A(1) = 10.E30
L		2	10.E+30			A(2) = 10.E30
O		3	10	3		A(3) = 10
O		4	10	3		A(4) = 12
P		5	9	5		A(5) = 10.E30
170 NEXT J						
190 B(I) = X					9	
80 FOR I = 1 TO N	4				[B(4)]	
100 X = 10.E+30			10.E+30			
110 FOR J = 1 TO N		1	10.E+30			A(1) = 10.E30
L		2	10.E+30			A(2) = 10.E30
O		3	10	3		A(3) = 10.E30
O		4	10	3		A(4) = 12
P		5	10	3		A(5) = 10.E30
170 NEXT J						
190 B(I) = X					10	
80 FOR I = 1 TO N	5				[B(5)]	
100 X = 10.E+30			10.E+30			
110 FOR J = 1 TO N		1	10.E+30			A(1) = 10.E30
L		2	10.E+30			A(2) = 10.E30
O		3	10.E+30			A(3) = 10.E30
O		4	12	4		A(4) = 10.E30
P		5	12	4		A(5) = 10.E30
170 NEXT J						
190 B(I) = X					12	

The Second Program

A more efficient sorting program, which reduces the maximum number of innerloop passes (lines 110 through 190) to $N^2/2$, is illustrated in this second sorting program. The program algorithm for sorting from the smallest element to the largest is summarized in the following three steps:

Step #1: Compare the first and the second element. If the first element is the larger one, switch the order of the elements.

Step #2: If no switch is made, proceed to the next element (third) in the array, and compare the element with the previous element, moving up toward the first element until no switch can be made.

Step #3: If no switch can be made, or if the top of the array is reached, proceed to the next element (fourth) in the array, go back to Step #2, and proceed to Step #3, until the last element in the array is considered and is put into place.

The flowchart and the BASIC program for this procedure follow. The DATA used in this program is identical to that of the previous program. The variable name **D** is a dummy variable and is used to switch elements and to avoid loss of memory of the numeric constant of one of the elements that is being exchanged for another. REM statements fully explain the program. The generated output of this arrangement is the same as for the previous program.

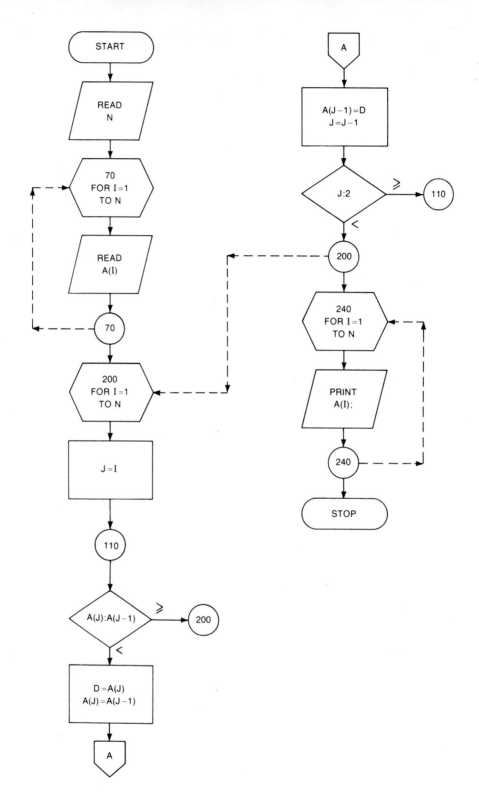

```
10 DIM A(50)
20 REM READ IN THE NUMBER ØF CØNSTANTS TØ BE ØRDERED
30 READ N
40 REM READ IN ALL N CØNSTANTS TØ BE ØRDERED
50 FØR I =1 TØ N
60 READ A(I)
70 NEXT I
80 FØR I =2 TØ N
90 J=I
100 REM CHECK WHETHER A SWITCH CAN BE MADE
110 IF A(J) >= A(J-1) ,THEN 200
120 REM SWITCHING TWØ ELEMENTS
130 D=A(J)
140 A(J) = A(J-1)
150 A(J-1) =D
160 REM DECREASE THE INDEX ØF CØMPARISØN BY ØNE
170 J=J-1
180 REM CHECK WHETHER THE TØP ØF THE ARRAY IS REACHED
190 IF J >= 2 ,THEN 110
200 NEXT I
210 PRINT "THE ØRDERED ARRAY IS AS FØLLØWS:"
220 FØR I=1 TØ N
230 PRINT A(I)
240 NEXT I
245 DATA 20
250 DATA 19.9,52.9,28.6,62.0,87.5,29.4,91.5,46.3,84.8,86.0
260 DATA 25.2,97.7,23.9,11.1,86.8,24.3,42.1,96.9,19.6,29.1
280 STØP


THE ØRDERED ARRAY IS AS FØLLØWS:
11.1
19.6
19.9
23.9
24.3
25.2
28.6
29.1
29.4
42.1
46.3
52.9
62
84.8
86
86.8
87.5
91.5
96.9
97.7
```

In Table 11.2, the program procedure is illustrated through the use of the same example as for the first sorting program. When switches are made, the constants are underlined.

TABLE 11.2
Illustration of the Second Sorting Program

A(I)	J — Values			
	2	3	4	5
7	1	1	1	1 1 1
1	7	7	7	7 7 7
10		10	10	10 9 9
12			12	9 10 10
9				12 12 12
	1 Comparison 1 Switch	1 Comparison No Switch	1 Comparison No Switch	3 Comparisons 2 Switches

Notice that six passes are made to accomplish the ordering. The use of the previous program resulted in $5^2 = 25$ passes. So, the second procedure is significantly more efficient than the first program.

EX. [1] FREQUENCY DISTRIBUTION OF CORN YIELD

The following data represents the yield of corn which each of several farmers obtained. The yield is specified in bushels per acre:

35	29	32	31	33
33	38	26	29	32
32	37	32	36	32
33	31	30	32	30
33	27	34	35	30
34	36	34	31	32
32	34	32	31	31
30	33	32	30	33
34	32	31	34	32
31	32			

The flowchart represents one of several procedures to output a frequency distribution table for the above data. A subroutine orders the above data in increasing yield values and assigns it to a vector A (lines 300 through 400). The counter F is set up to register the frequency for each yield class (line 160 and line 210). As the yields are ordered (in array A), adjacent yield values (going from first to last) are compared (line 180); if adjacent yields are equal, the frequency counter F is incremented by 1 (line 230). However, if they are not equal, then the frequency counter contains the frequency of the previously considered yield value, which is stored under the variable name Y, and the counter F is reset to 1, after the frequency information for the previous yield value is printed (lines 190, 200, 210). This process continues until all yields are considered and printed. Ordering the yields from the smallest to the largest value speeds up the process of defining the frequency distribution.

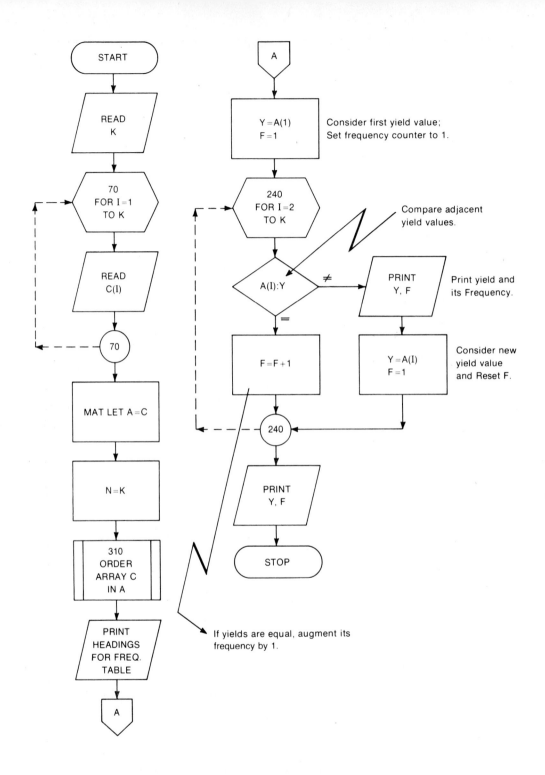

```
10 DIM C(50),A(50)
20 REM READ IN THE NUMBER ØF CØRNYIELDS TØ BE CØNSIDERED
30 READ K
40 REM READ IN ALL CØRNYIELDS
50 FØR I=1 TØ K
60 READ C(I)
70 NEXT I
80 REM DEFINE ARRAY A AND INDEX N FØR SØRT RØUTINE
90 MAT LET A=C
100 N=K
110 GØSUB 310
120 REM DEFINE FREQUENCY DISTRIBUTIØN
130 PRINT "FREQUENCY DISTRIBUTIØN ØF CØRNYIELD IN BUSHELS/ACRE"
140 PRINT "YIELD","FREQUENCY"
150 Y=A(1)
160 F=1
170 FØR I=2 TØ K
180 IF A(I) = Y ,THEN 230
190 PRINT Y,F
200 Y=A(I)
210 F=1
220 GØTØ 240
230 F=F+1
240 NEXT I
245 PRINT Y,F
250 STØP
300 REM ØRDERING RØUTINE
310 FØR I=2 TØ N
320 J=I
330 IF A(J) >= A(J-1) ,THEN 390
340 D=A(J)
350 A(J) = A(J-1)
360 A(J-1)=D
370 J=J-1
380 IF J >= 2 ,THEN 330
390 NEXT I
400 RETURN
450 DATA 47
460 DATA 35,29,32,31,33,33,38,26,29,32,32,37,32,36,32
470 DATA 33,31,30,32,30,33,27,34,35,30,34,36,34,31,32
480 DATA 32,34,32,31,31,30,33,32,30,33,34,32,31,34,32
490 DATA 31,32
500 END


FREQUENCY DISTRIBUTIØN ØF CØRNYIELD IN BUSHELS/ACRE
YIELD           FREQUENCY
26              1
27              1
29              2
30              5
31              7
32              13
33              6
34              6
35              2
36              2
37              1
38              1
```

Other Sorting Techniques

Sorting has traditionally been used mostly for business data processing. Nevertheless, it is a tool that any good programmer should master for use in a wide variety of situations.

A very comprehensive coverage of sorting techniques can be found in "The Art of Computer Programming—Volume 3/Sorting and Searching", by Donald E. Knuth of Standford University, published by Addison Wesley Publishing Company. In this text the author points out that computer manufacturers estimate that over 25% of running time on their computers is currently being spent on sorting and that there are many installations in which sorting uses more than half of the computing time. This is perhaps why efforts and research have gone in the development of efficient sorting techniques. The sorting examples presented in this chapter clearly illustrate the difference between a poor and a better sorting technique (program #1 versus program #2), in terms of running time.

There are major trade-offs between different sorting techniques, with respect to running time versus programming time. For short lists, the inefficient but easy-to-program routines, such as the ones illustrated in this chapter are preferred. However, when the list is long one should think about sort-merge routines which require significantly less steps.

Different types of internal sorting techniques are discussed in Knuth's text. These are: the inversion sort (where items are considered one at a time, and each new item is inserted into the appropriate position relative to the previous sorted item), the exchange sort (where two adjacent items which are out of order are interchanged), the selection sort (where the smallest item that is located is separated from the rest, then the next smallest, and so on . . .), the enumeration sort (where each item is compared with each of the others and where counting the number of smaller keys determines the item's final position), special purpose sorting methods, etc. . . . The book discusses approximately 25 such sorting techniques.

A useful summary of sorting algorithms can be found in a book published by Prentice Hall: "Computer Numerical Methods", by Maurer and Williams.

Exercises

PROBLEM #1

You are responsible for merging two arrays, array A and array B, into array C. Array A consists of M elements and array B consists of N elements.

Before you merge the two arrays into one array, C, order array A and B in increasing order by the use of an internal defined subroutine. To form the array C you cannot join A and B together to form C and then do a sort. Neither can you assume that you can perform the merge by simply alternating entries from A and B into C.

To merge A and B to form C set up three pointers: one pointer (I) to mark your current position in A, a second pointer (J) to mark your current position in B and, finally, a third pointer (K) to mark your current position in C. Note that pointer I can never exceed M, and pointer J can never exceed N.

PROBLEM #2

Murphy's downtown theater plans to offer a special movie. Reservations must be made by mail and you, being the theater manager, are asked to write a flowchart and a BASIC program that will assign seats according to the incoming requests.

The theater has M rows; K1 of these rows are considered lower level front rows, and K2 of the rows are considered lower level back rows. The remaining rows (M—K1—K2) are in the balcony. Each row contains N seats. The lower level front seats cost $7, the lower level back seats cost $5, and the seats in the balcony cost $3.

The following rules govern the filling of the reservations:

1. Within any of the three sections, satisfy reservations as far forward in that section as possible.
2. Each reservation must be filled within one row and within the requested section. Therefore, if there are not enough seats available within any row of the requested section, cancel the reservation.
3. Seats in a row are numbered from 1 to N, and you must fill the reservations in that order.
4. Accept reservations until all seats are sold (it will be a sellout).

INPUT

The input to your program consists of M (number of theater rows), N (number of seats per row), K1 (number of lower front rows), K2 (number of lower level back rows).

These four constants should be read in from a DATA statement and are:

$$M - 15, \qquad N = 8, \qquad K1 - 6, \qquad K2 = 5$$

The second set of data for your program consists of pairs of numbers. Each pair of numbers represents a reservation request. The first number in each pair indicates the number of seats requested (S) and the second number indicates the total amount paid for this request (A). Use these two numbers to define the location in which to make the reservation.

These pairs should be read in by the use of an INPUT statement. These pairs are:

S	A
3	15
2	6
14	70
6	42
6	18
5	25
7	35
3	21
2	14
5	15
5	35
2	10
4	28
4	12
5	35
2	14

S	A
6	30
1	3
4	20
4	28
4	28
3	9
2	6
1	3
6	30
3	21
4	20
3	15
4	12
3	9
8	56
2	6
1	5
2	14
1	7

In using this data do not assume that you know how many reservations will come in. The output must consist of the following:

For each reservation, your program should output the row and seat number(s) assigned to satisfy the reservation. If you cannot fill the reservation, output a courtesy message.

12

Formatted Output, Plotting and File Processing

Up to now we have discussed and used the **PRINT** statement as presented in Chapter 5. When the ⟨list⟩ of the ordinary **PRINT** statement consists of carriage controls, variable names, arithmetic expressions, strings of messages and/or output controls, we are often handicapped when we wish to align computer output. In this chapter, the **PRINT USING** statement is introduced to overcome this problem and others.

Plotting can be fairly straightforward in BASIC if it is approached correctly. The second section in this chapter will illustrate two simple plotting procedures.

Finally, we will discuss the use of files in **BASIC**. Files which are in the **BASIC** workspace can be read from, or results can be stored in them. The final section presents statements for creating files, using files, reading from and writing in files.

Formatted Output

THE PRINT USING STATEMENT

The programmer can exercise effective control when printing information via the **PRINT USING** statement, rather than the regular **PRINT** statement. Specifically, the **PRINT USING** statement enables us to line up decimal points, to place a dollar sign where it belongs, to specify the desired number of decimal places, and other things.

The **PRINT USING** statement is not used by itself. It calls either for an **IMAGE** statement or a string variable. The general form of the **PRINT USING** statement is as follows:

$$\text{PRINT USING} \begin{Bmatrix} \mathbf{n} \\ \textbf{string variable} \\ \textbf{format string} \end{Bmatrix}, \langle\text{list}\rangle$$

where: **n** is the line number of the **IMAGE** statement.

string variable is the character string variable that contains the desired format string.

format string is a string specifying the way in which the list is to be output.

list is an ordered list of variable names, expressions, messages and/or output controls.

The format of the **IMAGE** statement is as follows:

n :⟨image specifications⟩

where: The **colon (:)** is necessary to identify the statement as an **IMAGE** statement.

The ⟨**image specifications**⟩ can also be sandwiched between two double quotes and assigned to a string variable. In this case, the **PRINT USING** statement must reference that string variable rather than the **IMAGE** statement.

In order to properly and fully utilize the capabilities of the **PRINT USING** and **IMAGE** statements, the user of this text must familiarize himself with his computing system for additional details, since there are different versions in use. What follows is only a fundamental introduction to some of the existing image specifications. The following specifications are discussed and illustrated here:

—numeric image specifications
—edited numeric image specifications
—string image specification

These specifications are used to identify the following types of information:

—integer, decimal and exponential constants
—dollar signs, commas, asterisks and minus signs
—string constants
—alphanumeric printing characters

Let us now see how the above four types of information is formatted via the image specifications.

NUMERIC IMAGE SPECIFICATIONS

The formats of integer and decimal constants are specified via the use of numeric image specifications. The following format characters are used for this:

the pound or number sign (#)

one period (.)

four upward arrows (↑↑↑↑)

The following rules govern the use of the image specifications:

1. Numeric formats use one pound (#) sign for each digit to be printed, plus another one for the algebraic sign.
2. Only pound (#) signs are used for integer fields. When printed, the integer constants are right justified. If the constant is not an integer, then the constant is truncated.

3. Pound (#) signs and one decimal point is used to identify decimal fields. Decimal constants will be right adjusted and are rounded according to the number of places specified behind the decimal point.
4. Decimal fields followed by four upward arrows are used to identify exponential fields. The constants are written according to the decimal field rule.

The following BASIC program illustrates all four rules of the numeric **Image Specifications:**

```
10    READ A,B,C,D,E
20    :####    ###
30    PRINT USING 20, A,B
40    :###.##    ###.###    ###.##
50    PRINT USING 40, C,D,D
60    :###.##↑↑↑↑    ####.##↑↑↑↑ #####.##↑↑↑↑
70    PRINT USING 60, E,E,E
80    :###.##  ###.##  ####.#↑↑↑↑
90    PRINT USING 80, B,D,D
100   DATA 12,17.7,12,17.235,123.45
110   STOP
120   END
```

The formatted output of this BASIC program is as follows:

```
  12     17
  12.00    17.235     17.24
  12.35E+01    123.45E+00    1234.50E-01
  17.70   17   172.4E-01
```

Integer constants are printed via the image statement labeled 20 and the **PRINT** statement labeled 30. They illustrate rule (2). The first specification is one space larger than necessary (remember we need a space for the sign, which is suppressed because it is positive). Since the constant named **B** is not an integer, the constant is truncated because an integer format specification is used in the image statement.

Real constants are printed via the image statement labeled 40 and the **PRINT** statement labeled 50. They illustrate rule (3). Notice how zeros are added to fill up the decimal positions of variable **C**. The first **D** constant is fully printed, whereas the second **D** constant is rounded.

Constants with decimal exponents are printed via the image statement labeled 70. They illustrate rule (4). Notice the three different ways that the **E** constant is printed with decimal exponents!

Finally, the last image (80) and **PRINT** (90) statements illustrate a combination of the numeric image specifications. Study them! I am sure you will now understand the output they generate.

The image statements and associated **PRINT** statements of this example can be replaced by either of the following statement sets:

```
20   A$ = "####   ###"
30   PRINT USING A$, A, B
40   B$ = "###.##   ###.###   ###.##"
50   PRINT USING B$, C, D, D
and so on
```

Here string variables are used **(A$,B$)**.

```
30   PRINT USING "####   ###", A, B
50   PRINT USING "###.##   ###.###   ###.##", C, D, D
and so on
```

In this alternative format strings are within the **PRINT USING** statement.

In all other examples of this section, the **IMAGE (:)** statements will be used. The reader and user of this book may change them, using string variables or format strings within the **PRINT USING** statement-. Try this as an exercise!

EDITED NUMERIC IMAGE SPECIFICATIONS

These specifications are useful when one wishes to edit constants with a leading dollar sign **($)**, with commas **(,)**, to group a constant into hundreds, thousands, etc., with a trailing minus sign **(−)**, or with a leading asterisk **(*)**. These editing features are very helpful for creating accounting reports or for writing bank checks.

The rules governing the use of the edit specifications are the following:

1. A single leading dollar **($)** sign instead of the pound **(#)** sign outputs a dollar sign in that position. Two or more leading dollar signs instead of pound signs outputs a dollar sign immediately preceding the first digit of the number.
   Dollar signs can replace any or all of the pound signs. When a dollar sign is used to edit a negative constant, then there must be trailing minus sign (see rule 3).
2. Only one comma is needed for a number to be output with commas. The comma cannot be in the first two places. A pound sign or a comma must be present to reserve space for each comma to be output.

3. A trailing minus sign in a numeric specification results in placing the sign at the end of the constant. When a trailing minus sign is used, there is no need to save a position at the beginning of the numeric specification. A trailing minus sign for a positive constant causes a blank sign field.
4. Two or more leading asterisks (*) instead of pound signs outputs leading asterisks that fill up any unused positions in the output field. Again, a trailing minus sign is necessary to output negative constants.

The following BASIC program illustrates these rules:

```
10   READ A,B,C,D
20   REM ILLUSTRATION OF RULE#1
30   :$##.##   $###.##   $$###.##
40   PRINT USING 30, A,A,A
50   REM ILLUSTRATION OF RULE#2
60   :###,##.##
70   PRINT USING 60, B
80   REM ILLUSTRATION OF RULE#3
90   :##.##-   ##.##-
100  PRINT USING 90, C,(-1)*C
110  REM ILLUSTRATION OF RULE#4
120  :**#.##-   *****#.##
130  PRINT USING 120, C,D
140  DATA 17.12,1234.56,-1234.56,-12.35,1234.5
150  STOP
160  END
```

When carefully considering all four rules, the following output can easily be explained:

```
$17.12   $ 17.12   $17.12
1,234.56
12.35-   12.35
*12.35  *1234.50
```

Edited numeric image specifications can be combined as shown in the following example:

```
10    LET  A = 1234.56
20    :$$$$#,#.##
30    PRINT USING 20 ,A
40    :**###,#.##
50    PRINT USING 40 ,A
60    STOP
70    END
```

The output is:

```
 $1,234.56
***1,234.56
```

Note that the first **IMAGE** and **PRINT** statements combine the dollar (**$**) sign and the comma (**,**); whereas the second **IMAGE** and **PRINT** statements combine the asterisks (*****) with the comma (**,**). Use the previously established rules to understand the output!

STRING IMAGE SPECIFICATIONS

String constants can be formatted via the string image specifications. These specifications allow the programmer to right-justify (**R**), left-justify (**L**), or center (**C**) string constants in the output field that is specified. In addition, the extension specification (**E**) can be used to extend the width of the output field if the string constant is larger than what the image specifies. Finally, the first character of a string constant can be printed via the apostrophe (**'**).

The following rules govern the string image specification:

1. A string image specification starts with one apostrophe (**'**) and is followed with as many format characters (either **R**, **L**, **C**, or **E**) as are necessary to output the string constant. The apostrophe counts in determining the length of the output field.
2. A field of **R** characters is used to output a string constant right-justified. If the string constant is longer than the image specification, then the rightmost characters that overflow are truncated.
3. A field of **L** characters is used to output a string constant left-justified. If the string constant is longer than the image specification, then the rightmost characters that overflow are truncated.
4. A field of **C** characters is used to center the output of a string constant. If the string constant is longer than the image specification, then the rightmost characters that overflow are truncated.
5. A field of **E** characters is used to output a string constant left-justified. If the string constant is longer than the image specification, then the output field is widened to the right, so that all characters in the string can be accommodated.

These rules are now illustrated in the following example.

```
10   LET A$="STORM"
20   :'RRRRRR    'CCCCCC    'LLL    'EEE
30   PRINT USING 20, A$
40   STOP
50   END
```

The resulting output of this example is:

```
  STORM     STORM      STOR    STORM
|←------→| |←------→| |←----→| |←----→|
 1st field   2nd field   3rd field  4th field
```

In the image statement of this example, four string specifications are defined. The first one (**'RRRRRR**) defines a field width of seven characters in which the string constant must be right-justified. Since the string constant **STORM** contains five constants, the output contains two leading blanks. The second specification (**'CCCCCC**) defines a field width of seven characters in which the string constant must be centered. Notice that this results in leaving a leading and trailing blank in the second field. The third specification (**'LLL**) defines a field width of four characters in which the string constant will be left-justified. However, since the string constant **STORM** is one character longer than the specification, the last character is truncated. Finally, the last specification allows for extending a field of four characters to as many as needed to accommodate the string constant.

PRINTING CHARACTERS OR LITERAL FIELDS

If an image statement contains characters which are not control characters, then these characters are printing characters. These characters are then printed exactly as is:

```
10   LET A=12
20   LET B=A**2
30   :THE SQUARED VALUE EQUALS ####
40   PRINT USING 30,B
50   STOP
60   END
```

The output of this example is:

```
THE SQUARED VALUE EQUALS  144
```

Finally we must remember the following two basic rules when using the formatted **PRINT** statement:

1. If the **PRINT USING** statement contains more variables than the number of fields specified in the image, then the image statement is reused and a second output line is printed.

2. If the **PRINT USING** statement contains less variables than the number of fields specified in the image, then the extra specifications are ignored.

Plotting Procedures

Plotting in BASIC is a simple matter. Two plotting procedures are illustrated in this section; one for plotting the frequency distribution (Example [1]) and another procedure for the function plotting (Examples [2], [3], and [4]).

In this section we will not be discussing graphic processors (such as TEKTRONIX 4051) who have their own built-in graphics statements.

USE OF A STRING VARIABLE

A frequency distribution can be plotted by the use of a string variable. The string can contain as many alpha-numeric "*" characters as one wishes to assign to it as follows:

```
100    SS = ""
110    FOR I = 1 TO F
120    SS = SS + "*"
130    NEXT I
         •
         •
```

Note that in the above example an empty string is assigned to the string variable **SS** in line 100 (for other systems, **S$** would be an acceptable string variable). The assignment statement in line 120 enlarges the content of the string by an alpha-numeric "*" character. Line 120 is executed **F** times, resulting in a string **SS**, that contains **F** star (*) characters. If **F** represents the frequency count, then the **SS** string represents **F** stars for that frequency count. This technique is used in Example [1] for plotting the frequency distribution of corn yield (lines 181 through 190 and lines 241 through 245).

```
10 DIM C(50),A(50)
20 REM READ IN THE NUMBER OF CORNYIELDS TO BE CONSIDERED
30 READ K
40 REM READ IN ALL CORNYIELDS
50 FOR I=1 TO K
60 READ C(I)
70 NEXT I
80 REM DEFINE ARRAY A AND INDEX N FOR SORT ROUTINE
90 MAT LET A=C
100 N=K
110 GOSUB 310
120 REM DEFINE FREQUENCY DISTRIBUTION
130 PRINT "1 FREQUENCY DISTRIBUTION OF CORNYIELD IN BUSHELS/ACRE"
140 PRINT "YIELD","FREQUENCY"
150 Y=A(1)
160 F=1
170 FOR I=2 TO K
180 IF A(I) = Y ,THEN 230
181 SS=":"
182 FOR L =1 TO F
183 SS=SS+"*"
184 NEXT L
190 PRINT Y,SS
200 Y=A(I)
210 F=1
220 GOTO 240
230 F=F+1
240 NEXT I
241 SS =":"
242 FOR L=1 TO F
243 SS = SS+"*"
244 NEXT L
245 PRINT Y,SS
250 STOP
300 REM ORDERING ROUTINE
310 FOR I=2 TO N
320 J=I
330 IF A(J) >= A(J-1) ,THEN 390
340 D=A(J)
350 A(J) = A(J-1)
360 A(J-1)=D
370 J=J-1
380 IF J >= 2 ,THEN 330
390 NEXT I
400 RETURN
450 DATA 47
460 DATA 35,29,32,31,33,33,38,26,29,32,32,37,32,36,32
470 DATA 33,31,30,32,30,33,27,34,35,30,34,36,34,31,32
480 DATA 32,34,32,31,31,30,33,32,30,33,34,32,31,34,32
490 DATA 31,32
500 END
```

```
FREQUENCY DISTRIBUTIØN ØF CØRNYIELD IN BUSHELS/ACRE
YIELD          FREQUENCY
26             :*
27             :*
29             :**
30             :*****
31             :*******
32             :*************
33             :******
34             :******
35             :**
36             :**
37             :*
38             :*
```

USE OF THE OUTPUT TAB FUNCTION

The effect of the **TAB** function in a **PRINT** statement is explained in Chapter 5. It is this same **TAB** function that can be used to plot a function.

Recall that

TAB (exp)

causes the printer to tab to the column as indicated by the absolute truncated value of the expression, exp. The next character is then printed in that column. This is illustrated in Examples [2], [3], and [4].

EX. [2] PLOTTING THE SINE FUNCTION

```
10 DEF FNR(X) = X*3.14/180
20 PRINT "1PLØT ØF THE SINE FUNCTIØN "
30 FØR X =0 TØ 360 STEP 10
40 P=INT((SIN(FNR(X))+1)*20)
50 PRINT TAB(5+P);"*"
60 NEXT X
70 STØP
```

The user-defined interval function **FNR**, that converts degrees in radians, is defined in line 10. This function is used to calculate the SINE values in line 40.

Remember that: $-1 \leq SIN(FNR(X)) \leq +1$

Therefore: $0 \leq SIN(FNR(X)) +1 \leq 2$

and: $0 \leq (SIN(FNR(X))+1) *20 \leq 40$

or: $0 \leq P \leq 40$

This scaling is necessary to stretch the SINE plot over 40 printing areas. The **TAB** (5+P), in line 50, positions the printer in the (5+P)th position of the printing line, where the function value will be indicated by a "*", as this is the next character to be printed.

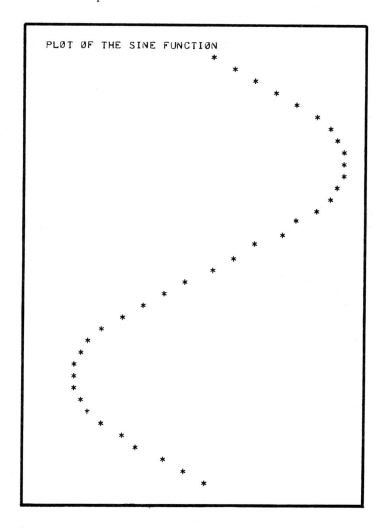

```
10 DEF FNR(X) = X*3.14/180
20 PRINT "1PLØT ØF THE SINE FUNCTIØN "
21 PRINT
22 PRINT TAB(7);"-1",TAB(27);"0";TAB(47);"+1"
23 SS="-"
24 FØR I=1 TØ 40
25 SS=SS+"-"
26 NEXT I
27 PRINT TAB(7);SS
30 FØR X =0 TØ 360 STEP 10
40 P=INT((SIN(FNR(X))+1)*20)
50 PRINT X,TAB(6);":",TAB(7+P);"*"
60 NEXT X
70 STØP
```

The plot that results from the above BASIC program is complete:

—The labels (**−1, 0, and +1**) are indicated on the **Y-axis** (line 22).

—The Y-axis is drawn by the use of a string (**SS**) to which 41 dashes (—) are assigned (lines 23 through 27).

—the **X** values (degrees), **X-axis** (:), and **SINE** plot (*) is the result of the PRINT statement in line 50.

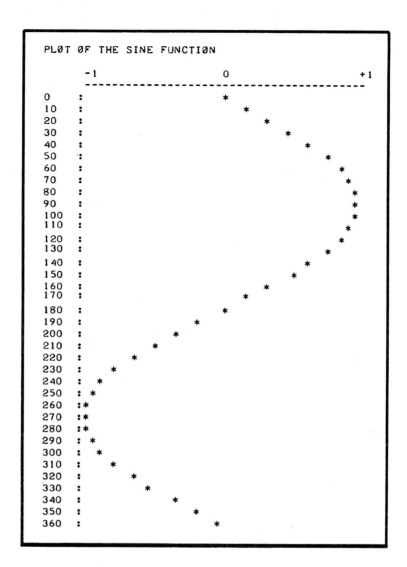

```
10 DEF FNR(X) = X*3.14/180
20 PRINT "1PLØT ØF THE SINE AND THE CØSINE FUNCTIØN"
21 PRINT
22 PRINT TAB(7);"-1",TAB(27);"0";TAB(47);"+1"
23 SS="-"
24 FØR I=1 TØ 40
25 SS=SS+"-"
26 NEXT I
27 PRINT TAB(7);SS
30 FØR X =0 TØ 360 STEP 10
40 P=INT((SIN(FNR(X))+1)*20)
45 Q=INT((CØS(FNR(X))+1)*20)
50 IF P<Q,THEN 54
51 IF P>Q,THEN 56
52 PRINT X,TAB(6);":",TAB(7+P);"*"
53 GØTØ 60
54 PRINT X,TAB(6);":",TAB(7+P);"*",TAB(7+Q);"+"
55 GØTØ 60
56 PRINT X,TAB(6);":",TAB(7+Q);"+",TAB(7+P);"*"
60 NEXT X
65 PRINT TAB(28);"SINE",TAB(48);"CØSINE"
70 STØP
```

When two functions have to be printed, it is necessary to check which function has to be tabbed first. This is done in lines 50 and 51:

50   IF P<Q, THEN 54

●

●

54   PRINT X, TAB(6); ":", TAB(7+P); "*", TAB (7+Q); "+"

If **P** is less than **Q**, then the **SINE** value has to be plotted before the **COSINE** value

51   IF P>Q, THEN 56

●

●

56   PRINT X, TAB(6); ":", TAB(7+Q); "+", TAB (7+P); "*"

If **Q** is less than **P**, then the **COSINE** value has to be plotted before the **SINE** value. However, if **P** and **Q** are equal, then only one point must be plotted

52   PRINT X, TAB(6); ":", TAB (7+P); "*"

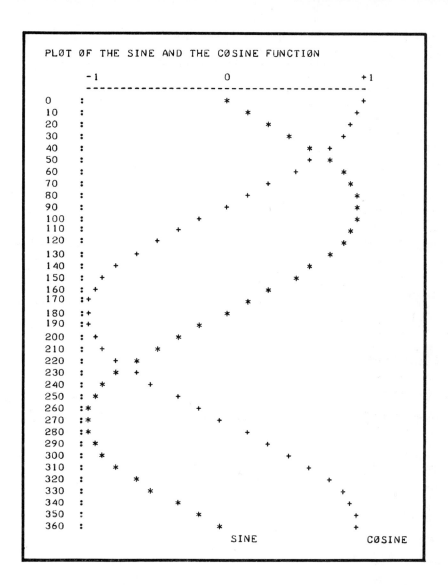

File Processing

BASIC has the capability of writing information in a file and getting data from a file. In order to use files to read from or to write in, these files must be assigned to channels. There is a limited number of channels available. As soon as a file has been assigned to a channel, it can be used in a **BASIC** program as will be discussed in what follows.

GENERAL DESCRIPTION OF FILES

Figure 12.1 is a general skeleton representation of a file.

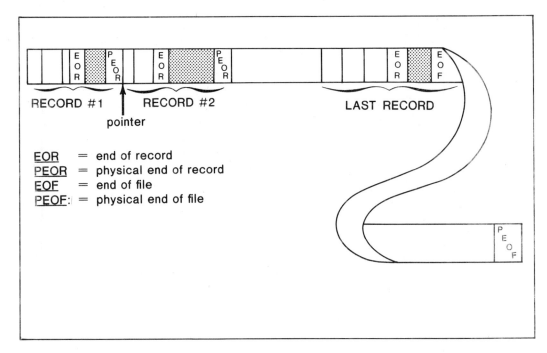

Figure 12.1   *File Representation*

A file is a named collection of all occurrences of a given type of logical records. Records in a file may have the same number of data items or they may have varying number of data items. Since the collection of records may take up less space than the actual size of the file, one must distinguish between the physical end of the file (**PEOF**) and the end of all records or the end of file (**EOF**). A physical record often contains multiple segment or data items. Since the length of a record is determined by the system programmer, or may be fixed, the actual end of a record (**EOR**) is often different from the physical end of a record (**PEOR**). A pointer is used to locate the next data element of a record under consideration.

Examples of records are: the inventory records in an inventory file, students' records in a student file, etc. The elements of an inventory record may be the identification (ID), amount of stock on hand, vendor's address, lead time, safety stock, reorder point, etc. Most likely, in such a type of inventory file all records have the same number of data items. The elements of a student file may consist of student identification, student name, major, grade point average, courses taken and grades received. In such a file, the records may exhibit varying numbers of data items.

SEQUENTIAL ACCESS AND RANDOM ACCESS FILES

A sequential access file is a file from which data is read or in which data is written sequentially, one item after the other. Such a file can either be in the read or the write mode. Even though it cannot be in both the read and the write mode simultaneously, it is possible to change the mode from the write mode to the read mode by the use of appropriate BASIC statements. Whenever the read mode is established, one starts reading at the beginning of the file. Similarly, whenever the write mode is established, the file is totally erased and writing starts at the very beginning of the file.

A random access file is a data file that is not necessarily read from or written in sequentially. Unlike sequential access files, random access files do not distinguish between the read or the write mode. Reading from or writing into a random file is done after first setting a pointer to the appropriate location of the file. Random access files can be handled in commonly available BASIC.

In what follows we will discuss the use of line-numbered sequential access files and random access files.

CREATING SEQUENTIAL ACCESS FILES

Line-numbered files are like **BASIC** programs that can be handled with any of the **BASIC** commands. They are created and changed as a **BASIC** program is created and changed. Here follow some of the basic rules to be followed when constructing a sequential access file.

1. Each line in a line-numbered file starts with a line number, followed by at least one **space**, a **tab**, the **letter D** or the key word **DATA**.
2. After the **space**, **tab**, **D** or **DATA**, any number of data items can be printed (up to a maximum total number of characters per line, say 142).
3. Data items are separated by commas, tabs or at least one space. No space, tab or comma is needed behind the last data item of each line.
4. Data items can either be numeric constants or string constants. String constants must be placed in quotes if they contain blanks, commas, or tabs.

In order to properly utilize what follows, the user of this text must replace all **BASIC** commands by the ones appropriate for his system. The **DEC10** **BASIC** commands are used here.

To close this section, let us set up a line-numbered sequential file at the editing level in **BASIC** via the teletype. Again, remember that all system and **BASIC** command (the underlined portion), are typically **DEC10** commands. It was previously suggested that you change them to the ones which are appropriate for your system.

```
R BASIC


READY, FOR HELP TYPE HELP.
NEW
NEW FILE NAME----PRIME

READY
10 "PRIME NUMBER"
20 1,3,5,7
30 11,13,17,19
40 23,29,31,37
SAVE

READY
```

Here a file is created at the editing level in **BASIC**. The name of the file is called **PRIME**. It consists of four numbered lines from 10 to 40. Notice the space behind the line number and the actual data. There is a total of thirteen (13) data items in this file: **"PRIME NUMBER", 1, 3, 5, 7, 11, 13, 17, 19, 23, 29, 31, 37.** The SAVE command saves that file, called PRIME, on disk. This sequential file will be used in the next two sections.

READING FROM SEQUENTIAL FILES

In this section five **BASIC** statements are discussed which are used in connection with reading from sequential files. These are: **FILES, READ, BACKSPACE, RESTORE,** and **IF END** statements. Before using these statements in a **BASIC** program a short description of each of them is in order.

The **FILES** statement is used to assign a data file to a channel. Data files must be assigned to a channel first before it can be used in the program. The **FILES** statement must therefore be in the beginning of the program. The general form of the **FILES** statement is as follows:

FILES filename1; filename2; filename3; . . .

where: **filenames** are separated by either commas (,) or semicolons (;); however, some systems will only accept semicolons.

When **FILES** is interpreted **filename1** will be assigned to **channel #1**, **filename2** will be assigned to **channel #2**, **filename3** will be assigned to **channel #3**, etc. . . .

Remember, all files whose name is mentioned in the **FILES** statement and who are used in the **BASIC** program must exist in the **BASIC** workspace. This will be re-emphasized later when a complete example is presented.

A special form of the **READ** statement is used to read data from a file. The general form of that **READ** statement is as follows:

READ #N, variable, variable, variable, . . .

where: —**N:** identifies the channel (say from 1 to nine)
—at **least one variable** must be present
—deliminator following N can either be a comma (,) or a semicolon (;)

The **READ** statement expects each line to start with a number. That line number of course is not read in by the **READ** statement; it is skipped or ignored.

This **READ** statement will read from a file as defined by its channel number **N**. The constants which are read are assigned to the variables defined in the **READ** statement.

The **BACKSPACE** statement backs up the referenced file one data item at a time. Only files in the read mode can be backspaced. The general form of the **BACKSPACE** statement is as follows:

BACKSPACE #N

where: **N** is the channel number of the file that must be backspaced

The **IF END** statement is used to transfer control to a statement other than the **READ** statement if the end of the file is reached. The general form of the **IF END** statement is as follows:

IF END #N THEN 1n

where: **N** is the channel number of the file that is being considered.
1n is the line number of that statement to which control must be transferred if there are no more unused data items stored in the file.

If there is more unused data in the file, the control will be transferred to the next executable statement.

Let us now illustrate some of these new **BASIC** statements in a program that does the following: It reads in prime numbers, one at a time, from a file called **PRIME**. The **PRIME** file was created earlier and is stored on disk. These prime numbers are squared and then printed out. Here is the **BASIC** program.

```
00010 FILES PRIME
00020 READ #1,A$
00030 PRINT "THE SQUARED VALUES OF PRIME NUMBERS"
00040 PRINT
00050 PRINT "NUMBER     SQUARED NUMBER"
00060 PRINT
00070 READ #1,N
00080 PRINT USING 90,N,N**2
00090 : ###             ######
00100 IF END #1 THEN 120
00110 GOTO 70
00120 STOP
00130 END
```

The above **BASIC** program consists of 13 lines (statements). When the **BASIC** program is going to use files, then the user must declare these files. Our **BASIC** program example declares one file, called **PRIME**. In line 10 the file **PRIME** is declared and is assigned to the **1st channel** and can be referenced in the program by **#1**. The second line reads a string constant from **channel #1** or from the **PRIME** file. This string constant is assigned to the string variable **A$**.

Study the statements in line numbers 30 and 40! They are very straightforward. The characters in the **PRINT** statement of line 50 are printed when the statement is executed. The **READ** statement of line 70 reads from the file on **channel #1**. The constant that is read is assigned to the variable **N** and is squared and printed via the **PRINT USING** statement in line 80, in accordance with the **IMAGE** statement of line 90. The **IF END** statement controls the repetition of lines 70, 80, 90, 100 and 110, until all data items of the file on **channel #1** have been used. When all data items have been used the execution of the program stops (**STOP**).

If this **BASIC** program is stored under the file name **TRY1**, then the following **BASIC** commands will execute it: (remember, adjust them to your system)

```
READY, FOR HELP TYPE HELP.
OLD
OLD FILE NAME----PRIME

READY
OLD
OLD FILE NAME----TRY1

READY
RUN
```

Notice that both the data file **PRIME** and the **BASIC** program **TRY1** must be brought in the **BASIC** working space via the **BASIC** command **OLD**. The resulting output of the **BASIC** program is as follows:

```
TRY1              14:29          07--JUN--79



THE SQUARED VALUES OF PRIME NUMBERS

NUMBER    SQUARED NUMBER

   1              1
   3              9
   5             25
   7             49
  11            121
  13            169
  17            289
  19            361
  23            529
  29            841
  31            961
  37           1369
```

WRITING IN SEQUENTIAL FILES

With respect to writing in sequential files, the following four statements are discussed in this section:

FILES
SCRATCH #N
WRITE #N
RESTORE #N

Again, the **FILES** statement is used to assign data files to channels. This must happen in the very beginning of the main **BASIC** program. When filenames are defined in the **FILES** statement, then these files will be assigned to channels; the first one to **channel #1**, the second one to **channel #2**, etc. . . . The general form of the **FILES** statement is as defined in the previous section:

FILES filename1; filename2; filename3; . . .

where: **filenames** are separated by either commas (,) or semicolons (;); however, some systems will only accept semicolons

Again, when **FILES** is interpreted by the system it will assign to **channel #1 filename1**, to **channel #2 filename2**, to **channel #3 filename3**, etc. . . .

All sequential files declared in the **FILES** statement are in the read mode. This can be changed to the write mode via the **SCRATCH** statement. A file must be in the write mode before one can write onto that file. The general form of the **SCRATCH** statement is as follows:

SCRATCH #N

where: **N** is the channel number of the file that must be put in the write mode

When a sequential access file is scratched all data is erased from that file and writing will start at the beginning of that file. Once a file is put in the write mode via the **SCRATCH** statement, that file cannot be referenced in a **READ** or an **IF END** statement.

The **WRITE** statement is used to write information in a file. The general form of the **WRITE** statement is as follows:

WRITE #N, variable; variable; variable; . . .

where: **N** identifies the channel number of the file that must be written in

A file is changed from the write mode to the read mode via the **RESTORE** statement as follows:

RESTORE #N

where: **N** identifies the channel of the file that is restored to the read mode.

Some of these statements are now illustrated by using the same example of the previous section. However, rather than printing the results on the terminal, they are written in the file called **PRIME**. The **BASIC** program is as follows:

```
00010 FILES PRIME;SQUARE
00020 SCRATCH #2
00030 READ #1,A$
00040 WRITE #2,"THE SQUARED VALUES OF PRIME NUMBERS"
00050 WRITE #2
00060 WRITE #2,"NUMBER    SQUARED NUMBER"
00070 WRITE #2
00080 READ #1,N
00090 WRITE #2,USING 100,N,N**2
00100 :  ###            #####
00110 IF END #1 THEN 130
00120 GOTO 80
00130 STOP
00140 END
```

Note that there are two files used in this program, the **PRIME** and the **SQUARE** file. Remember now that one must save both files and place them in the **BASIC** working area before the above program can be executed. The **PRIME** file will be referred to as **#1**, since it is assigned to **channel #1** and the **SQUARE** file will be referred to as **#2**. The statement in line 20 changes the **SQUARE** file from the read mode into the write mode. The **READ** statement in line 30 reads a string constant from the **PRIME** file and assigns it to the string variable **A$**. Statements in lines 40, 50, 60, 70, 90 and 100 writes information in the **SQUARE** file. Notice the use of the formatted **WRITE** and image statements!

If this **BASIC** program is stored under the file name **TRY2**, then the following **BASIC** commands will execute it:

```
.R BASIC

READY, FOR HELP TYPE HELP.
OLD
OLD FILE NAME----PRIME

READY
OLD
OLD FILE NAME----TRY2

READY
RUN

TRY2            14:32         07-JUN-79




TIME:  0.07 SECS.
```

Notice that the output file **SQUARE** is not opened. Observe, however, that on some systems all files declared in the **FILES** statement of the **BASIC** program must be placed in the **BASIC** working area before executing the **BASIC** program. Obviously, no output will be printed on the teletype since all information is written in the **SQUARE** file. A **BASIC** command such as **LIST** can be used to output the newly formed file **SQUARE**, as follows:

```
READY
OLD
OLD FILE NAME----SQUARE

READY
LIST


SQUARE              14:33              07--JUN--79



1000    THE SQUARED VALUES OF PRIME NUMBERS
1010
1020    NUMBER   SQUARED NUMBER
1030
1040        1                1
1050        3                9
1060        5               25
1070        7               49
1080       11              121
1090       13              169
1100       17              289
1110       19              361
1120       23              529
1130       29              841
1140       31              961
1150       37             1369
1160
```

RANDOM ACCESS FILES

Many **BASIC** systems can handle random access files; however there are vast differences among instructions from system to system. Therefore, it is recommended that the reader use this section only as a guide and consider consulting the manual of his system for proper manipulation of random access files.

A random access file is a data file that is not necessarily read from or written in sequentially. Unlike sequential access files, random access files do not distinguish between the read or the write mode. After setting a pointer to the appropriate location of the random access file one can read from or write into that file.

As with sequential access files, random access files must be established by the use of the **FILES** statement or the **OPEN** statement. When reading from a file or writing into a file, it is necessary to set a pointer at the exact location where we wish to read from or write into. With respect to reading and writing we will discuss the following statements: **READ:, WRITE:,** and **SET:,** and the following functions **LOC(m)** and **LOF(m)**.

The **FILES** statement is used to assign a random access data file to a channel. These files can either be **numeric files (%)** or **string files ($)**. The general form of the **FILES** statement is as follows:

FILES filename1; filename2; . . .

where: —**filenames** are separated by either commas (,) or semicolons (;); however, some systems will only accept semicolons.

—each **file name** must be followed by either **%** or **$** to identify a numeric or a string file respectively.

As with sequential access files, when **FILES** is interpreted **filename1** is assigned to **channel #1, filename2** is assigned to **channel #2,** etc. . . . Consider the following example:

10   FILES PAYROLL%,PEOPLE$

that defines **PAYROLL** as a numeric file and **PEOPLE** as a string file. The **PAYROLL** file is assigned to **channel #1** and the **PEOPLE** file is assigned to **channel #2.**

Some systems use the **OPEN** statement instead of the **FILE** statement. The general form is then

$$\textbf{OPEN filename, RANDOM} \begin{Bmatrix} \textbf{INPUT} \\ or \\ \textbf{OUTPUT} \\ or \\ \textbf{IO} \end{Bmatrix} \textbf{, N}$$

where: **RANDOM** means that "filename" is a random file
INPUT means that it is only an input file
OUTPUT means that it is only an output file
IO means that it is an input and output file
N is the channel to which the file is assigned.

Consider the following example:

30   OPEN PAY, RANDOM IO, 4

This statement assigns to **channel #4** the file called **PAY**. This file is a random access file from which we are able to read and in which we are able to write.

In order to read from a file or to write into a file, a pointer or key must be placed. When a file is opened the pointer is placed at the first record of the file; when that record is read or replaced (write) then the pointer moves to the second record, etc. . . . the programmer can set the pointer at any location he wishes by the use of the **SET** statement. The general format of the **SET** statement is as follows:

$$\textbf{SET:N, v}$$

where: **N** is the channel number

v is an arithmetic expression that defines the position where the pointer needs to be placed

Various methods can be used to define **v** in the above statements, including the following two functions:

$$\textbf{LOC(N)}$$

$$\textbf{LOF(N)}$$

LOC(N) is used to identify the current pointer value and **LOF(N)** defines the number of records in file **N**.

Once the pointer is set one can read from a file or write in the file as follows:

$$\textbf{READ: N, variable, variable, variable, . . .}$$

or

$$\textbf{WRITE: N, variable, variable, variable, . . .}$$

where: —: refers to a random access file

—**N** is the channel number

—at least one variable must be present

—deliminator following N can either be a comma (,) or a semi-colon (;)

To illustrate the use of random access files, consider the manipulation of two random access files: the **PAY** and the **NAMES** file. The **NAMES** file is a string file, whereas the **PAY** file is a numeric file. As a result of a new union contract the **PAY** file must be updated since all employees are receiving a 7% raise. After it is updated it is necessary to output the employee's name from the **NAME** file and his new hourly pay. The **BASIC** program is as follows.

In line 10 two files are opened, a numeric file called **PAY** and a string file called **NAMES**. Line 20 indicates that we will loop through all records of the files, from the first one to the last one as indicated by the function **LOF(1)**.

```
10   FILES PAY:,NAMES$
20   FOR K=1 TO LOF(1)
30   READ:1,P
40   LET P=P*1.07
50   SET:1,LOC(1)-1
60   WRITE:1,P
70   READ:2,N$
80   PRINT P,N$
90   NEXT K
100  END
```

Remember that when the files were opened in line 10, the pointers automatically point at the first record of each file. In line 30 of the **BASIC** program a constant is read from the first file and assigned to variable **P**. When this happens the pointer in that file moves to the second record. The **SET** statement backs up the pointer by one position, as indicated by **LOC(1)−1**. The new calculated pay value (**P**) is now written in the **PAY** file and replaces the previous one. The **READ** statement in line 70 reads an employee's name from the second file. Finally, the new hourly pay and the employee's name is printed via the **PRINT** statement in line 80.

Summary

In this chapter we have discussed some advanced **BASIC** techniques on formatted output, plotting and File Processing.

The **PRINT USING** and **IMAGE** statements are used for formatted input. The following specifications are used:

numeric image specifications:	the pound sign	#
	the period	.
	4 upward arrows	↑↑↑↑
edited numeric specifications:	the dollar sign	$
	the commas	,
	the trailing minus	−
	the leading asterisk	*
string image specifications:	for right justification	**R**
	for left justification	**L**
	for centering	**C**
	for extending	**E**

String variables and the output **TAB** function make plotting fairly straightforward in **BASIC**.

File processing is accomplished by the use of special **BASIC** statements which will either read from or write in files. The following statements are discussed in this chapter.

FILES	for assigning data files to channels
READ #N	for reading data from a sequential file
READ:N	for reading data from a random access file
BACKSPACE #N	for backing up one data element at a time in the reference file.
RESTORE #N	for permitting to read from a file from the beginning again or to change a file from the write mode to the read mode.
IF END	for transferring control to a statement other than the READ statement if the end of the file is reached.
SCRATCH #N	to change a file from the read mode to the write mode.
WRITE #N	to write information in the referenced sequential file.
WRITE:N	to write information in the referenced random access file.
SET:N	to set the pointer in a random access file.

Exercises

PROBLEM #1

Write the appropriate **PRINT USING** and **IMAGE** statements to output the following table:

INVENTORY INFORMATION

Item	Quantity	Value
234	1,243	$ 932.25
523	735	$18,375.00
124	321	$ 4,012.50

PROBLEM #2

Reconsider problem #2 or chapter 11. Elaborate on your program, so that in addition to the reservations you output two seating grids or plans as follows:

1. When approximately 50% of the theater is filled (approximately when M*N/2 seats are filled)
2. When all reservations have been considered. Indicate with a * (star) which seats are reserved, and leave all other seats blank. Label your grid.

PROBLEM #3

Rewrite the first ordering program taking the following items into consideration:

1. The data that needs to be ordered is in a data file called DATA:
2. After all the data is ordered, replace the data in file DATA by the ordered data.

13
Simulation

For some reason, one may want to have the capability of manipulating the real world and observing the effect of this manipulation without having to suffer the consequences of actual physical changes. This capability implies that the observer is able to construct a model which exhibits the properties of the real world.

The model need not necessarily be a duplication of the actual system. One merely has to try to create some operating function, or model, which can effect the same relationship between the inputs and the outputs that the real world exhibits. This model is called a "simulation model," because it simulates reality. High-speed computers have stimulated the progress of the use of simulation models in many research areas.

We should know in advance the nature and form of the input. The nature of the system may indicate that a deterministic or a stochastic input environment exists. If the input is stochastic, then it is necessary to use a random-number generator to generate random numbers which can then be used or transformed through a function to obtain the desired inputs. These inputs can now be "pushed" through the simulation model and, in a sense, the "reaction" of the model to these inputs can be observed through the analysis of the generated outputs.

The Random-Number Generator

A random-number generator is a process that generates uniformly distributed random numbers over the unit interval. Its cumulative distribution function can, therefore, be expressed as follows:

$$F(x) = \begin{cases} 0, & x \le 0 \\ X, & 0 < x < 1 \\ 1, & x \ge 1 \end{cases}$$

The sequence of random numbers, x, can be generated in a number of ways: manual methods, library tables, analog computer methods (yield truly random numbers), and digital computer methods.

The internal generation of random numbers by the use of a recurrence relation on a digital computer is used to generate random numbers in BASIC. The BASIC function **RND** uses Lehmer's method for producing pseudo-random numbers between 0.0 and 1.0. (*Communications of the ACM*, February 1969, pp. 85–86).

The general form of the **RND** function is as follows:

RND (v)

where: **RND** is the name of the function.

      v is a simple numeric variable name.

The argument is used for the storage of the random number base. **RND** supplies a starting value if the argument, **v**, is zero. However, if **v** is nonzero, the value of the argument is used as a starting base. This is extremely useful, when there is a need for generating separate, independent strings of random numbers, as is clearly illustrated in the following three BASIC programs.

The starting value in Program #1 is 99 (**20 B=99**); in Program #2 it is 89 (**20 B1=89**). Program #3 illustrates that same independent strings of random numbers can be obtained by using the same starting values.

GENERATING INDEPENDENT STRINGS OF RANDOM NUMBERS

Program #1	*Program #2*	*Program #3*

```
10 DIM X(20)          10 DIM Y(20)          10 DIM X(20),Y(20)
20 B=99               20 B1=89              20 B=99
30 FØR I=1 TØ 20      30 FØR I =1 TØ 20     30 B1=89
40 X(I)=RND(B)        40 Y(I)=RND(B1)       40 FØR I=1 TØ 20
50 PRINT X(I)         50 PRINT Y(I)         50 X(I)=RND(B)
60 NEXT I             60 NEXT I             60 Y(I)=RND(B1)
65 PRINT "1"          65 PRINT "1"          70 PRINT X(I),Y(I)
70 STØP               70 STØP               80 NEXT I
                                            85 PRINT "1"
0.7382552             0.127814              90 STØP
0.2836873             0.2164506
0.3098873             0.3949327             0.7382552      0.127814
0.880602              0.419162              0.2836873      0.2164506
0.325112              8.552366E-2           0.3098873      0.3949327
0.9191828             0.9515969             0.880602       0.419162
0.9049597             0.4583974             0.325112       8.552366E-2
0.7541427             0.13806               0.9191828      0.9515969
0.2565036             0.689732              0.9049597      0.4583974
0.8607842             0.5210748             0.7541427      0.13806
0.3848133             3.663009E-2           0.2565036      0.689732
0.8257723             0.2800358             0.8607842      0.5210748
0.1789809             0.3268508             0.3848133      3.663009E-2
0.2928331             0.3361068             0.8257723      0.2800358
0.7630803             0.8651094             0.1789809      0.3268508
0.523711              0.6157464             0.2928331      0.3361068
0.9764307             0.4701237             0.7630803      0.8651094
0.4605818             0.2520408             0.523711       0.6157464
7.587853E-3           0.5751453             0.9764307      0.4701237
0.3635267             0.2488472             0.4605818      0.2520408
                                            7.587853E-3    0.5751453
                                            0.3635267      0.2488472
```

How random numbers can be transformed through a function to generate the desired stochastic inputs is illustrated in the three simulation examples that follow.

Simulating the Inebriated Individual Crossing a Bridge

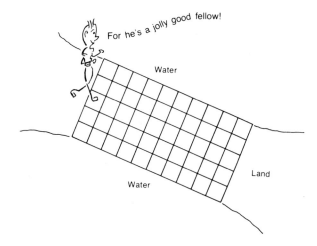

Consider the drunken individual who is attempting to cross a bridge five feet wide and ten feet long. Assume that the individual is standing between zero and the first-foot mark in the middle of the bridge passage as illustrated above.

Each step the individual takes is a one-foot step. Past records of our individual in his special condition show the following probability distribution for taking a one-foot step in either one direction.

Straight forward: 0.50

Straight backward: 0.10

Straight to the right: 0.20

Straight to the left: 0.20

In order to find the probability of the inebriate crossing the bridge, a simulation model is constructed which accomplishes the following:

1. Simulate in groups of 1,000 attempts the set of steps that the person takes until he falls off the bridge, crosses the bridge, or backs off the bridge.
2. Record the number of times he falls into the water, the number of times he crosses the bridge, and the number of times he backs off from the bridge.
3. Print out, after each 100 attempts the number of times he crossed the bridge, fell into the water or backed off from the bridge and the probability of his crossing the bridge.

Programming Procedure

The random number generator, **RND** function, is used to simulate the set of steps of the inebriated individual. **RND** generates real constants on the interval zero-one. These real constants are converted to integer constants from one (1) to ten (10) through the following BASIC assignment statement:

80   K=INT(10*RND(X)+1)

If **K** equals **1, 2, 3, 4, or 5,** a step forward is taken, and **I** is incremented by **1** (lines 90 and 100). This happens 50% of the time.

If **K** equals **6**, a step backward is taken, and **I** is decreased by **1** (lines 90 and 130). This happens 10% of the time.

If **K** equals **7** or **8**, a step to the right is taken, and **J** is increased by **1** (lines 90 and 160). This happens 20% of the time.

If **K** equals **9** or **10**, a step to the left is taken, and **J** is decreased by **1** (lines 90 and 190). This happens 20% of the time.

As the individual is standing between the zero and the first footmark in the middle of the bridge passageway, the initial value of **I** equals **1** and **J** equals **3** (lines 60 and 70).

Each time the drunk makes a step, the model checks where he is:

If a step in the forward direction was made, resulting in incrementing the counter **I(100 I=I+1)**, and if **I** has now become greater than **10** (line 110), then he crossed the bridge, and the counter for crossing the bridge is incremented by **1 (240   C=C+1)**.

If a backward step was made, resulting in decreasing the counter **I (130   I=I−1)**, and if **I** has now become less than **1** (line 140); then he backed off the bridge, and the counter for backing off from the bridge is increased by **1 (260   B=B+1)**.

If a step to the right (line 160) or to the left (line 190) was made and if **J** has now become greater than **5** (line 170) or less than **1** (line 200), then he fell into the water, and the counter for falling into the water must be incremented by **1 (220   F=F+1)**.

When the drunk crosses the bridge, falls into the water, or backs off from the bridge, this program places him again on the first footmark, in the middle of the bridge passageway (lines 60 and 70) until a sufficient number of attempts has been generated (lines 310, 320, 330).

This procedure is illustrated in the following flowchart and program.

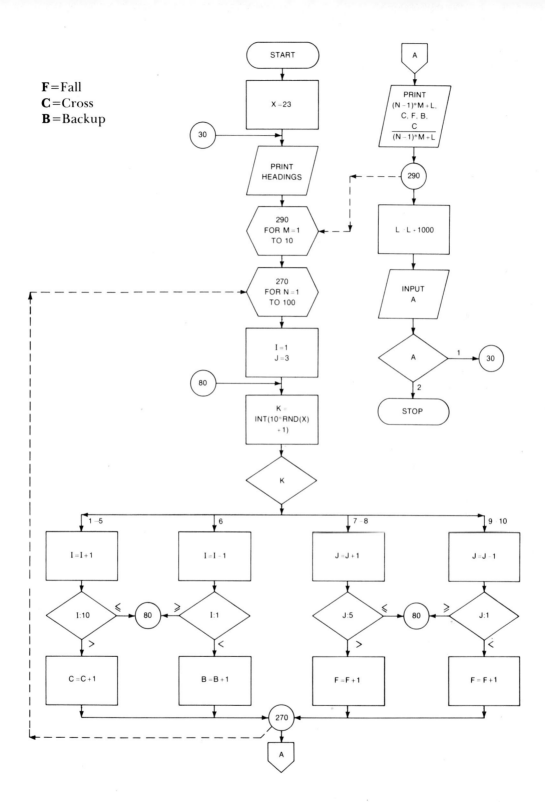

F = Fall
C = Cross
B = Backup

PROGRAM

```
10 REM SIMULATE THE DRUNK
20 X=23
30 PRINT "1ATTEMPTS","CRØSSINGS","FALLS","BACKINGS","P(CRØSSING)"
40 FØR M=1 TØ 10
50 FØR N=1 TØ 100
60 I=1
70 J=3
80 K= INT(10*RND(X)+1)
90 GØTØ (100,100,100,100,100,130,160,160,190,190),K
100 I=I+1
110 IF I>10 ,THEN 240
120 GØTØ 80
130 I=I-1
140 IF I<1 ,THEN 260
150 GØTØ 80
160 J=J+1
170 IF J>5 ,THEN220
180 GØTØ 80
190 J=J-1
200 IF J<1 ,THEN220
210 GØTØ 80
220 F=F+1
230 GØTØ 270
240 C=C+1
250 GØTØ 270
260 B=B+1
270 NEXT N
280 PRINT (N-1)*M+L,C,F,B,C/((N-1)*M+L)
290 NEXT M
300 L=L+1000
310 PRINT "MØRE ATTEMPTS? YES=1,NO=2"
320 INPUT A
330 GØTØ(30,340),A
340 STØP
```

ATTEMPTS	CRØSSINGS	FALLS	BACKINGS	P(CRØSSING)
100	33	46	21	0.33
200	67	89	44	0.335
300	107	133	60	0.3566667
400	138	188	74	0.345
500	174	236	90	0.348
600	200	297	103	0.3333333
700	233	352	115	0.3328571
800	261	411	128	0.32625
900	293	464	143	0.3255556
1000	326	514	160	0.326

MØRE ATTEMPTS? YES=1,NO=2
?1

ATTEMPTS	CRØSSINGS	FALLS	BACKINGS	P(CRØSSING)
1100	361	563	176	0.3281818
1200	393	611	196	0.3275
1300	423	668	209	0.3253846
1400	450	723	227	0.3214286
1500	483	771	246	0.322
1600	519	824	257	0.324375
1700	547	877	276	0.3217647
1800	586	919	295	0.3255556
1900	619	967	314	0.3257895
2000	654	1015	331	0.327

MØRE ATTEMPTS? YES=1,NO=2
?1

ATTEMPTS	CRØSSINGS	FALLS	BACKINGS	P(CRØSSING)
2100	685	1062	353	0.3261905
2200	719	1112	369	0.3268182
2300	753	1149	398	0.3273913
2400	787	1203	410	0.3279167
2500	818	1265	417	0.3272
2600	846	1318	436	0.3253846
2700	873	1372	455	0.3233333
2800	903	1425	472	0.3225
2900	933	1474	493	0.3217241
3000	966	1528	506	0.322

MØRE ATTEMPTS? YES=1,NO=2
?2

Computation of π Through Simulation

The Monte Carlo technique is used here to calculate π **(PI)**. Consider the circle which is inscribed inside a square, as illustrated in Figure 13.1.

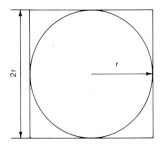

Figure 13.1. *Inscribed Circle*

The area of the circle equals $\pi r^2 = Y$, where **r** is the radius, whereas the area of the square equals $(2r)^2 = X$, where 2r is its side's length. The ratio of the area of the square to the area of the circle, therefore, is:

$$\frac{\textbf{Area of Square}}{\textbf{Area of Circle}} = \frac{\textbf{X}}{\textbf{Y}} = \frac{(2r)^2}{\pi r^2} = \frac{4r^2}{\pi r^2} = \frac{4}{\pi}$$

Therefore, π can be expressed as follows:

$$\pi = \frac{4Y}{X} = \frac{4 \text{ times the area of the circle}}{\text{the area of the square}}$$

So, in order to calculate π, one must be able to measure the areas of the circle and the square, or one must be able to calculate the ratio of the area of the circle to the area of the square. The following simulation technique, often referred to as the Monte Carlo method, will calculate that ratio.

Reconsider Figure 13.1 and inscribe the circle as in Figure 13.2.

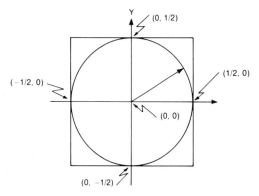

Figure 13.2. *Inscribed Circle Reconsidered*

Note that the radius is now equal to 1/2 and that the center of the circle coincides with the origin of the X-Y plane. If we can now devise a method whereby we can choose points at random which fall within the square, then 4 times the ratio of the number of these points which fall within the circle to the total number of points within the square equals π:

$$\pi = \frac{\textbf{4 times number of points within circle}}{\textbf{total number of points in square}}$$

These points can be generated by the use of two random number generators, since each point is represented by an X-Y coordinate.

RND(B) can be used to generate the X-coordinate and **RND(B1)** can be used to generate the Y-coordinate.

Note, however, that the **RND(B)** generates pseudo-random numbers between zero and one and that in our reconsidered Figure 13.2, X lies between $-1/2$ and $+1/2$. Therefore the random numbers have to be scaled as follows:

$$-1/2 < \textbf{RND(B)} -.5 < +1/2 \rightsquigarrow -1/2 < \textbf{X} < +1/2$$

A similar scaling is necessary for the Y-coordinate:

$$-1/2 < \textbf{RND(B1)} -.5 < +1/2 \rightsquigarrow -1/2 < \textbf{Y} < +1/2$$

The point that is thus defined by an X-Y coordinate:

$$\textbf{(X,Y)} \quad \textbf{(RND(B)} -.5, \textbf{RND(B1)} -.5)$$

will always lie within the square. It will also lie within the circle if it is within a distance (Z) of 1/2 from the origin:

$$\text{If } \textbf{Z} = \sqrt{\textbf{X}^2 + \textbf{Y}^2} \simeq \sqrt{(\textbf{RND(B)} - .5)^2 + (\textbf{RND(B1)} - .5)^2} < .5$$

This Monte Carlo procedure is used in the following BASIC program and is exhibited in the flowchart.

Procedure

Lines 20 and 21: supply the starting values for the two random number generators.

Lines 70 and 80: two random numbers between zero and one are generated.

Line 90: calculate the distance **Z**.

Lines 100 and 110: check whether the point is within the circle (**J=J+1**)

Line 130: each time 100 points are generated and located, the new π (**PI**) value is calculated, and

Line 140: printed.

FLOWCHART

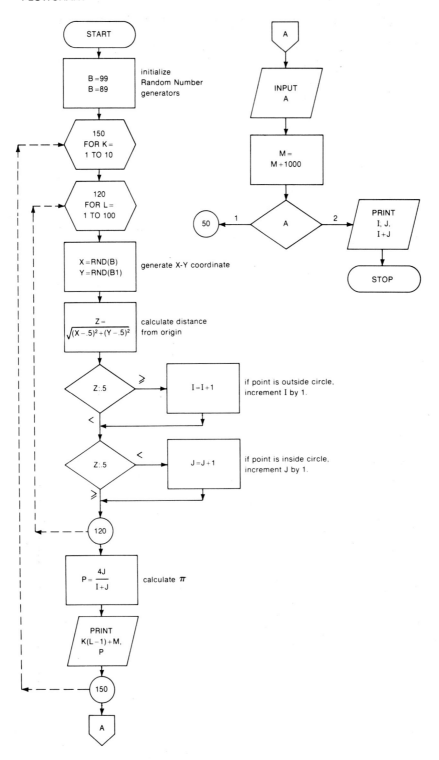

THE PROGRAM

```
10  PRINT "1CØMPUTE PI THRØUGH SIMULATIØN"
20  B=99
21  B1=89
40  PRINT "ITERATIØNS","PI"
50  FØR K=1 TØ 10
60  FØR L=1 TØ 100
70  X=RND(B)
80  Y=RND(B1)
90  Z=SQR((X-.5)**2+(Y-.5)**2)
100 IF Z>=.5 THEN:I=I+1
110 IF Z<.5 THEN:J=J+1
120 NEXT L
130 P=(4*J)/(I+J)
140 PRINT K*(L-1)+M,P
150 NEXT K
160 PRINT "1MØRE ITERATIØNS?  YES=1  NØ=2"
170 INPUT A
175 M=M+1000
180 GØTØ (50,190),A
190 PRINT "I,J,I+J",I,J,I+J
200 STØP
```

OUTPUT

```
CØMPUTE PI THRØUGH SIMULATIØN
ITERATIØNS      PI
100             3.28
200             3.2
300             3.066667
400             3.07
500             3.048
600             3.1
700             3.114286
800             3.135
900             3.12
1000            3.104
```

```
MØRE ITERATIØNS?   YES=1  NØ=2
?1
  1100            3.083636
  1200            3.093333
  1300            3.110769
  1400            3.122857
  1500            3.133333
  1600            3.13
  1700            3.141176
  1800            3.148889
  1900            3.128421
  2000            3.144




MØRE ITERATIØNS?   YES=1  NØ=2
?1
  2100            3.139048
  2200            3.143636
  2300            3.133913
  2400            3.141667
  2500            3.1328
  2600            3.14
  2700            3.139259
  2800            3.147143
  2900            3.137931
  3000            3.141333




MØRE ITERATIØNS?   YES=1  NØ=2
?2
  I,J,I+J        644           2356          3000
```

Transportation Cost Analysis: A Simulation

A manager of hypothetical company "Widget, Inc.," is interested in estimating the future cost of shipping a product via the most economical mode of transportation to each of his five distribution centers.

The future transportation costs are generated by simulating quantities, destination, and due dates for twenty orders every day over a two-day period.

In order to obtain "good will" within the distribution channel, Widget, Inc. always ships via whichever mode is necessary in order to meet the time requirements of its distribution centers.

Problem Statement and Procedure

Since "Widget, Inc." is a hypothetical company, most of the data is generated by a BASIC function RND. This pseudo-random number generator is used to generate for each order the following information:

1. destination of each order (**D1**)
2. quantity of each order (**Q1**)
3. due date of each order (**T1**)

The generated data is manipulated by the program to come up with workable data, as follows:

Destination. There are five distribution centers: **A**, **B**, **C**, **D**, and **E**. The pseudo-random-number generator generates real numbers between 0 and 1. Since there are five different destinations, these real numbers (0 to 1) are transformed to integer numbers from 1 to 5 (1 representing destination A, 2 representing destination B, 3 representing destination C, 4 representing destination D, and 5 representing destination E). The transformation function used is:

$$D1 = INT((RND(X)*5)+1)$$

where: **RND(X)** is the generated real constant.
 INT is the function that truncates.
 D1 contains the integer constant.

$$1 \leqslant D1 \leqslant 5$$

Quantity. The product can only be ordered in quantities of 20, 40, 60, 80, or 100 cases per shipment. In order to generate one of these cases for each order by the use of the pseudo-random-number generator, the following transformation function is used:

$$Q1 = INT((RND(Z)*5)+1)*20$$

where: $0 < RND(Z) < 1$
 $0 < RND(Z)*5 < 5$
 $1 \leqslant INT((RND(Z)*5)+1) \leqslant 5$
 Q1 = 20 or 40 or 60 or 80 or 100

Due Dates. As all due dates are within 20 days, a pseudo-random number is generated and transformed by the following function:

$$T1 = INT((RND(Y)*20)+1)$$

where: $0 < RND(Y) < 1$
 INT is the function that truncates.
 T1 contains the integer constant.

$$1 \leqslant T1 \leqslant 20$$

The inputted data consists of the distance in miles between "Widget Inc." and the five destinations (Table 13.1), the cost for each mode of transportation per case and per mile combined with the different destinations (Table 13.2), and the maximum number of days it takes for each mode to reach each destination (Table 13.3).

TABLE 13.1
Miles (M)

To	From Widget Inc.
A	500
B	1000
C	1500
D	600
E	2000

TABLE 13.2
Unit Transportation Cost (C(I,D1))

Mode (I)	Destination (D1)				
	A=1	B=2	C=3	D=4	E=5
Barge (1) (.005)	2.5	5.0	7.5	3.0	6.0
Rail (2) (.01)	5.0	10.0	15.0	6.0	12.0
Truck (3) (.015)	7.5	15.0	22.5	9.0	18.0
Air (4) (.03)	15.0	30.0	45.0	18.0	36.0

TABLE 13.3
Maximum Number of Traveling Days (D(I,D1))

Mode (I)	Destination (D1)				
	A=1	B=2	C=3	D=4	E=5
Barge (1)	4	6	8	4	17
Rail (2)	3	4	6	3	7
Truck (3)	2	2	2	2	2
Air (4)	1	1	1	1	1

STEPS TO BE PERFORMED

1. Input the **D** matrix, the **C** matrix, the **M** array, and the transportation mode **A** (lines 30, 31, 32, 33 (330 through 410)).
2. Generate the destination, **D1**, (line 140); due date, **T1**, (line 160); and order quantity, **Q1**, (line 180).
3. Check on the mode of transportation, **I**, to be used to maintain "good will" and to minimize the transportation cost (lines 200 through 230).

4. Calculate the transportation cost, **C1**, (line 240).
5. Repeat steps 1 through 4 for twenty orders over two days and accumulate daily totals for mileage covered **T(2,I3)**, cases shipped, **T(3,I3)**, and shipping cost, **T(1,I3)** (lines 260, 270, 280); then print out developed data (lines 290, 310, 320).

TABLE 13.4
Program Names

Program Variable Names	Definition	Dimension
A	An array where the different transportation modes are stored.	1
C	The unit transportation cost.	2
C1	Total shipping cost of an order.	0
D	Matrix indicating the maximum number of traveling days to each destination by each mode.	2
D1	Destination of an order.	0
M	Array for storing the miles from Company to destination.	1
Q1	Order quantity: number of cases to be shipped.	0
T1	Due date of an order.	0
T	Matrix for storing the daily shipping cost, miles covered, and cases sent.	2
X	Random-number base for RND of destination.	0
Y	Random-number base for RND of due date.	0
Z	Random-number base for RND of quantity.	0

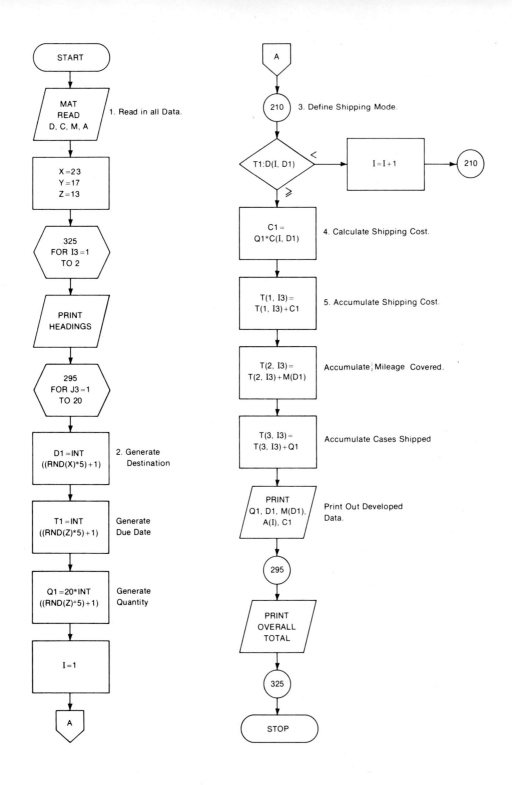

START

MAT
READ
D, C, M, A

1. Read in all Data.

X = 23
Y = 17
Z = 13

325
FOR I3 = 1
TO 2

PRINT
HEADINGS

295
FOR J3 = 1
TO 20

D1 = INT
((RND(X)*5)+1)

2. Generate
   Destination

T1 = INT
((RND(Z)*5)+1)

Generate
Due Date

Q1 = 20*INT
((RND(Z)*5)+1)

Generate
Quantity

I = 1

A

A

210   3. Define Shipping Mode.

T1 : D(I, D1)   <   I = I + 1   →   210

≥

C1 =
Q1*C(I, D1)

4. Calculate Shipping Cost.

T(1, I3) =
T(1, I3) + C1

5. Accumulate Shipping Cost.

T(2, I3) =
T(2, I3) + M(D1)

Accumulate Mileage Covered.

T(3, I3) =
T(3, I3) + Q1

Accumulate Cases Shipped

PRINT
Q1, D1, M(D1),
A(I), C1

Print Out Developed
Data.

295

PRINT
OVERALL
TOTAL

325

STOP

```
10 REM TRANSPØRTATIØN CØST ANALYSIS- A SIMULATIØN
20 DIM D(4,5),C(4,5),M(5),A(4),T(3,2)
30 MAT READ D
31 MAT READ C
32 MAT READ M
33 MAT READ A
40 REM INITIALIZE THE RANDØM NUMBER GENERATØRS
50 X=23
60 Y=17
70 Z=13
80 FØR I3= 1 TØ 2
90 PRINT "1",TAB(30);"WIDGET INCØRPØRATED"
100 PRINT
110 PRINT "QUANT.ORDERED","DESTINATIØN","MILES","MØDE","CØST"
120 FØR J3= 1 TØ 20
130 REM GENERATE DESTINATIØN
140 D1=INT((RND(X)*5)+1)
150 REM GENERATE DUEDATE
160 T1=INT((RND(Y)*20)+1)
170 REM GENERATE QUANTITY
180 Q1=INT((RND(Z)*5)+1)*20
190 REM CALCULATE SHIPPING CØST
200 I=1
210 IF T1>=D(I,D1) ,THEN 240
220 I=I+1
230 GØTØ 210
240 C1=Q1*C(I,D1)
250 REM CALCULATE DAILY SHIPPING CØST, MILES AND CASES SHIPPED
260 T(1,I3)=T(1,I3)+C1
270 T(2,I3)=T(2,I3)+M(D1)
280 T(3,I3)=T(3,I3)+Q1
290 PRINT Q1,TAB(5);"CASES",D1,M(D1),A(I),"$";C1
295 NEXT J3
300 PRINT
310 PRINT "*** DAILY TØTAL ***";T(3,I3);"CASES",T(2,I3);"MILES",
320 PRINT TAB(60);"$";T(1,I3)
325 NEXT I3
330 REM DATA FØR THE MAXIMUM NUMBER ØF TRAVELING DAYS (D)
340 DATA 4,6,8,4,17,3,4,6,3,7,2,2,2,2,2,1,1,1,1,1
350 REM DATA ØF UNIT TRANSPØRTATIØN CØST (C)
360 DATA 2.5,5.0,7.5,3.0,6.0,5.0,10.0,15.0,6.0,12.0
370 DATA 7.5,15.0,22.5,9.0,18.0,15.0,30.0,45.0,18.0,36.0
380 REM DATA FØR MILES TØ BE TRAVELED (M)
390 DATA 500,1000,1500,600,2000
400 REM DATA FØR TRANSPØRTATIØN MØDE (AA)
410 DATA 1,2,3,4
420 STØP
```

```
                        WIDGET INCØRPØRATED

QUANT.ORDERED    DESTINATIØN    MILES        MØDE         CØST
80    CASES      1              500          1            $ 200
80    CASES      5              2000         1            $ 480
80    CASES      2              1000         1            $ 400
20    CASES      4              600          1            $ 60
60    CASES      1              500          1            $ 150
20    CASES      4              600          1            $ 60
80    CASES      1              500          3            $ 600
80    CASES      5              2000         2            $ 960
80    CASES      2              1000         1            $ 400
40    CASES      2              1000         1            $ 200
40    CASES      2              1000         1            $ 200
60    CASES      3              1500         1            $ 450
20    CASES      4              600          3            $ 180
100   CASES      5              2000         2            $ 1200
100   CASES      2              1000         1            $ 500
80    CASES      5              2000         2            $ 960
20    CASES      3              1500         3            $ 450
40    CASES      5              2000         2            $ 480
80    CASES      2              1000         1            $ 400
40    CASES      4              600          1            $ 120

*** DAILY TØTAL *** 1200CASES   22900MILES

                                                          $ 8450



                        WIDGET INCØRPØRATED

QUANT.ORDERED    DESTINATIØN    MILES        MØDE         CØST
80    CASES      4              600          1            $ 240
20    CASES      4              600          3            $ 180
20    CASES      2              1000         1            $ 100
100   CASES      4              600          1            $ 300
80    CASES      1              500          1            $ 200
40    CASES      4              600          1            $ 120
20    CASES      3              1500         1            $ 150
80    CASES      1              500          1            $ 200
80    CASES      4              600          1            $ 240
20    CASES      5              2000         3            $ 360
40    CASES      4              600          1            $ 120
100   CASES      3              1500         1            $ 750
80    CASES      3              1500         3            $ 1800
60    CASES      5              2000         4            $ 2160
40    CASES      4              600          1            $ 120
80    CASES      3              1500         4            $ 3600
20    CASES      1              500          1            $ 50
100   CASES      4              600          1            $ 300
40    CASES      1              500          1            $ 100
100   CASES      5              2000         3            $ 1800

*** DAILY TØTAL *** 1200CASES   19800MILES

                                                          $ 12890
```

Exercises

PROBLEM #1

Simulate the game of tossing two dice and play that game 100 times. Record the outcomes of the simulated game in a file called GAME and make sure that each of the one hundred lines in that file contains two numbers, representing the two faces of the simulated game.

PROBLEM #2

There is a house, and anyone can play against it. The maximum bet which is allowed by the house is 500 dollars. The rules for the game are as follows:

1. If the sum of points of the two faces which turn up in the first toss is 2 or 12, the player wins three times as much as he bet.
2. If double 4 (this is, if the first and the second dice has the face with 4 points up), or double 5, or double 3 up, he wins twice as much as he bet.
3. If the sum or points of the two dice is 5 or 7, he wins as much as he bet.
4. If double 2 is up, he must toss the dice again. If this time the sum of the points on the two faces is 12 or 5 or 7 or 2, he wins as much as he bet; otherwise he loses.
5. In all other cases he loses.

Write a BASIC program that simulates this gambling in the house (no more than 20 games) and use the data that you have placed in file GAME when doing problem #1.

Your output must show for each game the amount of the bet, the outcome of the game, the amount won or lossed by the player.

14
Business Cases

Finance: Term Revolving Credit Plan

The objective of this program is to generate the customers' minimum monthly payments based on the end-of-the-month balance of their accounts.

The input of the program consists of a "master file" and a "sales file." The master file contains a set of data statements for each customer, containing the customer's number (**N**), the customer's name (**NN**), address (**AA**), and his old balance (**B**). The customer's file is ordered in increasing order of the customer number.

The sales file for each customer contains a set of data statements which are the copies of the customer's sales slips. Each copy of a sales slip contains the customer's number (**N**) and the sale's value (**S**). The last card of each set contains the customer's number (**N**), a possible sale's value (**S**) and an indicator (1), as an indicator for the last sales slip. These sales slips are ordered in increasing order of the customer number.

The steps used for computing the minimum monthly payment are as follows:

Step 1. Read in from the "master file" the customer's number (**N**), name (**NN**), address (**AA**), and the old balance (**B**).

Step 2. Read all sales slips for a customer, and add the sales (**S**) to the old balance (**B**) to obtain the new balance.

Step 3. Calculate the minimum monthly payment (**P**) as follows:
- if the new balance is less than or equal to $10, the payment equals the balance;
- if the new balance is larger than $10, but less than $100, the payment equals $10;
- if the new balance is larger than $100, but less than $150, the payment equals $15;

- if the new balance is larger than $150, but less than $200, the payment equals $20;
- if the new balance is larger than $200, the payment equals 10% of the new balance.

Step 4. Repeat steps 1, 2, and 3 for all customers of the master file.

The variable names used in the flowchart and the program, their meaning and dimension are:

TABLE 14.1
Program Names

Program Variable Names	Definition	Dimension
AA	Customer's city address	1
B	Balance of the customer's account	1
DD	Payment due date	1
K	Indicator	0
N	Customer's number on master file and sales slip	1
NN	Customer's name	1
P	Monthly minimum payment	1
S	Sale's value on the sales slip	1

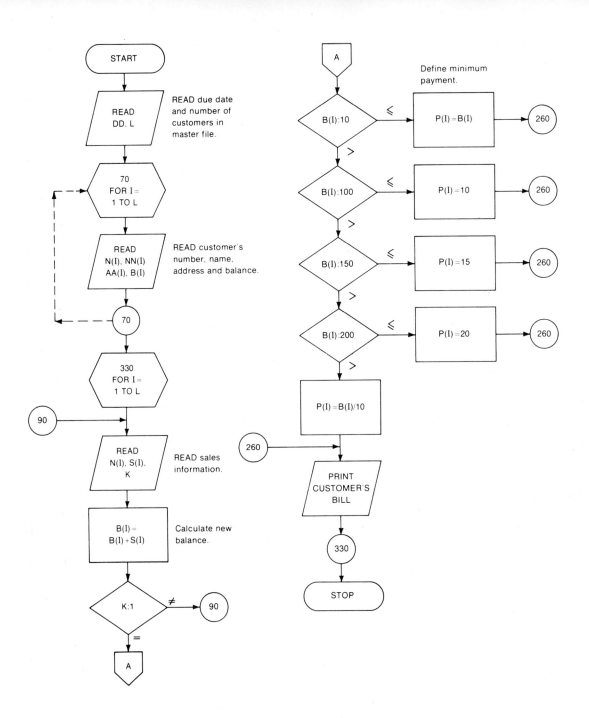

```
5 REM READ THE DUE DATE
10 READ DD
15 REM READ THE NUMBER OF CUSTOMERS
20 READ L
30 FOR I=1 TO L
35 REM READ THE CUSTOMER'S NUMBER AND NAME
40 READ N(I),NN(I)
45 REM READ THE CUSTOMER'S ADDRESS
50 READ AA(I)
55 REM READ THE CUSTOMER'S OLD BALANCE
60 READ B(I)
70 NEXT I
80 FOR I =1 TO L
85 REM READ CUSTOMER'S NUMBER, AMOUNT OF SALE AND INDICATOR
90 READ N(I),S(I),K
95 REM CALCULATE THE NEW BALANCE
100 B(I)=B(I)+S(I)
110 IF K=1 THEN 130
120 GOTO 90
125 REM CALCULATE THE MINIMUM PAYMENT
130 IF B(I)>10 THEN 160
140 P(I)=B(I)
150 GOTO 260
160 IF B(I)>100 THEN 190
170 P(I)=10
180 GOTO 260
190 IF B(I)>150 THEN 220
200 P(I)=15
210 GOTO 260
220 IF B(I)>200 THEN 250
230 P(I)=20
240 GOTO 260
250 P(I)=B(I)/10
260 PRINT "1 CUSTOMER BILL FOR"
270 PRINT "0",NN(I)
280 PRINT " ",AA(I)
300 PRINT "OCUSTOMER NUMBER";N(I)
310 PRINT " THE MINIMUM AMOUNT $";INT(P(I)*100+.5)/100;"  WILL BE DUE
*ON ";DD
320 PRINT " THANK YOU FOR YOUR ORDER(S)."
330 NEXT I
335 PRINT "1"
340 DATA "DECEMBER 31, 1971"
350 DATA 2
360 DATA 123456,"HENRY MILLER"
370 DATA "1234 WEST MORLAND DR., CINCINNATI, OHIO"
380 DATA 10.00
390 DATA 123457," JOHN A. WRIGHLEY"
400 DATA "202 HIGHLAND, CARLSBAD, NM.   92000"
410 DATA 20.75
420 DATA 123456,67.89,0
425 DATA 123456,67.89,0
430 DATA 123456,67.89,1
435 DATA 123457,67.89,0
440 DATA 123457,67.89,1
445 STOP
```

The first READ statement in line 10

10   READ DD

reads from one DATA statement the payment due date. The second READ statement in line 20 reads from the second DATA statement the number of customers to be considered.

20   READ L

The next three read statements (lines 40, 50 and 60) read in the "master file," containing for each customer, a number, name, address, and balance. The sales slips are read through the READ statement in line 90.

The new balance is calculated in the assignment statement in line 100.

100   B(I)=B(I)+S(I)

The IF statement in line 110 controls the adding of sales slips of the same customer to obtain the correct new balance of the customer (I) under consideration.

The remaining IF statements, assignment statements, and GOTO statements of the major FOR-NEXT loop accomplish Step 3 of the Term Revolving Credit Plan algorithm.

Finally, the PRINT statements (lines 260 through 320) generate the appropriate output: customer's name, address, number, minimum monthly payment, and due date.

Note that the program does not contain a DIMENSION statement, though six arrays are used. Since each of these six arrays does not contain more than ten elements, this is acceptable in BASIC since BASIC automatically assigns a maximum of ten storage locations to each nondimensioned array or 10×10 storage locations to each nondimensioned matrix.

```
   CUSTOMER BILL FOR

            HENRY MILLER
            1234 WEST MORLAND DR., CINCINNATI, OHIO

   CUSTOMER NUMBER 123456
   THE MINIMUM AMOUNT $ 21.37  WILL BE DUE ON DECEMBER 31, 1971
   THANK YOU FOR YOUR ORDER(S).




   CUSTOMER BILL FOR

            JOHN A. WRIGHLEY
            202 HIGHLAND, CARLSBAD, NM.  92000

   CUSTOMER NUMBER 123457
   THE MINIMUM AMOUNT $ 20   WILL BE DUE ON DECEMBER 31, 1971
   THANK YOU FOR YOUR ORDER(S).
```

Note that this example is a miniature file processing problem. Since BASIC is ill-equipped to perform multiple file processing, this language is normally not used for that purpose.

Insurance: Single-Premium Life Insurance

This example illustrates how to generate the savings accumulations for a single-premium life insurance policy. The single premium of $339.65 for $1,000 insurance is paid at the beginning of age 25 and thereafter accumulates 2½% interest. A net single premium of $339.65 for $1,000 in insurance is chosen since it results from a 2½% guaranteed interest.

Under the assumption that the premium is paid at age 25, at the beginning of the policy year, and that the death claims are paid at the end of the policy year, the accumulated fund at the end of any policy year, I, equals:

$$E(I) = J(I) + K(I) + S(I) - M(I), \qquad [1]$$

where: $E(I)$ is the accumulated fund at the end of year I.

$\quad\quad\quad J(I)$ is the accumulated fund at the beginning of year I.

$\quad\quad\quad K(I)$ is the interest of $J(I)$ at the end of year I.

$\quad\quad\quad S(I)$ is the survivor benefit at the end of year I.

$\quad\quad\quad M(I)$ is the mortality cost during year I.

The accumulated fund at the beginning of any year equals the fund at the end of the previous year:

$$J(I)=E(I-1) \qquad [2]$$

At age 25 the fund at the beginning of the year equals the premium of $339.65:

$$J(A)=P \qquad [3]$$

where: **A** is 25 or the beginning age.
P is $339.65 or the premium.

At the end of the policy year the interest accumulated during one year equals 2½% of the fund at the beginning of the year; or:

$$K(I)=J(I)*.025 \qquad [4]$$

The mortality cost ($M(I)$) can be obtained from the Commissioners 1958 Standard Ordinary Table (CSO) and is read in as data for the years 25 up to and including 75.

Since the CSO death rate at age 44 equals 4.92 people out of 1,000, and since $1,000 benefits are paid for each death claim, the mortality cost per person ($M(I)$) at age 44 equals:

$$\frac{\$1,000 \times 4.92 \text{ people}}{1,000 \text{ people}} \text{ or } \$4.92$$

Therefore the death rates per thousand people of the 1958 CSO table equals the mortality cost for $1,000 of life insurance.

The survivor benefit equals:

$$S(I) = \frac{[J(I)+K(I)-M(I)] \ D(I)}{L(I+1)} \qquad [5]$$

where: **L(I+1)** is number of people living at the end of the year **I**, or at the beginning of the year (**I+1**), in accordance with the 1958 CSO table.

$$D(I)=L(I)-L(I+1)$$

All people who die during year **I** (**D(I)**) cannot claim any of the accumulated savings (**J(I)+K(I)−M(I)**). This results in a total sum of

$$[J(I)+K(I)-M(I)] \ D(I),$$

relinquished savings, that becomes available to the survivors at the end of year **I**. Each survivor obtains, therefore, a survivor benefit equal to the total of the relinquished savings dividend by the number of survivors at the end of year **I**, which is reflected in the above survivor benefit equation [5].

The variable names used in the flowchart and the program, their meaning and dimension are:

TABLE 14.2
Program Names

Program Variable Names	Definition	Dimension
A	Initial age from which to calculate the accumulated savings for a single-premium life insurance policy.	0
B	Ultimate age for which to calculate the accumulated savings for a single-premium life insurance policy.	0
D	Number of people dying during a policy year.	1
E	Accumulated funds at the end of the policy year.	1
J	Accumulated fund at the beginning of the policy year.	1
K	Interest of J at the end of the policy year.	1
L	Number of people living at the beginning of the policy year.	1
M	Mortality cost during the policy year.	1
P	Single-premium payment.	0
R	Interest rate per unit.	0
S	Survivor benefit at the end of a policy year.	1

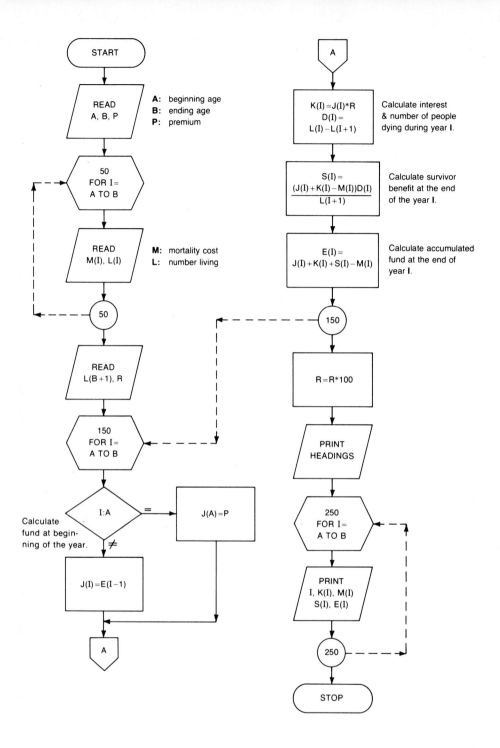

```
10 DIMENSIØN M(75),L(76),J(75),K(75),E(75),D(75),S(75)
15 REM READ BEGINNING AGE, ENDING AGE, PREMIUM
20 READ A,B,P
30 FØR I=A TØ B
35 REM READ IN THE MØRTALITY CØST AND NUMBER LIVING
40 READ M(I),L(I)
50 NEXT I
55 REM READ IN THE NUMBER ALIVE AT THE END AND THE INTEREST RATE
60 READ L(B+1),R
70 FØR I=A TØ B
75 REM FIND THE FUND AT THE BEGINNING ØF THE YEAR
90 IF I=A THEN:J(A)=P
100 IF I>A THEN: J(I)=E(I-1)
105 REM CALCULATE THE INTEREST
110 K(I)=J(I)*R
120 D(I)=L(I)-L(I+1)
130 S(I)=((J(I)+K(I)-M(I))*D(I))/L(I+1)
135 REM CALCULATE THE FUND AT THE END ØF THE YEAR
140 E(I)=J(I)+K(I)+S(I)-M(I)
150 NEXT I
160 R=R*100
170 PRINT "1SAVINGS ACCUMULATIØN"
180 PRINT " SINGLE PREMIUM LIFE INSURANCE PØLICY"
190 PRINT " 1958 CSØ AT ";R;"%, WITH A PREMIUM ØF $";P
200 PRINT "0**********************************************************
******"
210 PRINT " AGE INTEREST        MØRTAL         SURVIV        FUND AT DE
*C. 31"
220 PRINT " **********************************************************
******"
230 FØR I=A TØ B
240 PRINT "*";I;" ";INT(K(I)*100+.5)/100,"    ";M(I),"    ";INT(S(I)*10
*0+.5)/100,"    ";INT(E(I)*100+.5)/100
250 NEXT I
260 DATA 25,75,339.65                400 DATA 9.96,8610244
265 DATA 1.93,9575636                405 DATA 10.89,8524486
270 DATA 1.96,9557155                410 DATA 11.90,8431654
275 DATA 1.99,9538423                415 DATA 13.00,8331317
280 DATA 2.03,9519442                420 DATA 14.21,8223010
285 DATA 2.08,9500118                425 DATA 15.54,8106161
290 DATA 2.13,9480358                430 DATA 17.00,7980191
295 DATA 2.19,9460165                435 DATA 18.59,7844528
300 DATA 2.25,9439447                440 DATA 20.34,7698698
305 DATA 2.32,9418208                445 DATA 22.24,7542106
310 DATA 2.40,9396358                450 DATA 24.31,7374370
315 DATA 2.51,9373807                455 DATA 26.57,7195099
320 DATA 2.64,9350279                460 DATA 29.04,7003925
325 DATA 2.80,9325594                465 DATA 31.75,6800531
330 DATA 3.01,9299482                470 DATA 34.74,6584614
335 DATA 3.25,9271491                475 DATA 38.04,6355865
340 DATA 3.53,9241359                480 DATA 41.68,6114088
345 DATA 3.84,9208737                485 DATA 45.61,5859253
350 DATA 4.17,9173375                490 DATA 49.79,5592012
355 DATA 4.53,9135122                495 DATA 54.15,5313586
360 DATA 4.92,9093740                500 DATA 58.65,5025855
365 DATA 5.35,9048999                505 DATA 63.26,4731089
370 DATA 5.83,9000587                510 DATA 68.12,4431800
375 DATA 6.36,8948114                515 DATA 73.37,4129906
380 DATA 6.95,8891204                520 DATA 3826895
385 DATA 7.60,8829410                525 DATA 0.025
390 DATA 8.32,8762306                530 STØP
395 DATA 9.11,8689404
```

The BASIC program exhibits many BASIC features and is very efficiently written. The dimension statement in line 10 defines seven arrays and during compilation of this BASIC program seventy-five storage locations are set aside for each of the following seven arrays:

M: Mortality cost during each policy year;
L: Number of people living at the beginning of each policy year;
J: Accumulated funds at the beginning of each policy year;
K: Interest of J at the end of each policy year;
E: Accumulated funds at the end of each policy year;
D: Number of people dying during each policy year;
S: Survivor benefit at the end of each policy year.

The input statements are the READ statements, which read in the data from DATA statements (lines 260 through 525).
The first READ statement in line 20:

$$20 \quad \textbf{READ A,B,P}$$

provides for reading in three constants from the first DATA statement (line 260). These three constants are: the beginning age (**A=25**), the ending age (**B=75**), and the policy premium (**P=339.65**).
An explicit FOR-NEXT loop in line 30:

$$30 \quad \textbf{FOR I=A TO B}$$

results in reading in the next fifty-one DATA statements (lines 265 through 515), each containing a mortality cost and the number of people living at the beginning of each of the fifty-one policy years (years 25 through 75). The next READ statement in line 60 is self-explanatory.
In the next loop (lines 70 through 150), all necessary calculations are made for the Single-Premium Life Insurance Table, as previously explained:

J: the fund in the beginning of each policy year (lines 90 & 100)
K: the interest rate at the end of each policy year (line 110)
D: the number of people dying during each policy year (line 120)
S: the survivor benefit at the end of each policy year (line 130)
E: the accumulated funds at the end of each policy year (line 140)

Finally, all results are printed in a table by the PRINT statements in lines 170 through 250.
Note the use of the **INT** function in the PRINT statement in line 240! Because there is only a need for representing the results up to 2 digits behind the decimal point (cents), the **INT** function is used to accomplish this. After all, $346.88 makes more sense to the reader or user than $346.881654.
The generated results are indicated in the following:

```
SAVINGS ACCUMULATION
SINGLE PREMIUM LIFE INSURANCE POLICY
1958 CSO AT  2.5%, WITH A PREMIUM OF $ 339.65

*****************************************************************
  AGE  INTEREST      MORTAL        SURVIV         FUND AT DEC. 31
*****************************************************************
*  25   8.49          1.93          0.67            346.88
*  26   8.67          1.96          0.69            354.29
*  27   8.86          1.99          0.72            361.87
*  28   9.05          2.03          0.75            369.64
*  29   9.24          2.08          0.79            377.59
*  30   9.44          2.13          0.82            385.72
*  31   9.64          2.19          0.86            394.04
*  32   9.85          2.25          0.91            402.54
*  33  10.06          2.32          0.95            411.24
*  34  10.28          2.4           1.01            420.13
*  35  10.5           2.51          1.08            429.2
*  36  10.73          2.64          1.16            438.45
*  37  10.96          2.8           1.25            447.86
*  38  11.2           3.01          1.38            457.43
*  39  11.44          3.25          1.52            467.13
*  40  11.68          3.53          1.68            476.96
*  41  11.92          3.84          1.87            486.91
*  42  12.17          4.17          2.07            496.99
*  43  12.42          4.53          2.3             507.18
*  44  12.68          4.92          2.55            517.49
*  45  12.94          5.35          2.82            527.9
*  46  13.2           5.83          3.14            538.41
*  47  13.46          6.36          3.49            549
*  48  13.72          6.95          3.89            559.66
*  49  13.99          7.6           4.33            570.39
*  50  14.26          8.32          4.84            581.16
*  51  14.53          9.11          5.39            591.98
*  52  14.8           9.96          6               602.82
*  53  15.07         10.89          6.68            613.68
*  54  15.34         11.9           7.43            624.56
*  55  15.61         13             8.26            635.43
*  56  15.89         14.21          9.18            646.29
*  57  16.16         15.54         10.21            657.12
*  58  16.43         17            11.35            667.9
*  59  16.7          18.59         12.62            678.63
*  60  16.97         20.34         14.02            689.27
*  61  17.23         22.24         15.56            699.83
*  62  17.5          24.31         17.27            710.28
*  63  17.76         26.57         19.15            720.61
*  64  18.02         29.04         21.22            730.81
*  65  18.27         31.75         23.52            740.85
*  66  18.52         34.74         26.08            750.71
*  67  18.77         38.04         28.92            760.37
*  68  19.01         41.68         32.08            769.78
*  69  19.24         45.61         35.53            778.94
*  70  19.47         49.79         39.23            787.85
*  71  19.7          54.15         43.13            796.53
*  72  19.91         58.65         47.21            805.01
*  73  20.13         63.26         51.45            813.33
*  74  20.33         68.12         55.96            821.5
*  75  20.54         73.37         60.86            829.53
```

Management: Updating the Inventory Stock

A number, **N**, of different article groups are held in inventory. Each time one of these articles is withdrawn from stock, this information is recorded. This information accumulates and is processed at the end of the day.

Management has set up a safety stock level for each inventory group, a level which should not be diminished by withdrawals. Each time inventory has dropped beyond the safety level, or each time the safety level is reached, an order is placed to fill up the safety stock plus a certain constant minimum order quantity (economic quantity). When the ordered quantity exceeds a certain level, there is a price break. This level exists for all articles held in stock, but is different for each article.

A print-out for all ordered articles is the target of this program. The print-out consists of the stock number, quantity ordered, price per unit, and total price. The following program is designed to use as many basic BASIC features as possible and does not show the most rational way to compute the desired output.

The steps used for updating the inventory stock are as follows:

Step 1. Read in the number of inventory items to be updated (**N**);

Step 2. Read into arrays for each inventory item the safety stock quantity (**S**), the quantity in inventory (**I**), and the economic order quantity (**K**);

Step 3. Read into an array for each item to be updated the quantity withdrawn from inventory (**W**);

Step 4. For each inventory item to be updated, update the inventory and define the order quantity;

Step 5. For each inventory item to be updated, input into arrays the price break quantity (**Q**), the price per unit below the break volume (**H**), and the price per unit above the break volume (**L**);

Step 6. For each inventory item to be ordered define the unit price (**P4**), given the quantity to be ordered, and calculate the total order cost (**P**);

Step 7. Print out the inventory number, the ordered quantity, the unit price, and the total price.

The variable names used in the flowchart and the program, their meaning and dimension are:

TABLE 14.3
Program Names

Program Variable Names	Definition	Dimension
H	Unit price for small orders	1
I	Quantity in inventory	1
K	Economical order quantity	1
L	Unit price for large orders	1
N	Number of different stock items	0
O	Order quantity	1
P	Total price to be paid	1
Q	Price-jump quantity	1
S	Safety-stock quantity	1
W	Quantity withdrawn	1

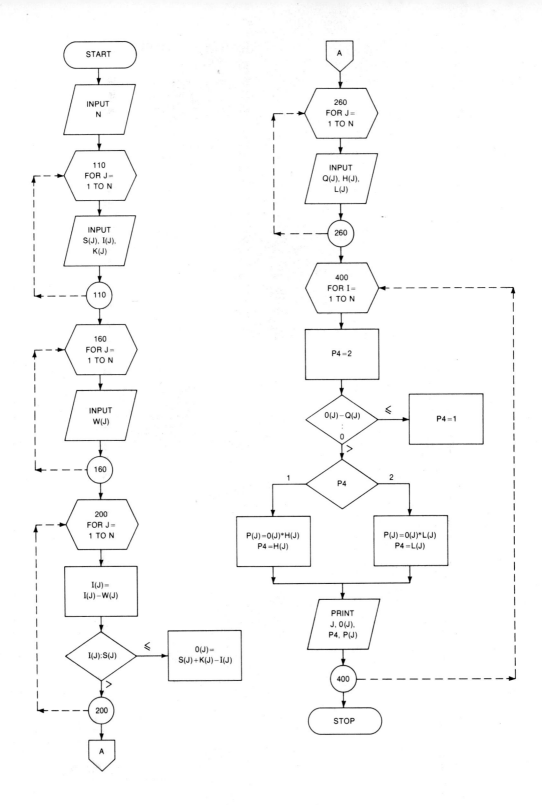

```
  10 DIMENSIØN I(100),W(100),Q(100),S(100),K(100),P(100),H(100),L(100),Ø
*(100)
  20 PRINT "1INVENTØRY UPDATE AND ØRDERING PRØGRAM"
  30 PRINT " ENTER THE NUMBER ØF INVENTØRY ITEMS TØ BE UPDATED."
  40 INPUT N
  50 PRINT " FØR EACH ITEM TØ BE UPDATED, ENTER IN THE FØLLØWING ØRDER,"
  60 PRINT " THE SAFETY STØCK QUANTITY, QUANTITY IN INVENTØRY AND THE"
  70 PRINT " ECØNØMIC ØRDER QUANTITY,"
  80 FØR J=1 TØ N
  85 PRINT "            ITEM",J
  90 INPUT S(J),I(J),K(J)
 110 NEXT J
 120 PRINT " FØR EACH ITEM TØ BE UPDATED, ENTER THE QUANTITY ØF THAT"
 130 PRINT " ITEM WITHDRAWN FRØM INVENTØRY."
 140 FØR J=1 TØ N
 145 PRINT "            ITEM",J
 150 INPUT W(J)
 160 NEXT J
 170 FØR J=1 TØ N
 175 REM DEFINE THE ØRDER QUANTITY FØR EACH INVENTØRY ITEM
 180 I(J)=I(J)-W(J)
 190 IF I(J)<=S(J) THEN: Ø(J)=S(J)+K(J)-I(J)
 200 NEXT J
 210 PRINT " FØR EACH ITEM TØ BE UPDATED, ENTER IN THE FØLLØWING ØRDER,
*"
 220 PRINT " THE PRICE BREAK QUANTITY, PRICE PER UNIT BELØW BREAK VØL-"
 230 PRINT " UME AND THE PRICE PER UNIT ABØVE BREAK VØLUME."
 240 FØR J=1 TØ N
 245 PRINT "            ITEM",J
 250 INPUT Q(J),H(J),L(J)
 260 NEXT J
 280 PRINT "1NUMBER          QUANTITY        PRICE          TØTAL"
 290 PRINT " ØF ARTICLE      ØRDERED         ØF ARTICLE     PRICE"
 295 REM DEFINE THE PRICE/ARTICLE AND THE TØTAL PRICE ØF THE ØRDERS
 300 FØR J=1 TØ N
 310 P4=2
 320 IF (Ø(J)-Q(J))<=0 THEN:P4-1
 330 GØTØ (340,370),P4
 340 P(J)=Ø(J)*H(J)
 350 P4=H(J)
 360 GØTØ 390
 370 P(J)=Ø(J)*L(J)
 380 P4=L(J)
 390 PRINT J,Ø(J),P4,P(J)
 400 NEXT J
 410 PRINT "1"
 430 STØP
```

The first INPUT statement (line 40) reads in the number of different inventory items which need to be updated.

The first FOR-NEXT loop (lines 80 through 110) reads the safety stock level, the inventory on hand, and the economical order quantity, for each article group.

The quantity withdrawn from inventory of each article group is read in the next FOR-NEXT loop (lines 140 through 160).

The quantity to be ordered for each article group is defined in the third FOR-NEXT loop (lines 170 through 200). It contains an assignment statement (line 180) that defines the updated inventory level for each article. It checks whether the new inventory level is below or equal to the safety-stock level and defines the order quantity if the inventory is less than or below the safety-stock level.

The INPUT statement in the next FOR-NEXT loop (line 250) defines for each article group the price break when the ordered quantity exceeds a certain level (**Q**).

The last FOR-NEXT loop (lines 300 through 400) checks the quantity to be ordered to define whether there will be a price break or not. If the quantity to be ordered is larger than **Q(J)**, then the total price equals **O(J)*L(J)**. If the quantity ordered is smaller than **Q(J)**, then the total price equals **O(J)*H(J)**.

This last FOR-NEXT loop can easily be rewritten without a conditional GOTO transfer.

Finally, the PRINT statement in line 390 prints out the inventory number (**J**), the quantity to be ordered (**O**), the price per unit (**P4**) and the total price (**P**).

```
INVENTORY UPDATE AND ORDERING PROGRAM
ENTER THE NUMBER OF INVENTORY ITEMS TO BE UPDATED.
?3
 FOR EACH ITEM TO BE UPDATED, ENTER IN THE FOLLOWING ORDER,
THE SAFETY STOCK QUANTITY, QUANTITY IN INVENTORY AND THE
ECONOMIC ORDER QUANTITY,
         ITEM    1
?100,200,150
         ITEM    2
?150,250,200
         ITEM    3
?200,300,250
 FOR EACH ITEM TO BE UPDATED, ENTER THE QUANTITY OF THAT
ITEM WITHDRAWN FROM INVENTORY.
         ITEM    1
?175
         ITEM    2
?225
         ITEM    3
?275
 FOR EACH ITEM TO BE UPDATED, ENTER IN THE FOLLOWING ORDER,
THE PRICE BREAK QUANTITY, PRICE PER UNIT BELOW BREAK VOL-
UME AND THE PRICE PER UNIT ABOVE BREAK VOLUME.
         ITEM    1
?190,20,10
         ITEM    2
?240,70,60
         ITEM    3
?290,120,110




NUMBER           QUANTITY        PRICE           TOTAL
OF ARTICLE       ORDERED         OF ARTICLE      PRICE
1                225             10              2250
2                325             60              19500
3                425             110             46750
```

Accounting: Asset Depreciation

The calculation of the yearly depreciation can be a tedious and sometimes a difficult process. The larger a firm grows, the more tedious the project becomes. A firm with many assets would be grateful for the help of a computer to perform this task.

Three depreciation methods are used here. These methods are straight line, double-declining balance, and sum-of-the-year's digits.

The straight-line depreciation method is a method that depreciates an equal amount each year. It has been argued that the straight-line depreciation method accounts for the asset as if it rendered the same economic or physical service each year. This is an erroneous assertion if the cost of the asset is viewed as a summation of the present values of the services to be rendered. In this case, the earlier consumed services have a higher value than do the later services, and therefore they should reflect this by having a higher cost depreciation.

The declining-balance and the sum-of-the-year's digits procedures are often referred to as pseudosophisticated tax-deferring devices. The only valid economic bases of applicability of these methods in the books of account are: (1) if the purchaser places a higher valuation on services which are immediately rendered than on services more remote in the future, and (2) if the depreciable assets provide less and less physical service per period as they become older.

DEPRECIATION PROCEDURES

In the development of the three depreciation methods, the following symbols are used:

F = day the asset is purchased

G = year the asset is purchased

C = cost of the asset

S = salvage value of the asset

U = useful life of the asset

H = 1978 is the end of the fiscal year

A = accumulated depreciation

STRAIGHT-LINE DEPRECIATION

The straight-line depreciation method is the simplest procedure for calculating the asset depreciation. With this method the annual depreciation is often expressed as a percentage of the depreciable basis; this percentage is the depreciation rate. For example, if an asset has a useful life of ten years, the depreciation rate is 10%.

The general formula used in straight-line depreciation is:

$$\frac{C - S}{U} = \frac{Cost - Salvage\ Value}{Useful\ Life}$$

If the asset was purchased prior to the 1978 fiscal year and has not ended its useful life during the 1978 fiscal year, or if it was purchased the first day of a fiscal year, the general formula is used for calculating the depreciation value for the asset. If the asset has ended its useful life during the 1978 fiscal year, the final depreciation value can be calculated with the following simple formula:

$$C - S - A = Cost - Salvage\ Value - Accumulated\ Depreciation$$

If the asset was purchased during the 1978 fiscal year, the depreciation value equals:

$$\left(1 - \frac{F}{365}\right)\frac{C - S}{U},$$

where $\left(1 - \frac{F}{365}\right)$ is that portion of the fiscal year that the asset was in use.

DOUBLE-DECLINING BALANCE

With the declining-balance method a fixed percentage of the book value at the beginning of the year is taken. The double-declining balance method takes twice the regular straight-line depreciation rate of the book value. Though both methods, double-declining-balance and straight-line, take a fixed percentage each year, the base is not the same in both cases. The depreciable basis, which remains the same during the life of the asset, is the base for the straight-line method. The book value is the base for the declining-balance method. This base changes from year to year, since it equals the cost of the asset minus the accumulated depreciation. Since the book value decreases from year to year, the yearly depreciation value will decrease also.

The general formula used in double-declining balance depreciation is:

$$\frac{2}{U}(C - A) = \frac{2}{useful\ life}(Cost - Accumulated\ Depreciation)$$

The above formula can be used if the asset was acquired the first day of the 1978 fiscal year, or if the asset was purchased prior to the 1978 fiscal year but has not ended its useful life during the 1978 fiscal year. If the asset has ended its useful life during the 1978 fiscal year, the final depreciation value is given by the following formula:

$$C - S - A = Cost - Salvage\ Value - Accumulated\ Depreciation$$

The asset will be depreciated over a portion of the fiscal year $\left(1 - \frac{F}{365}\right)$ if the asset was purchased during the 1978 fiscal year on day F of that year. In this case, the depreciation value amounts to:

$$\left(1 - \frac{F}{365}\right) \frac{2}{U} \left(C - A\right)$$

SUM-OF-THE-YEARS DIGITS—DEPRECIATION

As opposed to the straight-line and the declining-balance method, the sum-of-the-years-digits method applies a declining rate to a constant base— cost of asset minus salvage value.

If the asset was obtained the first day of a fiscal year, the following sum-of-the-years-digits depreciation formula is used:

$$\frac{(G + U - H)}{\frac{U(U + 1)}{2}} (C - S),$$

where $U(U + 1)$ is the sum-of-the-years digits and equals $\sum_{I=1}^{U} I$. If the asset was purchased the Fth day of the 1978 fiscal year, the depreciation value is:

$$\left(1 - \frac{F}{365}\right) \frac{U}{\frac{U(U + 1)}{2}} (C - S)$$

In case the asset was not purchased during the 1978 fiscal year and has not ended its useful life during the 1978 fiscal year, the sum-of-the-years-digits depreciation formula becomes:

$$\left(\frac{F}{365}\right) \frac{U + 1 - H + G}{\frac{U(U + 1)}{2}} (C - S) + \left(1 - \frac{F}{365}\right) \frac{U - H + G}{\frac{U(U + 1)}{2}} (C - S)$$

Finally, if the asset has ended its useful life during the 1978 fiscal year, the final depreciation value is $C - S - A$.

The variable names used in the flowchart and the program, their meaning and dimension are:

TABLE 14.4
Program Names

Program Variable Names	Definition	Dimension
A	Accumulated Depreciation	0
C	Cost of Asset	0
D	This Year's Depreciation	0
F	Day Purchased	0
G	Year Purchased	0
H	1978 (this fiscal year)	0
L	Asset Number	0
M	Depreciation Method 1. Straight Line 2. Double-Declining Balance 3. Sum-of-the-Year's Digits	0
NN	Asset Description	0
S	Salvage Value	0
U	Useful Life	0

L = Asset Number
NN = Asset Description
F = Day Purchased
G = Year Purchased
C = Cost of Asset
S = Salvage Value
A = Accumulated Depr.
U = Useful Life
M = Depr. Method

STRAIGHT-LINE DEPRECIATION METHOD

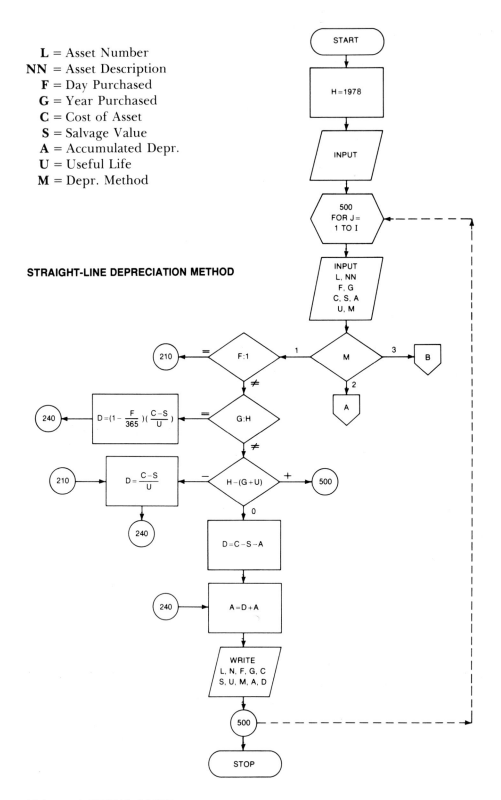

DOUBLE-DECLINING BALANCE

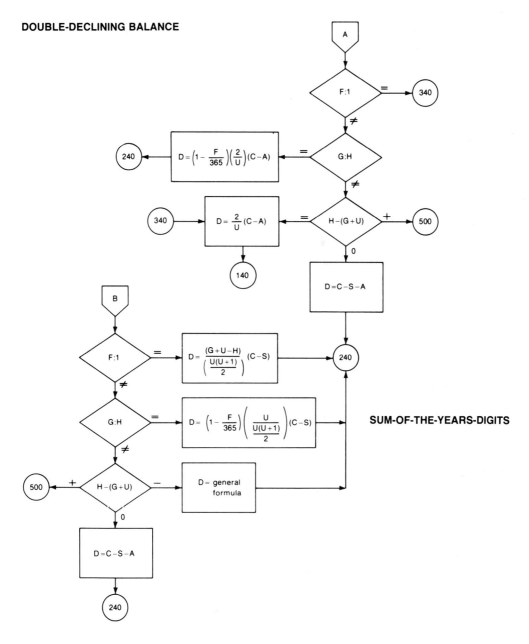

$$\text{general formula} = \left(\frac{F}{365}\right)\left(\frac{U+1-H+G}{\frac{U(U+1)}{2}}\right)(C-S) + \left(1-\frac{F}{365}\right)\left(\frac{U-H+G}{\frac{U(U+1)}{2}}\right)(C-S)$$

```
10 PRINT TAB(20);"ASSET DEPRECIATION"
20 LET H=1978
25 PRINT
26 PRINT
27 PRINT
30 PRINT "READ IN THE NUMBER OF ASSETS TO BE DEPRECIATED"
40 INPUT I
50 FOR J=1 TO I
55 PRINT
56 PRINT
57 PRINT
60 PRINT "THE ASSET NUMBER AND THE DESCRIPTION OF THE ASSET"
70 INPUT L,N$
80 PRINT "DAY AND YEAR PURCHASED"
90 INPUT F,G
100 PRINT "COST OF ASSET,SALVAGE VALUE AND ACCUMULATED DEPRECIATION"
110 INPUT C,S,A
120 PRINT "USEFUL LIFE AND DEPRECIATION METHOD (1,2 OR 3"
130 INPUT U ,M
140 ON M GOTO 150,280,380
145 REM STRAIGHT LINE DEPRECIATION METHOD (1)
150 IF F=1, THEN 210
160 IF G<>H,THEN 190
170 D=(1-F/365)*((C-S)/U)
180 GOTO 240
190 IF H=(G+U), THEN 230
200 IF H>(G+U), THEN 500
210 D=(C-S)/U
220 GOTO 240
230 D=C-S-A
240 A=D+A
250 PRINT "THIS YEARS DEPRECIATION =";INT(D)
260 PRINT "ACCUMULATED DEPRECIATION = ";INT(A)
270 GOTO 500
275 REM DOUBLE DECLINING BALANCE METHOD (2)
280 IF F=1, THEN 340
290 IF G<>H, THEN 320
300 D=(1-F/365)*(2/U)*(C-A)
310 GOTO 240
320 IF H=(G+U), THEN 360
330 IF H>(G+U), THEN 500
340 D=(2/U)*(C-A)
350 GOTO 240
360 D=C-S-A
370 GOTO 240
375 REM SUM OF THE YEARS DIGITS METHOD (3)
380 IF F<>1,THEN 410
390 D=(G+U-H)/(U*(U+1)/2)*(C-S)
400 GOTO 240
410 IF G<>H, THEN 440
420 D=(1-F/365)*(U/(U*(U+1)/2))*(C-S)
430 GOTO 240
440 IF H=(G+U), THEN 480
450 IF H>(G+U), THEN 500
460 D=((F/365)*((U+1-H+G)/(U*(U+1)/2))*(C-S))+((1-F/365)*((U-H+G)/(U*(U+
1)/2))*(C-S))
470 GOTO 240
480 D=C-S-A
490 GOTO 240
500 NEXT J
510 PRINT
520 STOP
530 END
```

The first INPUT statement (line 40) reads the number of items to be depreciated. That number **I**, is used as upper limit in the FOR-NEXT loop (line 50), where the depreciation is calculated using the correct called-for depreciation method.

Lines 70, 90, 110, and 130 input the necessary data for calculating the depreciation. This data is prompted for by the PRINT statements in lines 60, 80, 100, and 120 respectively.

The conditional GOTO statement in line 140:

140   ON M GOTO 150, 280, 380

transfers to the correct depreciation method as defined by **M**. If **M** equals one (1), then transfer is made to line 150, where the Straight-Line Depreciation method is used; if **M** equals two (2), then transfer is made to line 280, where the Double-Declining Balance method is used; if **M** equals three (3), then transfer is made to line 380, where the Sum-of-the-Years-Digits method is used.

BASIC statements in lines 150 through 230 reflect the above established procedure for the Straight-Line Depreciation method, as indicated in the first part of the flowchart; lines 280 through 370 contain the BASIC statements for the Double-Declining Balance method as pictured in the second part of the flowchart (continuation A); and finally, statements 380 through 490 represent the Sum-of-the-Years-Digits methods as shown in the third part of the flowchart (continuation B).

OUTPUT

```
                        ASSET DEPRECIATION


   READ IN THE NUMBER OF ASSETS TO BE DEPRECIATED
    ?5



   THE ASSET NUMBER AND THE DESCRIPTION OF THE ASSET
    ?1001,BUILDING
   DAY AND YEAR PURCHASED
    ?1,1968
   COST OF ASSET,SALVAGE VALUE AND ACCUMULATED DEPRECIATION
    ?500000,0,125000
   USEFUL LIFE AND DEPRECIATION METHOD (1,2 OR 3
    ?40,1
   THIS YEARS DEPRECIATION = 12500
   ACCUMULATED DEPRECIATION =  137500



   THE ASSET NUMBER AND THE DESCRIPTION OF THE ASSET
    ?1002,MACHINE
   DAY AND YEAR PURCHASED
    ?182,1975
   COST OF ASSET,SALVAGE VALUE AND ACCUMULATED DEPRECIATION
    ?20000,4000,4000
   USEFUL LIFE AND DEPRECIATION METHOD (1,2 OR 3
    ?10,1
   THIS YEARS DEPRECIATION = 1600
   ACCUMULATED DEPRECIATION =  5600



   THE ASSET NUMBER AND THE DESCRIPTION OF THE ASSET
    ?1006,BUILDING
   DAY AND YEAR PURCHASED
    ?1,1971
   COST OF ASSET,SALVAGE VALUE AND ACCUMULATED DEPRECIATION
    ?200000,0,106239
   USEFUL LIFE AND DEPRECIATION METHOD (1,2 OR 3
    ?20,2
   THIS YEARS DEPRECIATION = 9376
   ACCUMULATED DEPRECIATION =  115615
```

```
THE ASSET NUMBER AND THE DESCRIPTION OF THE ASSET
 ?1009,MACHINE
DAY AND YEAR PURCHASED
 ?133,1975
COST OF ASSET,SALVAGE VALUE AND ACCUMULATED DEPRECIATION
 ?2200,20,2152
USEFUL LIFE AND DEPRECIATION METHOD (1,2 OR 3
 ?3,2
THIS YEARS DEPRECIATION = 28
ACCUMULATED DEPRECIATION =  2180


THE ASSET NUMBER AND THE DESCRIPTION OF THE ASSET
 ?1013,BUILDING
DAY AND YEAR PURCHASED
 ?273,1977
COST OF ASSET,SALVAGE VALUE AND ACCUMULATED DEPRECIATION
 ?100000,5000,4318
USEFUL LIFE AND DEPRECIATION METHOD (1,2 OR 3
 ?10,3
THIS YEARS DEPRECIATION = 16837
ACCUMULATED DEPRECIATION =  21155
```

Exercises

PROBLEM #1

Write a BASIC program which will do the following:

a. Enter data into two arrays in storage from DATA cards. There
   are fifteen such DATA cards, each containing
   —an alphanumeric three digit utility code (I$ or II)
   —a utility rate per unit (R)

b. INPUT a second set of information by the use of an INPUT
   statement which contains customer data as follows:
   —customer's name and address (A$ or AA)
   —a two digit customer code (C)
   —a three-digit alphanumeric utility code (J$ or JJ)
   —the quantity (in units) of the utility needed (Q)
   There are twenty such customer requests.

c. Print a line for each customer, to contain name, address, and
   amount due according to the quantity requested, the rate, and the
   customer code as explained below.

C	Meaning
00	normal rate
01	3% discount
02	first 100 units at no charge
03	service temporarily discontinued—minimum charge of $2.50 to be billed to the customer
04	no charge

d. Print the total amount due the company (for all customers) (T)

INPUT

a.

Utility Code (I$)	Utility Rate/Unit (R)
APL	7.05
PER	11.15
GUM	2.00
LIP	33.27
DUM	5.02
APE	17.50
MOM	12.33
DAD	1.00
SON	99.00
ANN	10.00
POT	0.15
LOL	0.10
NOD	65.02
COT	50.00
ROT	2.50

b.

Name and Address	CCode	UCode	Quantity
Woods RR1 Lipton Ind	00	PER	999.95
Young 503 Vine Glenwood Ind	01	NOD	950.00
Bennett 1205 W 10th Lebanon Ind	00	APE	703.50
Begley Flint Dr. Connersv Ind	03	DAD	734.45
Bales 122 W 8th Connersv Ind	04	NOD	2.50
Craig 821 Fayette Denver Col	01	APL	4532.00
Creamer 604 Ranch Rd Connersv Ind	02	ROT	201.00
Hauk RR2 Lafayette Ind	02	LIP	95.50
Harris RR2 Connersv Ind	00	SON	220.00
Hansell 2251 Grand Av Oxford Oh	01	APE	25.00
Dorris 17 Grates Av Lola NY	01	ANN	715.00
Heeb 1517 Virginia Av Kokomo Ind	01	LOL	55.55
Liberty 3227 Beeson Av Cincinnati Oh	03	DUM	172.50
Kreep 1515 Conwell Buffalo NY	01	SON	12.50
Lambert 211 W 5th Lipton NJ	02	APE	717.50
Benson 3 County Rd Teapot Wy	00	COT	1215.20
Leming 17 Grand Av Connersv Ind	00	LIP	1300.00
Overbeck 208 S Market Liberty Ind	04	POT	500.00
Newell 13 Huston New Castle Ind	01	COT	123.00
Grimsel 1112 Burton Capetown Fl	00	GUM	7254.50

PROBLEM #2

Use the Single-Premium Life Insurance example and adjust it for a 20-year Premium Life Insurance Policy. During the years 25 up to 44 a premium of $21.68 is to be paid to the company at the beginning of the year. All other data is identical to the data used in the Insurance example.

PROBLEM #3

A small warehouse wishes to use a computer to maintain up-to-date inventory information for all parts in the warehouse. This data base includes the *part number, current inventory* (quantity on hand), and *quantity back-ordered* for all the different parts in inventory. The following rules apply to all parts in the warehouse.

1. If orders cannot be filled *completely,* they are back-ordered.
2. Multiple back orders are not allowed. Thus, if a part is currently back-ordered, new orders for that part will be filled only if the inventory "on hand" is sufficient to fill the order.
3. Back orders are always in multiples of 100. A back order should be as small as possible subject to the restriction that it be at least 750 units greater than the order that causes it.
4. If a part has been back-ordered, you may assume that the next shipment of that part that arrives will be the back order. Once this back-ordered shipment arrives, the back order is filled, the remainder of the shipment goes into inventory, and that part can again be back-ordered when necessary.

You are supposed to draw a flowchart and to write a BASIC program that will input the initial inventory as indicated under INPUT and that will process a series of transactions. If the transaction is negative, then assume that it is an order. If it is an order, one of three things may happen.

1. The order can be filled from the existing inventory.
2. The order cannot be filled from the existing inventory and can be back-ordered.
3. The order cannot be filled from the existing inventory and cannot be back-ordered because a back order is already outstanding.

If the transaction is positive, then assume that it is a shipment. If it is a shipment, then probably a back order needs to be satisfied; satisfy the back order and then update inventory.

INPUT

Initial Inventory

Part Number (N)	Inventory (Q)
70	5081
90	423
65	750
60	4
61	17
69	383
75	1280
77	976
78	33
79	275

Transaction

Part Number (N1)	Quantity (Q1)
78	−28
65	−1000
61	−35
70	−2000
65	−800
65	−800
61	−10
65	1800
90	−400
60	−10
61	−500
61	800
60	800

Transaction

Part Number (N1)	Quantity (Q1)
69	−375
69	−375
69	−375
75	−1400
75	−800
75	−800
75	2200
77	−600
79	−300
79	1100

1. Show Initial Inventory.

2. Show for all transactions in a labeled table the following updated inventory information.

   —Part number
   —Quantity ordered
   —Quantity received
   —Inventory in stock (after transaction is considered)
   —Back-ordered quantity (total amount of placed order)
   —Customer back order
   —Transaction comment

3. Show Final Inventory, including back orders.

15
Cases in Operations Research and Quantitative Methods

Goodness-of-Fit Test for the Random-Number Generator

The BASIC pseudo-random-number generator, **RND**, is used to generate stochastic inputs for the three simulation examples, discussed in Chapter 12. The hypothesis that **RND** is a reliable function for generating random numbers is tested here by means of a χ^2 test for goodness-of-fit.

THEORY OF THE χ^2 TEST OF GOODNESS-OF-FIT

The real sample values, as generated by **RND**, fall between 0 and 1. The values are called pseudo-random values because all numbers between 0 and 1 are supposed to have equal chance to occur when a number is generated.

To test this randomness, 1,000 numbers are generated and put into twenty classes, as follows:

class 1 contains all numbers between 0.00 and 0.04999 . . .
class 2 contains all numbers between 0.05 and 0.09999 . . .
class 3 contains all numbers between 0.10 and 0.14999 . . .
•
•
•
class 19 contains all numbers between 0.90 and 0.94999 . . .
class 20 contains all numbers between 0.95 and 0.99999 . . .

Since 1,000 pseudo-random numbers are generated, it may be expected that for each of the twenty classes, 50 numbers will be generated. Fifty numbers is the theoretical frequency if the function **RND** is a perfect pseudo-random-number generator. In general, and quite acceptably, a variation from this theoretical frequency is expected.

The relative total variation can be calculated as follows:

$$\sum_{I=0}^{20} \frac{(0(I) - 50)^2}{50}$$

where: **0(I):** is the observed frequency in class I.

50: is the theoretical frequency in all classes.

This relative total variation is a X^2 value, and a measure of goodness-of-fit between the random numbers generated by **RND** and the theoretical random frequencies (which the generated numbers are supposed to fit).

The larger the X^2 value, the worse the fit. To decide whether the generated data constitute a sample that is randomly distributed between 0 and 1, the calculated X^2 value is compared to a table X^2 value at a significance level, α, with n degrees of freedom. The degrees of freedom in this case equals the number of classes (20) minus one, and the significance level α is chosen at 5%. A 5% significance level means that 5% of the times one may reject randomness when indeed randomness occurs. The X^2 table value equals:

$$X^2_{(n = 19,\ \alpha = .05)} = \mathbf{30.14}$$

If the calculated X^2 value $\sum\limits_{I=1}^{20} \dfrac{(0(I) - 50)^2}{50}$ is smaller than the theoretical

$X^2_{(n = 19,\ \alpha = .05)}$ value (30.14), then **RND** is a good random-number generator; otherwise, if the calculated X^2 value is larger than $X^2_{(n = 19,\ x = .05)}$, **RND** does not generate reliable random numbers.

PROGRAMMING PROCEDURE

The following steps are used in the flowchart and program to test the random-number generator.

Step 1. Print all necessary headings for output table (lines 20 through 40).

Step 2. Initialize the random-number generator to 13 (line 70).

Step 3. Generate 1,000 random numbers by calling **RND** 1,000 times (line 100).

Step 4. For each generated number, define the class to which it belongs by assigning to the class "**J**" the expression **INT (Y*20) + 1** (line 120), where **Y** contains the generated random numbers and is a numeric constant between 0 and 1. After the class "**J**" is defined, augment the observed frequency for that class by 1 unit (line 140).

Step 5. For all twenty classes calculate the squared difference between the observed and the actual frequency, divided by the actual frequency (**A(I)** in line 190).

Step 6. Calculate the X^2 value by adding all **A(I)**'s for all classes (line 200).

Step 7. Print out the appropriate table (line 210), containing:
the observed frequency for all classes (**0(I)**).
the actual frequency for all classes ("**50**").

the squared difference between the observed and the actual frequency for all classes (**D(I)**).

the squared difference between the observed and the actual frequency divided by the actual frequency for all classes (**A(I)**).

the calculated χ^2 value (**C2**).

Step 8. If the calculated χ^2 value is smaller than the theoretical χ^2 value (30.14), print out "**RND** is a good random number generator," otherwise, print out "**RND** is not a good random-number generator."

Step 9. STOP.

TABLE 15.1
Program Names

Program Variable Names	Definition	Dimension
A	Squared difference between the actual and the observed frequency divided by the actual frequency.	1
C2	Calculated χ^2 value, which is the sum of the A's over all twenty classes.	0
D	Squared difference between the actual and the observed frequency.	1
O	Observed frequency from the random-number generator.	1
X	Random-Number base for RND.	0
Y	Random-Number between 0 and 1.	0

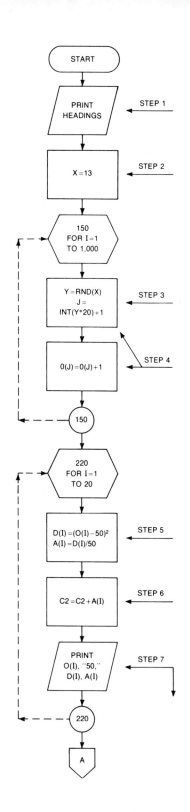

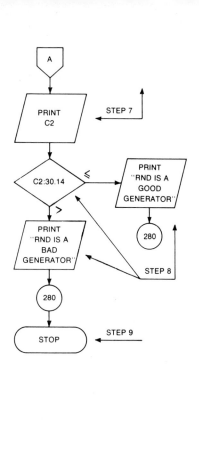

```
10 DIM D(20),0(20),A(20)
20 PRINT "1",TAB(15);"TESTING THE RANDØM NUMBER GENERATØR"
30 PRINT "0",TAB(15);"CHI-SQUARE VALUE IS 30.14 FØR DF=19"
40 PRINT "+ØBSERVED","ACTUAL","(ØBS-ACT)**2","(ØBS-ACT)**2/ACT"
50 PRINT
60 REM INITIALIZE RANDØM NUMBER GENERATØR
70 X=13
80 REM GENERATE 1000 RANDØM NUMBERS AND PUT THEM IN CLASSES
90 FØR I=1 TØ 1000
100 Y=RND(X)
110 REM DEFINE THE CLASS
120 J=INT(Y*20)+1
130 REM INCREMENT THE ØBSERVED FREQUENCY CØUNT ØF CØRRECT CLASS
140 0(J)=0(J)+1
150 NEXT I
160 REM CALCULATE THE CHI-SQUARE VALUE
170 FØR I=1 TØ 20
180 D(I)=(0(I)-50)**2
190 A(I)=D(I)/50
200 C2=C2+A(I)
210 PRINT 0(I),"50",D(I),A(I)
220 NEXT I
230 PRINT TAB(45);C2
240 IF C2 > 30.14, THEN 270
250 PRINT "RND IS A GØØD RANDØM NUMBER GENERATØR"
260 GØTØ 280
270 PRINT "RND IS NØT A GØØD RANDØM NUMBER GENERATØR"
280 PRINT "1"
290 STØP
```

```
                    TESTING THE RANDØM NUMBER GENERATØR

                    CHI-SQUARE VALUE IS 30.14 FØR DF=19
     ØBSERVED       ACTUAL           (ØBS-ACT)**2    (ØBS-ACT)**2/ACT

     52             50               4               0.08
     60             50               100             2
     73             50               529             10.58
     58             50               64              1.28
     49             50               1               0.02
     55             50               25              0.5
     51             50               1               0.02
     49             50               1               0.02
     58             50               64              1.28
     54             50               16              0.32
     38             50               144             2.88
     44             50               36              0.72
     52             50               4               0.08
     48             50               4               0.08
     43             50               49              0.98
     50             50               0               0
     41             50               81              1.62
     46             50               16              0.32
     42             50               64              1.28
     37             50               169             3.38
                                                     27.44

     RND IS A GØØD RANDØM NUMBER GENERATØR
```

Network Analysis: PERT-Program Evaluation Review Technique

The PERT method is a management-oriented technique for the scheduling of a series of nonrepetitive jobs so that the entire project can be completed in the shortest amount of time. This method serves to consider the series of interrelated activities and to determine the optimum planning and scheduling of the activities to obtain the desired goal. Information can also be obtained to show what jobs could be delayed without slowing down the completion of the total project. For the critical path analysis, the following information has to be obtained:

EARLY START AND EARLY FINISH

LATE START AND LATE FINISH

TOTAL SLACK FOR EACH JOB

This set of information is generated by the program and used in determining the critical path.

SETTING UP THE NETWORK

The preliminary step before executing the PERT algorithm is to develop the network model, representing the interrelationships between activities and the general flow of activities. This development can be accomplished as follows:

Step 1. Develop the logical sequence in which the activities have to be performed for completing the project. An activity is the performance of a specific task, and consequently it is the effort of manpower and machinery resources.

Step 2. Draw the arrow diagram network using activities and events. An event is represented by a node, representing the occurrence of a checkpoint in time. This is the accomplishment of a task, rather than the performance of a task (activity). The event represents the start of an activity(ties) and/or the completion of an activity(ties).

Step 3. Assign an activity time to each activity. These times must be developed by qualified people—supervisors or foremen in charge of the project, engineers, and others.

Step 4. Number the nodes in such a way that:

1. each job has a unique set of node numbers assigned to it.
2. all activities entering a node have identical followers.
3. all activities leaving a node have identical predecessors.
4. a node represents the complete relationship between all entering and exiting jobs.
5. they are in ordered sequence, such that the **I** node (beginning node) is smaller than the **J** node (ending node).

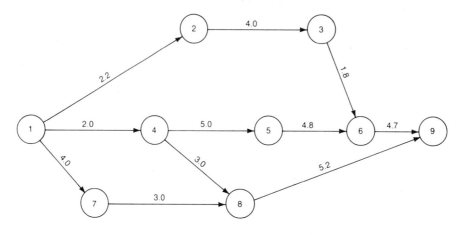

ACTIVITY

INode	JNode	Job Description	Job Time
1	2	Order Fixtures	2.2
1	4	Excavation	2.0
1	7	Order Trees and Shrubs	4.0
2	3	Manufacture Furniture	4.0
3	6	Deliver Furniture	1.8
4	5	Erect Steel Structure	5.0
4	8	Back Filling	3.0
5	6	Masonry Work	4.8
6	9	Install Furniture	4.7
7	8	Plant Trees and Shrubs	3.0
8	9	Final Grading	5.2

PERT-ALGORITHMIC PROCEDURE

The algorithm steps can be executed using the following procedure:

Step 1. Initialize data tables. This step involves loading the arrays which are required by the critical path algorithm. The data include: the starting (**I**) node and the ending (**J**) node for each job, a job description, and activity time (**T**) (lines 40, 70 through 90).

Step 2. Calculation of the early start (**E**) and early finish (**F**) times. The early start time is that time at which an event can be started, providing all events preceding it have been started and completed as early as possible. The simplest method of calculating the early start (**E**) for all activities is to use the Forward Scan Rule as outlined here:

- Give each node a bucket value: **B(I)**
- Initialize these buckets to zero (line 110)
- Now for each activity **K** proceed by assigning **(B(I1) + T(K))** to **B(J1)** if and only if **(B(I1) + T(K))** is greater than the previous **B(J1)** value (lines 180 through 220):

B(J1)′←B(I1) + T(K)
iff B(J1)′≥B(J1)

where: **I1** is the Inode of activity **K**
J1 is the Jnode of activity **K**
T(K) is the activity time

- The early start for activity **K** is then:
E(K) = B(I1) (line 200)
- After all **E(K)s** are calculated, the **F(K)s** (early finish) can be calculated as follows for each activity **K**
F(K) = E(K) + T(K)

Step 3. Calculation of the late start (**L**) and late finish (**C**). The latest finish time is that time at which an event must be accomplished so as not to cause slippage in the project-completion date. The simplest way of calculating the late start (**L**) for all activities is to use the Reverse Scan Rule as outlined here:

- Give each node a bucket value: **B(I)**.
- Initialize the buckets to the project-completion date (**T1**).
- Now for each activity **K**, starting with the last activity, proceed by assigning **(B(J1) − T(K))** to **B(I1)** if and only if **(B(J1) − T(K))** is smaller than the previous **B(I1)** value (lines 340 through 400).

B(I1)′←B(J1) − T(K)
iff B(I1)′<B(I1)

where: **I1** is the Inode of activity **K**
J1 is the Jnode of activity **K**
T(K) is the activity time

- The late start for activity **K** is then:
L(K) = B(J1) − T(K)
- After all **L(K)s** are calculated, the **C(K)s** (late finish) can be calculated as follows for each activity **K**
C(K) = L(K) + T(K)

Step 4. Calculation of the total slack (**S**) times. The total slack is a relationship between the early start (**E**) and the late start (**L**) and indicates how long an activity may be postponed without affecting the due date. It is calculated for each activity as follows: (lines 440 through 444).

S(K) = L(K) − E(K)

Step 5. Critical activities. The critical activities are the activities which cannot be delayed in order to finish the job as early as possible. Thus, if the total slack (**S**) of an activity (**K**) is zero, then the **K**th activity is a critical activity (line 470). This procedure is outlined in the following flowchart and BASIC program.

TABLE 15.2
Program Names

Program Variable Names	Definition	Dimension
B	Bucket for each mode	1
C	Late finish time	1
E	Early start time	1
I	Beginning node	1
I1	Inode of activity K	0
J	Ending node	1
J1	Jnode of activity K	0
L	Late start time	1
N	Number of activities	0
N1	Number of the highest node	0
S	Total slack time	1
T	Activity time	1
T1	Total project time of the Job	0

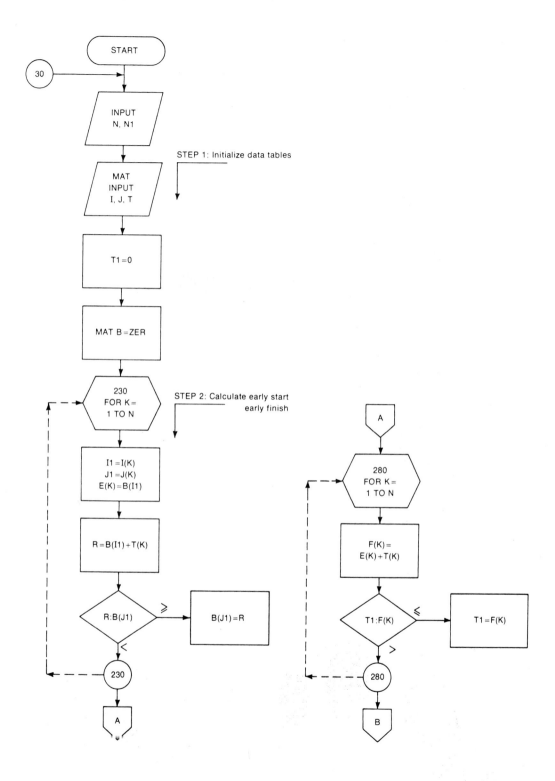

FLOWCHART (Continued)

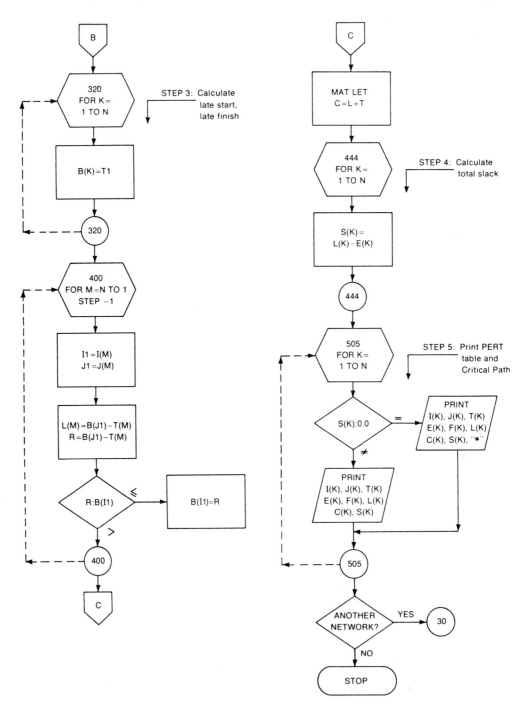

```
10 DIM I(50),J(50),T(50),E(50),F(50),L(50),C(50),S(50),B(50)
20 REM READ IN THE TØTAL NUMBER ØF ACTIVITIES AND HIGHEST NØDE NUMBER
30 PRINT "1INPUT NUMBER ØF ACTIVIYIES AND HIGHEST NØDE NUMBER"
40 INPUT N,N1
50 REM READ IN ALL ØRDERED ACTIVITIES
60 PRINT "INPUT BEGINNING NØDE(I),ENDING NØDE(J),ACTIVITY,AND TIME(T)"
70 FØR K=1 TØ N
80 INPUT I(K),J(K),SKP(1),T(K)
90 NEXT K
100 T1=0
110 MAT LET B=ZER
120 REM PRINT HEADINGS
130 PRINT "1"
140 PRINT "ACTIVITY",TAB(12);"JØB",TAB(19);"EARLY",TAB(27);"EARLY",TAB(
*36);"LATE",TAB(44);"LATE",TAB(53);"TØTAL",TAB(61);"CRIT."
150 PRINT TAB(3);"I",TAB(7);"J",TAB(13);"TIME",TAB(20);"START",TAB(28);
*"FINISH",TAB(37);"START",TAB(45);"FINISH",TAB(54);"SLACK",TAB(62);"PATH
*"
160 REM USE FØRWARD SCAN RULE FØR DETERMINING THE EARLY START
170 FØR K=1 TØ N
180 I1=I(K)
190 J1=J(K)
200 E(K)=B(I1)
210 R=B(I1)+T(K)
220 IF R>=B(J1), THEN:B(J1)=R
230 NEXT K
240 REM CALCULATE THE EARLY FINISH AND THE TIME TØ CØMPLETE THE JØB
250 FØR K=1 TØ N
260 F(K)=E(K) + T(K)
270 IF T1<=F(K),THEN:T1=F(K)
280 NEXT K
290 REM INITIALIZE THE BUCKETS (B) TØ THE CØMPLETIØN TIME ØF THE JØBS
300 FØR K=1 TØ N
310 B(K)=T1
320 NEXT K
330 REM USE THE REVERSE SCAN RULE FØR DETERMINING THE LATE START
340 FØR M=N TØ 1 STEP -1
350 I1=I(M)
360 J1=J(M)
370 L(M)=B(J1)-T(M)
374 REM CHECK FØR LATE START EQUAL TØ -0.0
375 IF L(M)<0.0, THEN:L(M)=0.0
380 R=B(J1)-T(M)
390 IF R<=B(I1),THEN:B(I1)=R
400 NEXT M
410 REM CALCULATE THE LATE FINISH (LATE START +TIME)
420 MAT LET C=L+T
430 REM CALCULATE THE TØTAL SLACK (LATE START-EARLY START)
440 FØR K=1 TØ N
441 S(K)=L(K)-E(K)
442 REM CHECK FØR SLACK EQUAL TØ -0.0
443 IF S(K)<0.0, THEN: S(K)=0.0
444 NEXT K
```

```
450 REM ØUTPUT PERT RESULTS
460 FØR K=1 TØN
470 IF S(K)=0.0,THEN 500
480 PRINT TAB(2);I(K),TAB(6);J(K),TAB(12);T(K),TAB(19);E(K),TAB(27);F(K
*),TAB(36);L(K),TAB(44);C(K),TAB(53);S(K)
490 GØTØ 505
500 PRINT TAB(2);I(K),TAB(6);J(K),TAB(12);T(K),TAB(19);E(K),TAB(27);F(K
*),TAB(36);L(K),TAB(44);C(K),TAB(53);S(K),TAB(63);"*"
505 NEXT K
510 PRINT "1DØ YØU WISH TØ RUN ANØTHER NETWØRK?YES=1,NØ=2"
520 INPUT A
530 GØTØ(30,540),A
540 STØP
```

OUTPUT

```
 INPUT NUMBER ØF ACTIVITIES AND HIGHEST NØDE NUMBER
?11,9
 INPUT BEGINNING NØDE(I),ENDING NØDE(J),ACTIVITY,AND TIME(T)
?1,2,"ØRDER FIXTURES",2.2
?1,4,"EXCAVATIØN",2.0
?1,7,"ØRDER TREES AND SHRUBS",4.0
?2,3,"MANUFACTURE FURNITURE",4.0
?3,6,"DELIVER FURNITURE",1.8
?4,5,"ERECT STEEL STRUCTURE",5.0
?4,8,"BACK FILLING",3.0
?5,6,"MASØNRY WØRK",4.8
?6,9,"INSTALL FURNITURE",4.7
?7,8,"PLANT TREES AND SHRUBS",3.0
?8,9,"FINAL GRADING",5.2
```

ACTIVITY		JØB TIME	EARLY START	EARLY FINISH	LATE START	LATE FINISH	TØTAL SLACK	CRIT. PATH
I	J							
1	2	2.2	0	2.2	3.8	6	3.8	
1	4	2	0	2	0	2	0	*
1	7	4	0	4	4.3	8.3	4.3	
2	3	4	2.2	6.2	6	10	3.8	
3	6	1.8	6.2	8	10	11.8	3.8	
4	5	5	2	7	2	7	0	*
4	8	3	2	5	8.3	11.3	6.3	
5	6	4.8	7	11.8	7	11.8	0	*
6	9	4.7	11.8	16.5	11.8	16.5	0	*
7	8	3	4	7	8.3	11.3	4.3	
8	9	5.2	7	12.2	11.3	16.5	4.3	

```
 DØ YØU WISH TØ RUN ANØTHER NETWØRK?YES=1,NØ=2
?2
```

Moving Averages of the Dow-Jones Industrial Stocks

Patterns in time series vary widely but can be classified under the following groups: averages, trends in the averages, cyclic effects, seasonal effects, and random variations. In most forecasting models, averages are meaningless, since trends, cycles, and seasonal patterns may prevail. A variation of simple averages is moving averages. These averages emphasize recent values and therefore estimate trend effects. The method of moving averages is also useful in isolating cyclical components; it has the advantage that there is no need for computing any trend. In general, moving averages tend to lag a trend, raise the valleys, and depress the peaks of cyclic patterns.

When calculating moving averages, only data from more recent time periods are used. The number of data used in calculating a moving average needs to be determined very carefully, since the magnitude of the lag and the smoothing of cyclic patterns depend on the number of data used.

In this case the moving-averages technique is applied to a series of one hundred Friday closings of the Dow-Jones Industrial Stocks, in order to picture a general trend and cycle effect, if any.

THEORY AND PROCEDURE

The following is the basis for applying the moving-averages forecasting method to the Friday closings of the Dow-Jones Industrial Stocks. The irregular fluctuations of these stocks in the past cannot, as such, be used for future stock estimates. Rather, one wishes to isolate continuing changes. Therefore, we desire to separate the continuing from the temporary effects which can be accomplished by taking, for example, ten-week moving average. As continuing influences, such as trends, tend to steer the stock values of all Friday closings in the same direction, it will appear in the moving averages. The temporary influences which raise the price of a stock today and lower it tomorrow, will not appear in the moving averages.

However, as the ten-week moving averages include data from ten weeks back, a lag in the forecast occurs. The moving average will lag behind the current stock level if there is a steady rise or fall in the stock price; and it will lag further behind the future stock price level that it is trying to forecast.

The calculation procedure for the K weeks moving averages of the Dow-Jones Industrial Stocks (DJIS) is as follows:

1. Add the Friday closing prices of the DJIS for the first **K** consecutive weeks (week **#1** through week **#K**) (lines 130 through 150).
2. Divide the sum(s) by K to obtain the first moving average to predict or forecast for the (**K + 1**)st week.
3. Repeat the above two steps for weeks #2 through #(**K + 1**), #3 through #(**K + 2**), ..., for weeks #(**101 − K**) through #101 (lines 190 through 240).

The program, as written here, provides for a print-out of the actual Friday closing prices, the predicted Friday closing prices, and for requesting the "**K**."

The variable names used in the flowchart and the program, their meaning and dimension are:

TABLE 15.3
Program Names

Program Variable Names	Definition	Dimension
K	Constant indicating the number of weeks over which to calculate the moving averages.	0
L	Integer constant referring to the week under consideration.	0
M	Mean of K-Friday closings of Dow-Jones Industrial Stocks.	1
S	Sum of K-Friday closings of Dow-Jones Industrial Stocks.	0
Y	Actual Stock price of the Friday closings of Dow-Jones Industrial Stocks.	1

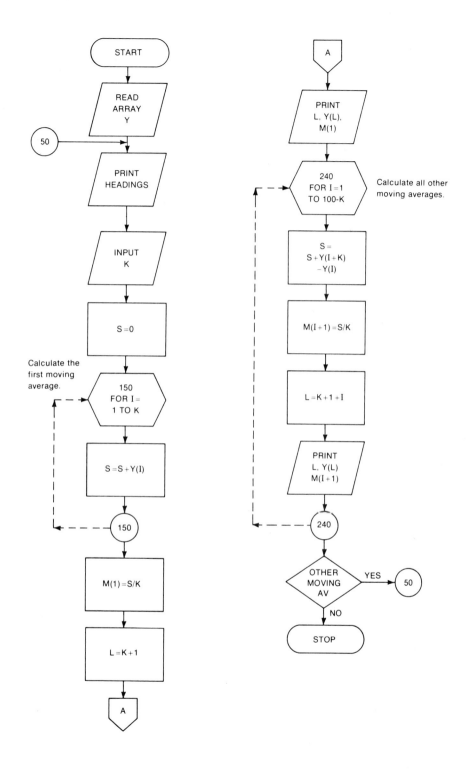

```
10 DIM M(101),Y(101)
20 REM READING 101 STØCK VALUES
30 MAT READ Y
40 PRINT "1"
50 PRINT " MØVING AVERAGES ØF THE DØW-JØNES INDUSTRIAL STØCKS"
60 PRINT " NUMBER ØF WEEKS ØVER WHICH TØ CALCULATE MØVING AVERAGES:"
70 INPUT K
80 PRINT
90 PRINT "WEEK","ACTUAL","PREDICTED"
100 PRINT
110 S=0
120 REM CALCULATE THE K-WEEKS MØVING AVERAGES
130 FØR I=1 TØ K
140 S=S+Y(I)
150 NEXT I
160 M(1)=S/K
170 L=K+1
180 PRINT L,Y(L),M(1)
190 FØR I=1 TØ (101-K-1)
200 S=S+Y(I+K)-Y(I)
210 M(I+1)=S/K
220 L=K+1+I
230 PRINT L,Y(L),M(I+1)
240 NEXT I
250 PRINT "1DØ YØU WISH TØ RECALCULATE MØVING AVERAGES?YES=1,NØ=2"
260 INPUT A
270 GØTØ(50,400),A
280 DATA 913.62,900.93,897.80,903.51,922.46,913.92,888.47,871.27
281 DATA 869.65,885.89,892.34,896.01,921.25,917.21,924.42,933.80
282 DATA 952.95,949.59,967.49,961.28,948.41,958.98,965.88,967.06
283 DATA 985.08,978.24,981.29,966.99,952.51,951.89,925.53,935.54
284 DATA 938.59,946.05,947.85,951.95,916.65,905.21,911.18,904.28
285 DATA 920.00,935.48,927.30,933.46,924.82,924.00,957.17,961.61
286 DATA 967.30,947.45,937.56,924.77,894.84,876.16,869.76,886.12
287 DATA 852.25,845.92,818.06,826.59,824.46,820.88,837.25,836.72
288 DATA 819.50,824.25,830.39,824.18,808.41,806.96,836.06,862.26
289 DATA 855.99,860.48,849.26,823.13,812.30,793.03,786.69,789.86
290 DATA 797.65,809.20,798.11,782.60,775.54,744.06,752.77,753.30
291 DATA 757.46,777.59,784.12,772.11,763.66,791.05,791.84,794.46
292 DATA 775.94,747.29,733.63,717.73,702.22
400 STØP
```

OUTPUT

```
MØVING AVERAGES ØF THE DØW-JØNES INDUSTRIAL STØCKS
NUMBER ØF WEEKS ØVER WHICH TØ CALCULATE MØVING AVERAGES:
?10

WEEK            ACTUAL              PREDICTED

11              892.34              896.752
12              896.01              894.624
13              921.25              894.132
14              917.21              896.477
15              924.42              897.847
16              933.8               898.043
17              952.95              900.031
18              949.59              906.479
19              967.49              914.311
20              961.28              924.095
21              948.41              931.634
22              958.98              937.241
23              965.88              943.538
24              967.06              948.001
25              985.08              952.986
26              978.24              959.052
27              981.29              963.496
28              966.99              966.33
29              952.51              968.07
30              951.89              966.572
31              925.53              965.633
32              935.54              963.345
33              938.59              961.001
34              946.05              958.272
35              947.85              956.171
36              951.95              952.448
37              916.65              949.819
38              905.21              943.355
39              911.18              937.177
40              904.28              933.044
41              920                 928.283
42              935.48              927.73
43              927.3               927.724
44              933.46              926.595
45              924.82              925.336
46              924                 923.033
47              957.17              920.238
48              961.61              924.29
49              967.3               929.93
50              947.45              935.542
51              937.56              939.859
52              924.77              941.615
53              894.84              940.544
54              876.16              937.298
55              869.76              931.568
56              886.12              926.062
57              852.25              922.274
58              845.92              911.782
59              818.06              900.213
60              826.59              885.289
```

61	824.46	873.203
62	820.88	861.893
63	837.25	851.504
64	836.72	845.745
65	819.5	841.801
66	824.25	836.775
67	830.39	830.588
68	824.18	828.402
69	808.41	826.228
70	806.96	825.263
71	836.06	823.3
72	862.26	824.46
73	855.99	828.598
74	860.48	830.472
75	849.26	832.848
76	823.13	835.824
77	812.3	835.712
78	793.03	833.903
79	786.69	830.788
80	789.86	828.616
81	797.65	826.906
82	809.2	823.065
83	798.11	817.759
84	782.6	811.971
85	775.54	804.183
86	744.06	796.811
87	752.77	788.904
88	753.3	782.951
89	757.46	778.978
90	777.59	776.055
91	784.12	774.828
92	772.11	773.475
93	763.66	769.766
94	791.05	766.321
95	791.84	767.166
96	794.46	768.796
97	775.94	773.836
98	747.29	776.153
99	733.63	775.552
100	717.73	773.169
101	702.22	767.183

```
DØ YØU WISH TØ RECALCULATE MØVING AVERAGES?YES=1,NØ=2
?2
```

Exercises

PROBLEM #1

Some PERT networks utilize a Beta Distribution for the development of the average times (A). These average times are then used instead of the assigned activity times used in the text. Three specific times are used to describe the Beta Distribution for each activity, these are: P (the pessimistic time), M (the most probable time), and O (the optimistic time).

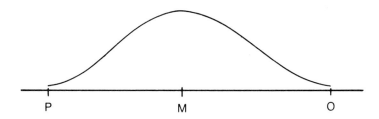

The pessimistic time is the minimum possible period of time in which an activity can be accomplished; it is that time in which an activity can be completed if everything goes exceptionally well. The assumption is made that an activity does not have more than one chance in a hundred of being completed in that time. The optimistic time is the time required for an activity under adverse conditions. It is estimated that the activity would have no more than one chance in a hundred of exceeding this amount of time. The most probable time estimate is the most realistic estimate of the time the activity might consume. It is assumed that this time would occur most often if the activity is repeated under the same conditions. Assuming a Beta Distribution of the time variable, the average time (A) for activity K can now be calculated as follows:

$$A(K) = \frac{O(K) + 4M(K) + P(K)}{6}$$

Given the following revised data for the example used in the text, adjust the BASIC PERT program to consider the O, M, and P times to calculate the A time to be used in the PERT analysis.

ACTIVITY

Inode	Jnode	Job Description	P	M	O
1	2	Order Fixtures	1	2	4
1	4	Excavation	1	2	3
1	7	Order Trees and Shrubs	3	4	5
2	3	Manufacture Furniture	3	4	5
3	6	Deliver Furniture	1	2	2
4	5	Erect Steel Structure	4	5	6
4	8	Back Filling	1	3	5
5	6	Masonry Work	3	5	6
6	9	Install Furniture	1	5	7
7	8	Plant Trees and Shrubs	1	3	5
8	9	Final Grading	4	5	7

In calculating the average time, do not go beyond one place of the decimal point.

PROBLEM #2

Reconsider the Moving Averages of the Dow-Jones Industrial Stocks! Change the BASIC program as outlined in that section so that you plot the actual and predicted averages for weeks 11 through 101, rather than printing them. Choose an acceptable transformation formula for the actual and predicted values, since you can not have more than seventy printing positions per line. Label your plot.

16
Interactive Programming in BASIC

With the cost of computers and computer time rising, more and more programs will be written to run on terminals, tied in to a central computer. The user of the terminal will, in many cases, not know anything about the program except what can be learned from a user's manual. For the user to run the program correctly and get meaningful data processing done, a program written for terminal application will have to be carefully written to lead the user through the problem to its solution. In practice, the program will have to be foolproof, or serious problems will plague the program and, therefore, the user.

Three key areas that need to be attended to are input error processing, output identification, and logical flow. In each area, if a program is carefully written, fewer human errors will be processed and those that are will be flagged for attention before serious damage can be done to the program, the data set, or the solution of the problem.

The programmer or systems analyst will understand that the rule book to be written is an ideal, a way of programming to be striven for. Unfortunately, the ideal is all too infrequently reached. The set of rules won't be the only set or even the best one. It won't be an exhaustive list of do's and don'ts, but it should lead to more accurate data processing when programs must be run on a computer terminal.

Input Error Processing

A program written to be executed on a computer terminal is different from a program written to be run in batch mode. It is different in that some of the data will be entered by a human operator at a terminal keyboard. A batch program normally accepts data only from cards, magnetic tape or disk, or some other off-line storage device. If needed, this data may be listed, verified, and corrected before the information is processed by the computer program. When data is entered by hand from a computer terminal, the user has one chance to review each line and correct it before sending it to the computer to be processed. When the user is processing a large data set, it is easy to mistype a data item, or transpose digits, or forget a decimal point. There are far more possibilities for error than one might assume. What kind of errors can the program recognize? How should the program process the errors when they are recognized?

There are two categories of errors to be concerned with. Category 1 is the input of invalid data. The validity of data depends very much upon the computer language in which one is writing; so does the programmer's ability to handle this type of error properly. For example, FORTRAN distinguishes between data modes; that is, "integers" are different from "real numbers." In BASIC, however, no distinction is made between real numbers and integers. In both computer languages, as in most others, inserting an alphabetic character in a number, or entering a word when a number is expected, will be considered invalid.

In general, the effect of an input error on the execution of a program will be quite disastrous. One of two possibilities will usually occur. The program will come to an immediate halt and print that an error has occurred during input. The program then terminates without yielding the information needed. Figure 16.2 is a sample of what would happen if the program in Figure 16.1 were executed with a Category 1 error.

```
10 PRINT "1COMPUTE BREAKEVEN POINT"
20 PRINT "0ENTER FIXED COST, UNIT VARIABLE COST & UNIT PRICE,"
30 PRINT " SEPERATED BY COMMAS(,)."
40 INPUT F,V,S
50 REM CALCULATE CONTRIBUTION MARGIN
60 C=S-V
70 REM CALCULATE BREAKEVEN POINT
80 B=F/C
90 PRINT " BREAKEVEN POINT IS";B;" UNITS."
100 STOP
```

Figure 16.1. *BASIC program to calculate breakeven point*

```
COMPUTE BREAKEVEN POINT

ENTER FIXED COST, UNIT VARIABLE COST & UNIT PRICE,
SEPERATED BY COMMAS(,).
?100,45.63,70.6E
```

Figure 16.2. *Sample output, Category 1 input validity error*

If the user of the terminal is familiar with the program he is using or is familiar with the computer language in which the program is written, the effect of a type 1 input processing error will be minimal.

If, however, the user is inexperienced, he is left with the indefinite message from the computer that an error occurred at a particular line of the program and that the computer is now "READY!" "Ready for what?" he is likely to respond, and after an undetermined amount of time waiting and probably several unsuccessful attempts to find out what the computer is ready for, he is going to go away muttering to himself. If the inexperienced user can get away with it, he will never make another attempt to use a terminal to tie in to a computer. He will never have the opportunity to become experienced. He will never be able to use the computer to help him solve problems.

If a program, designed to be used from a computer terminal, is written carelessly so as not to take into account possible errors in data input, it is inferior to a program that is taking these problems into account. To write superior programs, one must keep certain things in mind while writing the program.

There is no easy way in BASIC to undo a Category 1 error. We can only give the user, who is not familiar with the language, instructions in how to interpret and handle the message. Figure 16.3 illustrates one way of doing this. Lines 36 and 37 are PRINT statements, which convey a message to the user on how to handle an error that is flagged by the computer during the execution of the program.

The second category of error is data out of range. This, of course, presupposes that in a given problem there is a range in which at least one item is valid, and out of that range, that item is invalid. In Figure 16.1 which is a listing or a program written in BASIC to calculate breakeven points, the data needed are fixed cost (F), variable cost (V), and selling price (S). To achieve accurate results from the program, the following constraints must be observed on the data:

—Fixed cost must be greater than zero

—Variable cost must be greater than zero

—Price must be greater than zero

—Price must be greater than variable cost

If these conditions are not present when the program executes statements 60 and 80, the program will not function properly.

The effect of a Category 2 error cannot be determined in advance, but will be either of two types. In the one case, the error will cause a processing error somewhere in the program. Figure 16.4 is an example of what happens in this case. In this example, variable cost equals price violating the fourth constraint on the data. When the program attempts to execute statement 80, it will attempt to divide the fixed cost by zero. This is mathematically impossible and an error results.

```
10 PRINT "1CØMPUTE BREAKEVEN PØINT"
20 PRINT "0ENTER FIXED CØST, UNIT VARIABLE CØST & UNIT PRICE,"
30 PRINT " SEPERATED BY CØMMAS(,)."
36 PRINT "IF YØUR DATA IS FLAGGED HAVING AN ILLEGAL CHARACTER,"
37 PRINT "THEN RESPØND BY 'STØP' AND RUN THE PRØGRAM AGAIN!"
40 INPUT F,V,S
50 REM CALCULATE CØNTRIBUTIØN MARGIN
60 C=S-V
70 REM CALCULATE BREAKEVEN PØINT
80 B=F/C
90 PRINT " BREAKEVEN PØINT IS";B;" UNITS."
100 STØP




COMPUTE BREAKEVEN PØINT

ENTER FIXED CØST, UNIT VARIABLE CØST & UNIT PRICE,
SEPERATED BY CØMMAS(,).
IF YØUR DATA IS FLAGGED HAVING AN ILLEGAL CHARACTER,
THEN RESPØND BY 'STØP' AND RUN THE PRØGRAM AGAIN!
?100,200,500
+ ILLEGAL NUMERIC CØNSTANT.
+ AT LINE "40" IN PRØGRAM "CASE2"
+READY!
>STØP
& AT LINE "40" IN PRØGRAM "CASE2"
& PRØGRAM ENDS
:%RUN CASE2




COMPUTE BREAKEVEN PØINT

ENTER FIXED CØST, UNIT VARIABLE CØST & UNIT PRICE,
SEPERATED BY CØMMAS(,).
IF YØUR DATA IS FLAGGED HAVING AN ILLEGAL CHARACTER,
THEN RESPØND BY 'STØP' AND RUN THE PRØGRAM AGAIN!
?100,200,250
BREAKEVEN PØINT IS 2 UNITS.
```

Figure 16.3. *Warning for Category 1, input validity error*

If a processing error does not occur, a more insidious error results. In the examples so far, the computer (not the program) has discovered an error and suspended execution of the program. In some cases, the computer will accept data out of range and process it. If this occurs, the results of the program will be inaccurate. Figure 16.5 is an example of such a situation. The value of −15

```
    CØMPUTE BREAKEVEN PØINT

    ENTER FIXED CØST, UNIT VARIABLE CØST & UNIT PRICE,
    SEPERATED BY CØMMAS(,).
   ?100,45.63,45.63
   + ATTEMPT TØ DIVIDE BY ZERØ.
   + AT LINE "80" IN PRØGRAM "CASE1"
   +READY!
   >
```

Figure 16.4. *Sample output for Figure 16.1, processing error due to data out of range*

```
    CØMPUTE BREAKEVEN PØINT

    ENTER FIXED CØST, UNIT VARIABLE CØST & UNIT PRICE,
    SEPERATED BY CØMMAS(,).
   ?100,-15,35
    BREAKEVEN PØINT IS 2 UNITS.
```

Figure 16.5. *Sample output of Figure 16.1 nonprocessing error due to data out of range*

violates the second constraint on the data, yet this violation goes unnoticed and an erroneous breakeven point is printed. The program performed the proper manipulation of the data, but incorrect input data yields meaningless output.

When one writes a computer program, one is communicating. The thing many programmers seem to forget is that they are communicating to two different audiences. The first is an audience of one, the computer. The programmer must communicate his instructions to the computer in order for it to function. This is necessary and so important that many novice programmers stop here. The second audience is really more important. The audience is the human user. If the user makes an error when he inputs data, it should be the function of the computer program to advise, in as much detail as is practical, what the error was and how to correct it. In order to do this, the program must test all data for errors. The extent of this test depends to some extent on the language used, and on the consequences of passing through data that is incorrect. If the test shows an item of data to be in error, the program should advise the user of the error and allow him the option of correcting it.

Figure 16.6 illustrates the dramatic results one may obtain when tests are made on the variables to be sure they are within specified ranges. None of the second type of errors (data out of range) cause stoppage of the program or unnoticeable erroneous breakeven points. All data is carefully tested. If any of the aforementioned data constraints are violated, the user is notified of the type of input error and has a chance to correct it.

```
10 PRINT "1COMPUTE BREAKEVEN POINT"
20 PRINT "OENTER FIXED COST, UNIT VARIABLE COST & UNIT PRICE,"
30 PRINT " SEPERATED BY COMMAS(,)."
36 PRINT "IF YOUR DATA IS FLAGGED HAVING AN ILLEGAL CHARACTER,"
37 PRINT "THEN RESPOND BY 'STOP' AND RUN THE PROGRAM AGAIN!"
40 INPUT F,V,S
41 IF F>0, THEN 44
42 PRINT "THE FIXED COST MUST BE LARGER THAN ZERO!TRY AGAIN"
43 GOTO 20
44 IF V>0, THEN 47
45 PRINT "THE VAR. COST MUST BE LARGER THAN ZERO! TRY AGAIN"
46 GOTO 20
47 IF S>0, THEN 50
48 PRINT "THE PRICE MUST BE LARGER THAN ZERO!TRY AGAIN"
49 GOTO 20
50 IF S>V, THEN 60
51 PRINT "THE PRICE MUST BE LARGER THAN THE VARIABLE COST!TRY AGAIN"
52 GOTO 20
55 REM CALCULATE CONTRIBUTION MARGIN
60 C=S-V
70 REM CALCULATE BREAKEVEN POINT
80 B=F/C
90 PRINT " BREAKEVEN POINT IS";B;" UNITS."
100 STOP


COMPUTE BREAKEVEN POINT

ENTER FIXED COST, UNIT VARIABLE COST & UNIT PRICE,
SEPERATED BY COMMAS(,).
IF YOUR DATA IS FLAGGED HAVING AN ILLEGAL CHARACTER,
THEN RESPOND BY 'STOP' AND RUN THE PROGRAM AGAIN!
?100,45.63,45.63
THE PRICE MUST BE LARGER THAN THE VARIABLE COST!TRY AGAIN

ENTER FIXED COST, UNIT VARIABLE COST & UNIT PRICE,
SEPERATED BY COMMAS(,).
IF YOUR DATA IS FLAGGED HAVING AN ILLEGAL CHARACTER,
THEN RESPOND BY 'STOP' AND RUN THE PROGRAM AGAIN!
?100,-15,35
THE VAR. COST MUST BE LARGER THAN ZERO! TRY AGAIN

ENTER FIXED COST, UNIT VARIABLE COST & UNIT PRICE,
SEPERATED BY COMMAS(,).
IF YOUR DATA IS FLAGGED HAVING AN ILLEGAL CHARACTER,
THEN RESPOND BY 'STOP' AND RUN THE PROGRAM AGAIN!
?100,200,250
BREAKEVEN POINT IS 2 UNITS.
```

Figure 16.6.   *Warning for Category 2, input validity error*

In summary, to improve input processing by the elimination of errors, follow these rules when writing a program for terminal application.

1. Given the language used, if possible, test for the validity of all input into the program before it is processed.
2. Test those variables that have a specific range to be sure that each is within its legal range.
3. If a variable is found to be invalid, advise the user that an error has occurred. Tell him what the error was (if it can be determined) and give him the opportunity to correct the error. Advise in a similar manner for data out of range.

If these simple rules are followed, nearly all input error processing problems may be virtually eliminated.

Output Identification

A computer program must have three functions to be useful. It must accept input data, it must process the data in some manner, and it must communicate the results of the processing. It is important that both batch and terminal runs be clearly labeled so that the output from a program may stand alone and still be meaningful.

The problem has two facets. The first has to do with simply labeling the output. If a programmer is writing a "quick and dirty," one shot program, he is likely to not label the output. But is also likely to use the output immediately. He is also familiar with the program and what output to expect. He is essentially different from the person sitting at a terminal. That person may or may not make immediate use of the information. If a significant period of time elapses between the terminal program run and the use of the data, unlabeled output will be meaningless. No one can remember what the data means. Also, more programs are being written to be run by people who aren't familiar with the program and therefore don't know what output to expect. A jungle of figures pouring off of a computer terminal is meaningless to such a person.

Let us look at some examples to illustrate the concepts presented concerning output identification only. Figures 16.7 and 16.8 show two parallel BASIC programs that functionally do the same thing. Each is complete and functional, assuming valid and correct input (not necessarily a good assumption to make!). However, compare the output of both exhibits! See how much more self-contained the second output is?

```
10 PRINT "1GIVE ME INPUT"
20 INPUT F,V,S
30 PRINT F/(S-V)
40 STOP



GIVE ME INPUT
?100,25,50
 4
```

Figure 16.7. *Program illustrating bad output identification*

```
10 PRINT "1COMPUTE BREAKEVEN POINT."
20 PRINT " ENTER FIXED COST, UNIT VARIABLE COST AND UNIT PRICE"
30 INPUT F,V,S
40 PRINT " BREAKEVEN POINT IS ";F/(S-V)
50 PRINT " OUTPUT IS IN UNITS."
60 STOP


COMPUTE BREAKEVEN POINT.
ENTER FIXED COST, UNIT VARIABLE COST AND UNIT PRICE
?100,25,50
 BREAKEVEN POINT IS  4
 OUTPUT IS IN UNITS.
```

Figure 16.8. *Program illustrating better output identification*

In Figure 16.8, the problem is stated, the input is identified, and the output is labeled. Six months from now one could look at the output from the second program and tell exactly what it means. Not so with the first example. Ten minutes after it was printed, the user will forget its meaning.

The second facet of the problem is the representation of internal precision in the output. For example, in a program to calculate retail markup, the internal representation of the final price could be $48.55679267. Should that be printed on the output as $48.55679267 or would $48.55 or $48.56 be better choices? In this case, there is probably no significant difference between any of the three. In some cases the difference could be important. Fortunately, this problem is relatively easy to correct as illustrated in the several examples within Chapter 14:

> —Term Revolving Credit Plan (TRCP), line 310
>
> —Single-Premium Life Insurance (SPLI), line 240
>
> —Asset Depreciation (ASSET), lines 250 and 260

In all of these examples an appropriate function, the INT function, is used to obtain desired and meaningful precision.

Thus, with respect to output identification and precision, all the programmer has to keep in mind is his audience. He must ask himself: "Who will use the program?" and "For what purpose is it being run?" To continue the list already begun as the summary of rules to follow when writing a program for terminal application (page 323), let us add . . .

4. In program output, the program should print, so far as is feasible, what the program is designed to do, the input data identified as such, and all output also identified as such, including the relevant unit of measure if appropriate.
5. All computations within the program should be carried at the greatest level of accuracy practical or affordable.
6. When information is printed, it should be printed with only the accuracy demanded by the use of the data, or the greatest accuracy practical or affordable, whichever is the lesser.

Only number 6 is likely to cause any second thoughts. The reason for this prescription is to prevent attributing more accuracy to a computer than it deserves. If a figure is accurate to five significant digits, show it as such. To allow the computer to add random digits is misleading. For the other case, why give a person more information than he can use. In our previous example, $48.56 is to be preferred to $48.55679267 because the last six digits of the second choice will never be used. $48.56 is shorter, less open to further human error and therefore more accurate.

Logical Flow

The concept of logical flow is important if one programs a computer, but few people give it much thought in the context in which it will be used here. In a long program, there will typically be many steps. Some of these steps will each require data from the user. The question to ask is, "In what order should the program request data, and in what order should it accept data?" And of course, the answer is, "In a natural, logical order for the program and the user." In a program, some data is typically required before a computation is made. It belabors the obvious to state that the program must have the data before it is needed. However, in most cases, the programmer is free to choose when to input data within the aforementioned constraint.

Since the programmer is partially free in his choice of timing in data input, he should design the program suiting the convenience of the user, within efficiency constraints.

To take a minor example, let us look at the flow when computing a discounted cash flow. The data needed before processing is done would be the dollar amounts of the flows and the rates to apply in each year. So far as the program is concerned, as long as all data is internal when processing is begun, there is no optimal order to receive the data. For the case when three years are considered, which of the two flows in Figure 16.9 makes the most sense to the user? I think most will agree that data input in logical flow B makes more sense to the operator, although both follow a pattern of input that is logical and consistent. The whole point seems trivial in this context, but in a long, complicated program, the ordering of data input can make a considerable difference.

Flow A	Flow B
1. Cash flow year 2	1. Cash flow year 1
2. Rate year 3	2. Cash flow year 2
3. Cash flow year 1	3. Cash flow year 3
4. Rate year 1	4. Rate year 1
5. Cash flow year 3	5. Rate year 2
6. Rate year 2	6. Rate year 3

Figure 16.9. *Two logical flows leading to discounted cash flow calculations*

In the case of ordering data input, the prescription is simple and should be easy to follow. All that needs to be done is to consider yourself as the computer. If one was about to work a problem, he would need data. The natural order in which the human mind requests is the order that the computer should request data from a human user. To complete the rule book for improving input processing . . .

7. All data necessary for computation by a program should be entered before it must be used.
8. When the programmer is free to choose the order in which to request data from the terminal user, he should request it in the same sequence that he would request it for himself if he were going to work the problem in his head.

Philosophy

The alert reader has understood what has been stated and realizes that to program for terminal applications, the analyst must lead the user through a program because that user cannot be familiar with it and probably won't be familiar with the language it is written in. To understand it, the program must be so written that the user is never surprised. All the data must be called for in logical order, tested for validity and range; and when results are printed they should be clearly identified and labeled accordingly.

In order to accomplish the guided tour through a problem, the programmer should follow a sequence when he writes a time-sharing program.

• Given the language used, test for validity of all input into the program *before* it is processed, if possible.
• Test all variables that have a legal range to be sure they are in that range.

- If a variable is found to be invalid or out of range, advise the user and give him an opportunity to correct the data before processing is begun.
- In program output, identify as completely as is feasible the problem the program is designed to solve, the input data entered and processed, and all output, including the unit of measure.
- All computations within a program should be carried at the greatest level of accuracy practical or affordable.
- When information is printed, it should be printed with the accuracy demanded by the use of the data, or the greatest accuracy present in the program, whichever is the lesser.
- All data necessary for computation by the program should be entered before it must be used.
- When the programmer is free to choose the sequence in which to request data from the terminal user, it should be requested in the order a human mind would request it if called upon to perform the same processing as the machine.

If the prescription is followed, the analyst's programs will perform better. The user will be more satisfied with the service the computer gives him. His data processing will be more accurate.

A
Flowcharting Symbols

1. Processing Group

PROCESS   Any processing function; defined operation(s) causing change in form, value, or location of information.

2. Decision Group

DECISION   A decision or switching-type operation that determines which of a number of alternative paths to follow.

3. Input/Output Group

INPUT/OUTPUT   General I/O function; information available for processing (input), or recording of processed information (output).

PUNCHED CARD   Input/output function in card medium (all varieties).

DOCUMENT   Output on paper medium.

ONLINE STORAGE   Input/output using any kind of online storage—magnetic tape, drum, disk.

MANUAL INPUT   Information input by online keyboards, switch settings, pushbuttons.

4. Connector and Terminal Group

TERMINAL, INTERRUPT   A terminal point in a flowchart—start, stop, halt, delay, or interrupt; may show exit from a closed subroutine.

CONNECTOR   Exit to, or entry from, another part of the chart.

PAGE CONNECTOR

5. Linkage Group

ARROWHEADS and *FLOWLINES*   In linking symbols, these should show operations sequence and dataflow direction.

COMMUNICATION LINK   Function of transmitting information by a telecommunication link.

6. Predefined Process Group

PREDEFINED PROCESS   One or more named operations or program steps specified in a subroutine or another set of flowcharts.

7. Preparation Group

PREPARATION   Instruction modification to change program—set a switch, modify an index register, initialize a routine.

8. Comment Group

COMMENT   Additional descriptive clarification, comment. (Dotted line extends to symbols as appropriate.)

B

Summary of BASIC Statements and Implementation

This text discusses the BASIC language as it is implemented at the University of Michigan for the IBM 360-67. There are, however, other implementations of the BASIC language. This appendix summarizes the BASIC statements as discussed in this book and indicates their various implementations. To keep this list as brief as possible, but nevertheless complete, the different implementations will be referred to by the following code:

Code	Implementation
1	Burroughs B5500 System
2	Control Data Corporation (CDC 3300)
3	Com-Share Scientific Data 940
4	Dartmouth BASIC
5	Digital Equipment (PDP 10)
6	GE Models
7	Hewlett-Packard 2000A
8	IBM 1130
9	IBM 360
10	RCA (Spectra 70/46)
11	Scientific Data Sigma 5 and 7
12	UNIVAC 1108
13	University of Michigan BASIC

Arithmetic Assignment Statement (p. 49)

(LET) Variable Name = Arithmetic Expression

LET optional keyword for [2], [3], and [9].
Variable Name: one letter of the alphabet
                   one letter followed by one decimal digit.

Arithmetic Expression: Constants
                        Operators $(+, -, *, **, \uparrow)$
                        Variable Names

Implementation: Most systems use "$\uparrow$" for exponentiation.
                   Implementation [1] uses "**" and implementations [10],
                   [12], and [13] use both.

Backspacing Statement (p. 233)

BACKSPACE #N

N: channel identification
Implementation: all

Computed GOTO Statement (p. 87)

GOTO $(n_1, n_2, n_3, \ldots, n_m)$, exp

implementation [2] and [13]

On exp GOTO $n_1, n_2, n_3, \ldots, n_m$

implementation [1], [2], [3], [5], [6], [10], [11]

$n_1, n_2, n_3, \ldots, n_m$: line numbers
exp: an arithmetic expression whose truncated numeric value is used to
    select a line number.
n_1: if the truncated value of the expression equals 1, then transfer is made
     to n_1.
n_m: if the truncated value of the expression equals m, then transfer is made
     to n_m.

Data Statement (p. 61)

DATA ⟨list⟩

⟨list⟩: contains an ordered set of constants, separated by commas.
implementation: all

Dimension Statement (p. 143)

DIMENSION v, v, v, . . .

v: variable names followed by parentheses, enclosing 1 or 2 integer constants, giving the maximum size of each subscript.
implementation: implementation [5] does not allow two subscripts

Files Definition Statement (p. 233)

FILES filename1; filename2; . . .

filenames: separated by either commas or semicolons.
implementation: all

FOR-NEXT Loop (p. 115)

FOR i=e_1 to e_2 STEP e_3

-
-
-

NEXT i

i: a numeric nonsubscripted loop variable
e_1, e_2, and e_3: arithmetic expressions
e_1: initial value of i
e_2: ultimate value of i
e_3: increment value of i
FOR: beginning of the loop
NEXT: end of the loop
implementation: all

Function Definition Statement (p. 186)

DEF FNα(d)=exp

α: a letter of the alphabet; there are a maximum of 26 functions
d: dummy variable or argument
exp: arithmetic expressions to be evaluated; it may or may not contain the arguments
implementation: implementation [8] and [10] do not use DEF

Halt Statements (p. 72)

STOP (all implementations)
PAUSE (implementation [2], [4], [8], [9], [11], [13])
END (all implementations)

IF-THEN, Type 1 Statement (p. 91)

If exp1 reln exp2 THEN n

exp1 & exp2: arithmetic expressions
reln: relational operator
exp1 reln exp2: logical expression
n: a line number to which control is transferred if the logical expression is true

Meaning	Relational Operators (implementation 1)	Relational Operators (other implementations)
equal to	/EQ	=
greater than	/GT	>
less than	/LT	<
not equal to	/NE	< >
less than or equal to	/LE	< =
greater than or equal to	/GE	> =

IF-THEN, Type 2 Statement (p. 99)

IF exp1 reln exp2 THEN (n$_1$, n$_2$, n$_3$, . . ., n$_m$), exp3

exp1, exp2, & exp3: arithmetic expressions
reln: relational operator
exp1 reln exp2: logical expression
n$_1$, n$_2$, n$_m$: control is transferred to one of these line numbers according to the truncated value of exp3 if the logical expression is true.
implementation: this is implemented on [13]

IF END File Statement (p. 233)

IF END #N THEN ln

N: channel identification of file
ln: line number
Implementation: all

Image Statement (p. 216)

n :⟨image specifications⟩

: is necessary to identify the statement as an image statement.
specifications are:

numeric specifications: #   pound sign
                           .   period
                       ↑↑↑↑ four upward arrows

edited numeric specifications:$ dollar sign
                           ,   commas
                           − trailing minus
                           * leading asterisk

string specifications: R right justification
                     L left justification
                     C centering
                     E extending

Input Control (p. 63)

SKP(exp)

exp: an arithmetic expression

Input Statement (p. 64)

INPUT ⟨list⟩

⟨list⟩: contains an ordered list of variable names and/or controls, separated by
commas.
implementation: not implemented on [12]

Internal Subroutine (p. 190)

GOSUB n

n: line number of the first executable statement of the subroutine to which
control is to be given.
implementation: all

Matrix Addition Statement (p. 150)

MAT LET C=A+B

A, B, and C: different matrix names
+: matrix addition operator
LET: optional assignment keyword
implementation: not implemented on [8], [9], and [12]

Matrix Assignment (p. 157)

MAT LET B=A

A and B: different matrix names
LET: optional assignment keyword
implementation: not implemented on [8], [9], and [12]

Matrix CON Assignment (p. 162)

MAT LET A=CON
MAT LET A=CON (exp1, exp2) implemented on [13]

CON: matrix function that assigns ones (1) to all elements of a matrix
A: matrix name
exp1 and exp2: expressions for redimensioning
LET: optional assignment keyword
implementation: not implemented on [8], [9], and [12]

Matrix IDN Assignment (p. 162)

MAT LET A=IDN
MAT LET A=IDN (exp1, exp2) implemented on [13]

IDN: matrix function that defines a square matrix as an identity matrix
A: matrix name
exp1 and exp2: expressions for redimensioning
LET: optional assignment keyword
implementation: not implemented on [8], [9], and [12]

Matrix Input Statement (p. 148)

MAT INPUT ⟨list⟩

⟨list⟩: represents a list of BASIC array names, separated by commas. A
    dimension statement indicates the size of the array. Matrixes are read in
    row by row.
implementation: is implemented on [3], [5], [11], and [13] only

Matrix Inverse (p. 158)

MAT LET B=INV(A)

A and B: different matrix names
INV: matrix function that defines the inverse of A
LET: optional assignment keyword
implementation: not implemented on [8], [9], and [12]

Matrix Multiplication (p. 154)

MAT LET C=A*B

A, B, and C: different matrix names
*: multiplication operator
LET: optional assignment keyword
implementation: not implemented on [8], [9], and [12]

Matrix Print Statement (p. 148)

MAT PRINT ⟨list⟩

⟨list⟩: represents a list of BASIC array names, separated by commas or semi-colons. Matrixes are printed row by row, with each row starting a new line.
implementation: not implemented on [8], [9], and [12]

Matrix Read Statement (p. 148)

MAT READ ⟨list⟩

(with DATA statement)
⟨list⟩: represents a list of BASIC array names, separated by commas. A dimension statement indicates the size of the array. Matrixes are read in row by row.
implementation: not implemented on [8], [9], and [12]

Matrix Redimensioning (p. 161)

MAT LET A=RDM(exp1, exp2)

A: matrix name
RDM: redimensioning function
exp1, exp2: expressions
LET: optional assignment keyword
implementation: is implemented on [13]

Matrix Scalar Multiplication Statement (p. 153)

MAT LET B=(exp)*A

A and B: different matrix names
exp: expression which becomes the multiplier
*: multiplication operator
LET: optional assignment keyword
implementation: not implemented on [8], [9], and [12]

Matrix: Simultaneous Linear Equations (p. 156)

MAT LET X = A/B

X: an nX1 matrix
A: an nX1 matrix
B: an nXn nonsingular square matrix
/: division operator
LET: optional assignment keyword
implementation: this matrix operation is implemented on [13]

Matrix Subtraction Statement (p. 151)

MAT LET C = A − B

A, B, and C: different matrix names
−: matrix subtraction operator
LET: optional assignment keyword
implementation: not implemented on [8], [9], and [12]

Matrix Transpose (p. 160)

MAT LET B = TRN(A)

A and B: different matrix names
TRN: matrix function that defines the transpose of A
LET: optional assignment keyword
implementation: not implemented on [8], [9], and [12]

Matrix Unary Negation Statement (p. 152)

MAT LET B = −A

A and B: different matrix names
−: unary minus operator
LET: optional assignment keyword
implementation: this matrix is implemented on [13]

Matrix ZER Assignment (p. 162)

MAT LET A = ZER
MAT LET A = ZER (exp1, exp2) implemented on [13]

ZER: matrix function that assigns zero (0) to all elements of a matrix
A: matrix name
exp1 and exp2: expressions for redimensioning
LET: optional assignment keyword
implementation: not implemented on [8], [9], and [12]

Print, Carriage Controls (p. 66)

" ": single spacing
"0": double spacing
"−": triple spacing
"1": skip to top of next page on batch
  skip six lines on the terminal

Print, Output Controls (p. 69)

TAB: output tab function
; : for packed output
, : for zoned output
: : output carriage return

Print Statement (p. 66)

PRINT ⟨list⟩

⟨list⟩: contains an ordered list of carriage controls, variable names, arithmetic
  expressions, messages, and/or output controls
implementation: not implemented on [2] (WRITE statement)

Print Using Statement (p. 215)

PRINT USING $\begin{Bmatrix} \textbf{n} \\ \textbf{string variable} \\ \textbf{format string} \end{Bmatrix}$, ⟨list⟩

n: is the line number of the IMAGE statement
string variable: character string variable that contains the desired format
  string
format string: a string specifying the way in which the list is to be output
⟨list⟩: ordered list of variable names, expressions, messages and/or controls

Read Statement (p. 61)

READ ⟨list⟩

(in conjunction with a Data statement)
⟨list⟩: contains an ordered list of variable names and/or input controls, separated by commas
implementation: all

Read From File Statement (p. 233, 240)

READ #N, variable, variable, variable, . . .
READ :N, variable, variable, variable, . . .

#N: channel identification of sequential file to be read from, there must be at least one variable

:N: channel identification of random access file to be read from, there must be at least one variable

Restore Statement (p. 236)

RESTORE #N

N: channel identification of file to be restored
implementation: all

Remark Statement (p. 39)

REMARK
REM

implementation: all

Return Statement (p. 190)

RETURN

implementation: all

Set the Pointer (p. 240)

SET :N,v

:N: is the identification of the random access file where a pointer must be set
v: variable or an expression for the pointer value

Scratching File Statement (p. 236)

SCRATCH #N

#N: channel identification of the file to be scratched
implementation: all

String Assignment (p. 57)

(LET) String Variable = String Expression

String Variable: Single letter followed by a $ sign, or two (2) identical letters (impl. [13]).
String Expression: string addition for linking two strings.
LET: optional keyword for [2], [3], [9], [13]

Unconditional GOTO Statement (p. 82)

GOTO n

n: is the statement number or line number of an executable statement in the program to which control must be made
implementation: all

Writing in File Statement (p. 236, 340)

WRITE #N, variable, variable, variable, . . .
WRITE :N, variable, variable, variable, . . .

#N: is the identification number of the sequential file in which one wishes to write
:N: is the channel identification of the random access file in which one wishes to write

C
List of Flowcharts

Index

DIM
END
FOR
GOSUB
GOTO
IF-THEN
INPUT
LET
MAT LET
NEXT
ON
PAUSE
PRINT
READ
REM
RETURN
STOP